The Transformation of Political Culture in Cuba

Stanford Studies in Comparative Politics, 2

The Transformation of Political Culture in Cuba

Richard R. Fagen

Stanford University Press, Stanford, California 1969

Stanford University Press
Stanford, California

Printed in the United States of America
L.C. 77-83117
SBN 8047-0702-2

Preface

MEN, EVEN social scientists, are moved by events of great sweep and drama. I must confess to being so moved by the Cuban Revolution. Like many others who were intrigued when reports began to trickle out of the Sierra Maestra in 1957 that Fidel Castro and a small group of followers had launched a guerrilla action against Batista, I began to follow the Cuban story, more because of the romance and mystery that surrounded it than because I thought a truly revolutionary transformation was in the making. By the end of 1959, however, after the revolutionaries had been in power for a year, it was quite obvious that what was going on in Cuba involved social, economic, and political changes far beyond those normally associated with reformist regimes in Latin America. It was also about then that I began to lose my innocence with respect to the Cuban Revolution. That is, I began to realize that if the revolutionary leadership was as committed as it seemed to be to achieving a fundamental reorganization of Cuban society, then some very difficult political and moral issues were going to be raised. To be more precise, I began to feel that the historic importance of the Cuban case would revolve not around the guerrilla struggle but around the way the revolutionary leadership was going about accomplishing the massive redistribution of goods, services, and opportunities implied by its early programmatic statements and actions.

The realization that what Fidel Castro and his followers were doing in Cuba truly deserved to be called revolutionary awakened in me the ambivalence that well-fed children of the enlightenment so often suffer when confronted with such profound transformations. On the one hand, I was attracted by the audacity and creativity with which the revolutionaries were attacking the old order and building the new. On the other hand, I was disturbed by the ruthlessness and the thoroughness with which civil liberties and conventional freedoms were swept aside whenever they were seen by the revolutionary elite as inhibiting the developmental effort. That this ambivalence was shared by the larger community is attested to by the rash of polemical and semipolemical literature generated in response to the revolution. Much of this polemic is skillful, and some of it is even enlightening, but my own resolve was that I could offer to the debate little that was not being argued better by others. Therefore I began to work, as well as I could from a distance, on trying to understand some of the changes wrought by the Castro government in the Cuban educational system, supposing that this was a subject matter at least one step removed from the heat of the polemic and yet still central to an understanding of Cuban development. I found, of course, that although it was removed from the polemic, it was by no means removed from the political, organizational, and moral issues raised by the revolution.

Education in Cuba is so broadly understood by the revolutionary elites and so intimately a part of their programs for the transformation of the social, economic, and political orders that I was rather rapidly drawn to consider other aspects of the revolutionary style of governance and planned change. Thus what began as a book on revolutionary education in Cuba soon grew into a book about political socialization and cultural change under the Revolutionary Government. The metamorphosis was not as tortuous as one might expect, for political socialization and the transformation of political culture are first-order goals of revolutionary education. What happened was that my attention was directed away from the system of formal education in Cuba and toward those new revolutionary institutions that were at the same time both the most visible manifestations of the new political culture and the settings for the formation of new citizens.

These settings are so numerous in revolutionary Cuba and they change so rapidly that I could not hope to deal with more than a few of them in sufficient depth to give a meaningful picture of their evolution, functioning, and consequences. Furthermore, barred by the State Department from visiting Cuba until the summer of 1966, and plagued by the difficulties of securing Cuban materials in the United States, I was forced to choose settings that could be studied from a distance. Thus the three case studies that comprise the central section of this book—studies of the campaign against illiteracy, the Committees for Defense of the Revolution, and the Schools of Revolutionary Instruction—may be thought of as a sample chosen for both pragmatic and theoretical reasons. The pragmatic consideration was that all three of these experiences generated sufficient public and semipublic documentation to allow them to be analyzed without traveling to Cuba, seeing unpublished reports, or generating interview data. The theoretical consideration was that the three cases cover a range of revolutionary settings that, if they do not represent the entire Cuban experience of socialization and cultural change, at least touch on its most distinctive aspects. The campaign against illiteracy was perhaps the most successful and important of the one-time mobilization efforts directed toward a specific developmental goal. The Committees for Defense of the Revolution are the most innovative and far-reaching of all the revolutionary mass organizations. And the Schools of Revolutionary Instruction were the most ambitious of all the formal or semiformal programs for political education and citizenship training.

Finally, a word is in order about the subjective and qualitative aspects of research on a subject like this one. Although in the summer of 1966, in the spring of 1968, and again in the summer of 1969 I was able to visit Cuba, travel to some of the environments I had been studying, talk to people about my research, and secure the photographs included in this book, it would be misleading to claim that I have done research in Cuba. I have used the Cuba trips to fill in a few gaps in the written materials available, to embolden myself to make certain evaluations and estimates that I might otherwise not have made, and above all to "soak" as fully as possible for a few months in the *ambiente* of the revolution. The consequences of this soaking for the final manuscript are not easy for me to determine, but the first trip convinced me that it would be very difficult to convey in a book of this sort any feeling for the textures of cultural change as experienced by those actually living through it. Therefore, to ameliorate somewhat the facelessness of my scholarship, I decided to include as an appendix a report written from field notes on my visits to three rural settings that constitute part of the larger, diffuse socialization environment. Hopefully, this report will contribute to giving some flesh and human scale to an effort that otherwise might seem more mechanical and institutionalized than it actually is. Additionally, for each of the case studies I have translated and abridged a relevant speech of Castro's. His words and his presence are so central to the governance and transformation of Cuba that a reader must appreciate why and how his rhetoric continues to motivate and mobilize broad sectors of the Cuban population in order to understand one of the prime strengths of the revolution. Thus the speeches stand not only as important substantive documents in their own right, but as a kind of qualitative data on the ambiente and tenor of the revolution. They are as much bearers of the political culture of revolutionary Cuba as are the institutions and programs in which socialization and civic training take place.

When one works for five years on a book, albeit intermittently, one incurs a vast fund of indebtedness. I have depended for financial support on a joint grant from the Social Science Research Council and the American Council of Learned Societies, and on grants at Stanford University from the Center for Research in International Studies, the Committee on Latin American Studies, and the Institute of Political Studies. My debt to these organizations is twofold—it is not only for the funds given, but also for the investment of trust implied by their willingness to continue to support an endeavor that for a long time was yielding no visible written return.

When I began working on the Cuban Revolution I was blessed with two diligent and knowledgeable research assistants, Sally Harms and David Ronfeldt. When they left for greener pastures, Jeanne Friedman helped mightily in organizing and typing the manuscript. My colleagues Gabriel Almond and Alexander George read and commented extensively on various drafts. They are both critics in the best sense of the word, and they have strengthened the manuscript in numerous ways. Additionally, Jess Bell, Editor of the Stanford University Press, and John Daniel, Assistant Editor, have struck manful blows for coherence and literacy—Jess because he has counseled me on book-writing from the very outset of this project, and John because he constantly reminded me with his pencil that a manuscript and a book are not the same. Finally, I find myself with a diffuse but profound debt to all those Cubans who have shared the triumph and the tragedy of their lives and their revolution with me. In dozens of conversations and shared experiences they have exposed me to aspects of contemporary Cuba that must remain closed to those who study only books and documents. Their imprint is on this book in ways that I know to be important and that I hope the reader can sense.

R.R.F.

Contents

Eight pages of photographs follow page 84.

On January 1, 1959, many people thought they had stepped into a world of riches. What they had really done was to win the opportunity to start creating—in the midst of underdevelopment, poverty, ignorance, and misery—the wealth and well-being of the future.

FIDEL CASTRO

1 Toward a New Political Culture

> The radical has a passionate faith in the infinite perfectibility of human nature. He believes that by changing man's environment and by perfecting a technique of soul forming, a society can be wrought that is wholly new and unprecedented.
>
> *Eric Hoffer*

beaut.

WHAT IS the Cuban Revolution? The triumph of true democracy in the hemisphere, say its leaders. A repudiation of Yankee imperialism, say its supporters. The inevitable outcome of historical forces, say its ideologues. A betrayal of the Cuban people, say its exiles. The prime threat to hemispheric peace and stability, say its political opponents. The stimulus behind the Alliance for Progress, say the cynics. Each of these definitions has its attractions. None of them, however, really answers the question, for the significance of the Cuban Revolution lies not in the many ways its consequences can be viewed, but rather in the nature of the social and political transformations it has wrought. These changes have been so basic, so massive, and so rapid that the revolution is rightfully called, by friend and foe alike, the most radical in the history of the Americas. It is this radicalism that has given rise to the many interpretations of the revolution, for sociopolitical transformations of this magnitude can be neither ignored nor evaluated with equanimity by those whose lives they affect.

Thus, to answer the question "What is the Cuban Revolution?" we must first examine what might be called the evolution and content of Cuban radicalism—those fundamental changes in the structure and operation of society and politics that define the revolutionary experience. A preliminary checklist is easy to assemble: in ten years Cuba has seen the advent of Leninist politics, agrarian reform, educational reorganization, economic transformations, and international realignments—all force-drafted at a rate that leaves outsiders as well as many Cubans bewildered. But it is not just the magnitude and pace of the transformations that makes the Cuban experience radical; the manner in which change is effected is also important. For although the Cuban elite makes the decisions and dictates the timing of change, it is the Cuban masses who must reorder their belief systems and their lives in the service of the revolution. Thus there arises a pervasive and continuous effort to mobilize the people and enlist their energies, loyalties, and skills in creating the new Cuba. Where existing energies, loyalties, and skills are found wanting by the revolutionaries, they have taken upon themselves the job of creating new ones.

It is this effort to create a new Cuban man, a man equal to the tasks set for him by the revolutionary elite, that will engage our attention on the following pages. The transformation of Cuban man into revolutionary man is at the heart of Cuban radicalism; it is seen by the leadership as a requisite for the success of the new institutional order, and the regime spares no energies in its pursuit. In the Cuban view, there can be no successful and lasting Leninist politics, agrarian reform, economic transformations, or international realignments without the education and reeducation of the Cuban masses. As Castro has said, "All revolution is an extraordinary process of education.... Revolution and education are the same thing."[1]

Political Socialization and the Revolution

Switching from the language of the revolution to the language of contemporary social science, we may say that the regime's central concern is with political socialization. By political socialization we mean the inculcation of political information, values, and practices, whether formally or informally, in planned or unplanned fashion.[2] When Castro said that all revolution is an extraordinary process of education, he was saying that in a relatively short time Cubans must learn an almost totally new set of political values and practices.

The Cuban elite, of course, is not alone in giving "the making of citizens" a high priority.[3] As students of politics have been pointing out at least since the time of Plato, all viable political systems develop procedures for creating the types of citizens thought necessary for their survival and growth. In various political systems, many different kinds of institutions play a part in citizenship training, among them the family, the church, the mass media, schools, peer groups, youth organizations, religious and social clubs, and political parties. Thus at the highest level of abstraction Cuba's efforts at political socialization are comparable to those of such remote societies as Periclean Athens and Tudor England. A much more directly relevant comparison, however, would be with other contemporary modernizing nations.

As indicated above, the overriding theme of the Cuban Revolution is change. Its leaders seek a new society, one organized from the ground up on principles different from and often diametrically opposed to those of the preceding regime. One need not concede either the morality or the workability of the new order to admit that the social, economic, and political bases of Cuban life have been fundamentally transformed. The pre-Castro system of land ownership is gone; private enterprise has been destroyed; education has been nationalized and restructured; the politics of Batista have given way to the politics of Castro and the Cuban Communist Party; dependence on the United States has been replaced by a special relationship with the Socialist countries; more than 5 percent of the population—including many of the most highly skilled—have fled; and the pre-Castro system of status and economic rewards has been almost completely replaced. Perhaps the only major holdover from the old order has been Cuba's economic dependence on sugar, a dependence that the regime tried unsuccessfully to break in the early 1960's.

Few nations have ever undergone such massive transformations in so short a time. Certainly no non-Communist system has been changed at such a pace. Thus neither the specific transformations wrought in Cuba nor the rate at which they have been pressed upon the populace could be called representative of developmental or even radical political practice in the postwar world. Rather, the key likeness to be found when comparing Cuba with other developmental or revolutionary systems is in the philosophy of politics and social change that motivates the leaders. Simply stated, the

Cuban leaders believe, or act as if they believe, the following argument. (1) The social, economic, and political institutions inherited from the old regime are fundamentally unjust, immoral in practice, and unequal to the tasks of national development. (2) It falls upon the leadership to seize the instrumentalities of power, define the content of the new order, and then use the full resources of the state to bring the new order into being. (3) It falls upon the masses to follow the dictates of the leaders, to participate fully in the building of the new order (which is, after all, for them), and to endure willingly the many sacrifices that must be made during the period of national reconstruction.

This argument, it will be recognized, is congenial, if not fundamental, to Leninist politics. But, as the history of the last two decades attests, it also enjoys much wider appeal. It was operative in Cuba under Castro before he publicly proclaimed himself a Marxist-Leninist, and certainly any number of indigenous non-Communist leaders in ex-colonial areas would embrace its basic tenets. The argument is elitist in spirit and populist in rhetoric; the new order is to be statist in organization and authoritarian in practice. None of these characteristics is exclusively Leninist.

The Transformation of Political Culture

Programs of political socialization in systems where the leadership follows this philosophy of social change exhibit certain similarities. Above all, there is inevitably a great deal of planning and a great deal of state control. Because the elite is committed to the destruction of the institutional framework of the old order, a frontal attack is made on the beliefs, values, symbols, and kinds of behavior thought to sustain it. Similarly, because the official version of the new order stresses progress, harmony, and obedience, attempts are made to inculcate patterns of belief, evaluation, and behavior that will contribute to these goals. In extreme cases, what is sought is nothing less than the directed destruction of the old political culture and the creation of a new one.*

* The second half of this chapter offers a partial specification of what the Cuban leaders have rejected in the old culture and what they seek in the new. Much more detail is woven into Chapters 3–5.

It is important to get a clear picture of what is meant here by the concept of political culture. One widely used definition runs as follows: "The political culture of a society consists of the system of empirical beliefs, expressive symbols, and values which defines the situation in which political action takes place. It provides the subjective orientation to politics."[4] Political culture so viewed is an aggregate or patterning of individual "states of mind." By design, the definition excludes other elements of "the common, learned way of [political] life" so central to many anthropological formulations of the concept of culture.[5] More specifically, it purposely excludes recurring patterns of manifest political behavior, treating these as consequences or outcomes partially determined by the political culture but not analytically a part of it. Thus the fact that large numbers of citizens in country X habitually cheat on their income tax returns is not, according to the definition, part of the political culture of X.[6] The beliefs, symbols, and values that lead citizens to behave in this fashion, that make such behavior legitimate or possible, are part of the cultural package; but the behavior itself is not. Psychological variables are used to explain recurring patterns of political behavior and the operation of political institutions, but the patterns themselves are not considered part of the system of political culture.[7]

This definition is useful in investigating and explaining how and why certain political institutions function or fail to function in specific national settings. It is much less useful, however, when the focus of inquiry is on the directed transformation of the institutions themselves. Anthropologists interested in planned change do not limit their definition of culture to psychological variables; they include patterned ways of life and action as well as the states of mind that sustain and condition these patterns. Similarly, those interested in directed political change would cast their net too narrowly by excluding patterns of manifest political behavior from their definition of political culture. When the Cuban elite engages in planned political change, it is attempting (in ways that will be explained below) to transform both the cognitive and the overt behavior of Cuba's citizens. The old political system was a "way of life" or cultural system in the anthropological sense; what the elite seeks to put in its place is also a way of life, a new interlocking system of political values and behaviors, a new political culture.[8]

The necessity in the Cuban case (and in others like it) of freeing the definition of political culture from exclusive reliance on psychological variables can be appreciated if we return for a moment to the notion of political socialization, i.e. the processes by which political information, values, and practices are inculcated in the population. These, of course, are learning processes, and the definition underlines the fact that not only information and evaluations are learned, but new practices and new ways of behaving. The outcomes of political socialization are not viewed as confined to certain ways of thinking and feeling about politics; rather, they include certain ways of behaving or failing to behave. In the Cuban case, as in many others, to view planned political socialization activities solely within a psychological frame of reference is to see the efforts of the regime as a mixture of informational and exhortative communication, a kind of political advertising. These elements are present, but they certainly do not capture either the essential content or the primary purpose of political socialization in Cuba.[9]

Thus the Cuban elite has not in the main been interested in socializing citizens to preexisting values and ways of behaving. Rather, the socialization process has been directed toward an attempt to create new values and behaviors in the context of new political settings. Political socialization under the Revolutionary Government has not been used primarily for settling citizens into the ongoing system. It has been a directed learning process through which the elite seeks to create a new political culture. As we shall see, the process is very different from socialization in more settled and well-institutionalized systems, whatever their political coloration. In Cuba there has been a planned attack on the cultural fabric itself.[10]

Participation, New Institutions, and Political Socialization

In the case studies that make up the bulk of this book we shall be concerned with strategies and processes of political socialization and cultural change as manifested in three institutional settings.

In all three settings, great emphasis was or is placed on participation as both motive and motor of the revolutionary effort. Since this same emphasis is found in almost all institutions generated by the revolution, a few preliminary remarks on the relationship between participation and political socialization may be in order.* The first point to be made is that a primary aim of political socialization in Cuba is to produce a participating citizen, not just one who can recite the revolutionary catechism perfectly. The test of the new Cuban man is how he behaves—whether or not he works, fights, studies, cooperates, sacrifices, and contributes in the prescribed manner. Of course he should think "right thoughts," but such thoughts are at best a necessary, never a sufficient, condition for revolutionary militancy.

Viewed only in this manner, political socialization might be thought of as simply a prelude to political participation. This unilinear view of the process, however, does not do justice to the complexity of the Cuban case. In both theory and practice, participation is viewed as organically related to socialization. As we shall see again and again in the case studies, the regime seeks to forge the new political culture in the crucible of action. In the mass organizations, the armed forces, the Party, and the schools, great emphasis is placed on the creative, corrective, and salutary effects of immersion in revolutionary activity. With the exception of the Party, one need not be "pure" in order to join; it is precisely through participation that cultural change and individual purification take place. Revolutionary institutions are both the training ground and the testing ground for the participatory citizen.

The relationship between participation and political socialization is clarified by emphasizing three reasons why high levels of directed participation are found in developing systems organized

* In this initial discussion of participation, new institutions, and political socialization, no special attention is paid to the central problem of training enough cadres to staff the new institutions and act as "bearers" of the new political culture to the masses. As the case studies make abundantly clear, however, the revolutionary strategy of cultural transformation gives high priority to the shaping of cadres who in thought, word, and deed will serve as "first generation" examples of revolutionary man.

predominantly—but not exclusively—on Leninist principles. Levels of participation in such systems cannot be explained entirely in terms of the need to form new citizens. Other arguments not always articulated by the elites but almost always a factor in their thinking help us to understand the high value that is placed on participation. The first we can call the self-protection argument, the second the mobilization argument, and the third the culture and personality change argument.* Only the third is fundamentally and directly related to political socialization.[11]

The self-protection argument is based on the elite's realization that radical social change imposed on the masses may generate sufficient discontent to endanger both the planners and the movement. Only by directed participation can this tendency be controlled. Lipset has stated the case well:

> As a general hypothesis, one might suggest that the greater the changes in the structure of society that a governing group is attempting to introduce, . . . the more likely the leadership is to desire or even to require a high degree of participation in various groups by citizens or members. The radical changes that accompany social revolution . . . put severe strains on group loyalties and create a potential for strong membership hostility toward the leadership. A high level of controlled and manipulated rank-and-file participation is perhaps the only way, given the leadership's purpose, of draining off or redirecting the discontent created by violent changes in traditional patterns and relationships.[12]

This mechanism seems to have been relatively unimportant in Cuba during the first years of the revolution. The high legitimacy of the Castro government, the draining off of discontent by the exodus of tens of thousands of exiles, and the rapid and marked improvement in life-style for large sectors of the population were more important than controlled participation was in minimizing the danger of a counter-dynamic.[13]

* I have called these "arguments" because the purposes served by structured participation are at least implicitly recognized and sometimes openly articulated by the Cuban elite. With slight modifications in language and emphasis, these arguments could be restated more formally as middle-range hypotheses—free of references to the Cuban experience—as in fact Lipset has done in the first case.

The mobilization argument is in one sense the obverse of the self-protection argument. Self-protection is negative, a matter of keeping potentially mischievous hands out of trouble; mobilization, by contrast, is overwhelmingly positive, a matter of enlisting potentially supportive hands in the service of national goals. Much of the organized activity since the revolution has been of this kind, activity designed to support the regime and its leaders on the one hand, and specific political and economic programs on the other. This is akin to what Nettl calls "stalactite mobilization": it originates at the top of the political structure and moves downward organizationally.[14]

Mobilization as used here means "getting out the troops" to do whatever the leadership feels needs to be done. It involves participation in support of the revolutionary effort, including, of course, protection of the revolution from its enemies. By attendance at schools and membership in mass organizations, the armed forces, and the Party, most Cubans at least nominally participate in the revolutionary system. Mobilization involves turning this membership into effective support for the regime and its programs. As distinct from the culture and personality change argument, mobilization does not depend on the prior internalization by the citizenry of the new norms and values sponsored by the political elite. Skilled leadership, the restructuring of opportunities, social and political pressures, and various types of rewards, incentives, encouragements, deprivations, and punishments are the ingredients of successful mobilization campaigns.

The culture and personality change argument is based on the elite's awareness that the relationship between change of attitude and change of behavior is very complex. The Cuban position can be stated as follows. Limited changes in behavior can be accomplished by fiat: for instance, all men of a certain age must register for military service. More extensive changes in behavior, those most crucial to the revolutionary movement, are less easily ordered. For example, voluntary labor during weekends and leisure time can only partially be legislated and policed on a national scale.

Success depends on people "wanting" to volunteer, and it is the "wanting" that becomes the object of the elite's attention and manipulation. Other important changes in attitude seem at first to have no direct behavioral component, for example hatred of capitalism and love of socialism. In such cases the behavioral payoff is diffuse—expressed through enthusiasm and loyal support for revolutionary programs. Attitudes, values, and beliefs leading to both extensive and diffuse behavioral change are best shaped by participation in those revolutionary institutions where direction, social suggestion, and peer group pressures are greatest. Furthermore, in revolutionary institutions where participation in a wide range of activities is encouraged, behavior is frequently modified even when there is no initial change in attitude. Such behavioral changes may lead in turn to new ways of perceiving and evaluating the world, and thus a permanent nexus for relating the two types of change is established. In short, participatory activity—not in itself dependent on the internalization of new norms—may eventually lead to very basic changes in the value and belief systems of those who are swept into participation. In this manner, easy formulas such as "attitudes shape behavior" or "behavior shapes attitudes" give way to a system that is organized to sustain a dynamic relation between behavioral change and attitudinal change.[15]

Thus, revolutionary institutions exist not only to form citizens for the new Cuba, but also to encourage and facilitate participation in revolutionary activities. It is expected that almost all such activities will contribute, in the long run, to the characterological transformation of those who are drawn into them. Training in revolutionary participation on the one hand and opportunities for continued participation on the other are built into such institutions, which are themselves both new and changing. The case studies, therefore, although they focus on mobilization, political socialization, and cultural change, must of necessity also be studies of the design, operation, and transformation of the institutional and participatory life of the revolution. In Cuba, the study of directed change in political culture cannot be isolated from the study of citizen participation and institutional change.

Ideology, Symbols, and the New Man

If we seek to discover the Cuban elite's vision of the new order, we encounter what seems at first to be a great deal of contradictory rhetoric and behavior. In Castro's speeches there is grist for many mills, and the first years of the revolution were certainly characterized by rapid shifts in policies, personnel, tactics, alliances, and expressed goals.[16] Some admirers of the Cuban style profess to see in this turbulence the organic growth and maturation of the movement, the victory of the "true" revolution over the forces originally impeding and qualifying it. But such explanations ignore the leadership's tendency toward pragmatism, and experimentation. The turbulence and the contradictions are there, both in rhetoric and in action, and no amount of post-facto analysis can erase them.

This does not mean, however, that the revolution has had no continuity in thought or in programs. There has been considerable consistency through time, particularly in the core of symbols around which the motivating vision of the new order has been organized and in the socialization practices instituted to bring this new order into being. In the remainder of this chapter we shall concentrate on this vision of the new order and the new Cuban man who, it is hoped, will be its architect, its bearer, and its beneficiary.

At the core of the ideology of the Cuban Revolution lie two intertwining themes: the theme of *lucha,* or struggle, and the theme of utopia, or the millennium.[17] Struggle has been central to the revolutionary rhetoric since Castro first took up arms against Batista. The summons to struggle directs attention to larger and continuing problems as well as to concrete and immediate difficulties. Over the last decade, the Cuban people have been called upon to struggle against colonialism, neocolonialism, imperialism, counterrevolution, bureaucratism, sectarianism, discrimination, illiteracy, absenteeism, low productivity, and much, much more. Although the tactics and targets change, the lucha itself, with its emphasis on personal and collective sacrifice, never ceases.

The millennial vision provides the necessary counterpoint to the theme of struggle.[18] The persons, conditions, problems, and attitudes that Cubans are called on to struggle against are precisely the factors that impede the coming of the political kingdom (and therefore the coming of the social and economic kingdoms). The millennial vision justifies the hardships of the moment, for the political kingdom is not easily won; many must suffer and some must die before the promised land is reached. By holding up a gilded image of the future, the leadership seeks to give universality and a spiritual quality to affairs of the workaday world. "These are no ordinary times," is the message. The joy of belonging to the movement, the joy of being righteous in action, and ultimately the joy of victory are within the reach of all who are willing to struggle now to bring closer tomorrow's utopian order.

This utopian order is characterized, in part, as the antithesis of the old. In the beginning, negative images—especially of the United States—loomed very large in the new utopian vision. The new Cuba, child of the revolution, was to be the antithesis of the old Cuba, bastard child of the United States. The old economy had been dominated by foreign corporations; thus the new economy would have no place for corporate investment. Politics under Batista had been corrupt, class-based, and influenced by the United States; thus politics under Castro would be incorruptible, mass-oriented, and influenced only by Cubans. In the old regime the rural sectors had had fewest opportunities and benefits; thus in the new regime they would be given every possible opportunity and benefit—including many not available to city dwellers.

This macro-vision of the new society as it evolved in the first few years of the Cuban Revolution had two shortcomings: what it rejected was clearer than what it aspired to, and it lacked an articulated program for moving from the present toward the future. By no means have the Cubans yet worked out an ideological system that is elegant or complete, but they have been steadily developing an image of the new society and ideas about how that society is to be realized. Almost from the beginning the key mechanism of change has been seen not in this or that specific institution, policy, or program, but rather in the fundamental transformation of the sociopolitical character of the Cuban citizen; without such transformation at the individual level, there would be no utopian collectivity. During the 1960's the formation of a "new Cuban man" became so central to revolutionary rhetoric and action programs as to constitute the ideological and operational mainspring of the revolution. In the Cuban view, getting from the past through the present to the idealized future depends on the formation of a new modal personality.[19] No one has stated this view more frequently and forcefully than Castro:

> It is not a man of the jungle that we want to develop; a man of the jungle cannot be of any benefit to human society. It is not that self-centered, savage mentality that can in any sense benefit human society. The more human society fights against those self-centered, savage, and anti-social attitudes, the closer it will come to embodying a way of life that is ideal and good for all.
>
> And the old society fostered exactly those sentiments, exactly those attitudes. And if today there are still many who have those attitudes, unquestionably it is because of that heritage. . . .
>
> We want the coming generations to receive the heritage of a very different attitude toward life, to receive the heritage of an education and a formation that is totally devoid of selfish sentiments, that is totally devoid of the sentiments appropriate to a man of the jungle.[20]

> We cannot encourage or even permit selfish attitudes among men if we don't want man to be guided by the instinct of selfishness, . . . by the wolf instinct, the beast instinct. . . . The concept of Socialism and Communism, the concept of a higher society, implies a man devoid of those feelings, a man who has overcome such instincts at any cost, placing above everything his sense of solidarity and brotherhood among men. . . . If we fail because we believe in man's ability, in his ability to improve, then we shall fail, but we shall never renounce our faith in mankind![21]

It is worth stressing that although the new man thesis was not formally articulated until after the Revolutionary Government had been in power for a number of years, the operation of the revolutionary system has almost from the outset depended on such a model of change. Long before the debate about how to motivate men introduced frequent discussions of the new man into the public rhetoric, revolutionary institutions were consciously being turned to the task of shaping new patterns of motivation and behavior. In Cuba there is usually a considerable time lapse before

the language of the revolution is brought into line with its operative characteristics as inferred from patterns of action and institutional change. As we shall see again and again in the case studies, the Cubans were acting like Leninists long before they knew it.[22]

Focusing on the individual rather than the collectivity has certain advantages for the regime. Action programs flow more naturally from a vision of radical reconstruction that has as the immediate object of change the individual rather than the entire social order. The good citizen is defined as one who engages in activities X, Y, and Z, who struggles to raise production, who studies in his spare time, who is responsive to calls from the authorities. Such definitions of the good citizen, rooted as they are in behavior, are clearly easier to formulate than definitions of the good society; and certainly they provide a more immediate and flexible guide to action. As the case studies will demonstrate, the specific content of revolutionary behavior has been defined in various ways depending on the institutional setting in which it is supposed to take place. Nevertheless, there are important constants like cooperation, egalitarianism, sacrifice, service, hard work, self-improvement, obedience, and incorruptibility—qualities both general enough to be tied together in a single ideological package and specific enough to be translated into meaningful prescriptions for behavior.* Neither millennial visions nor patriotic slogans transform virgin land into plowed fields or cane into refined sugar. But when, as in the Cuban case, the visions and the slogans can be applied directly to the work at hand, they do constitute a potential resource that should not be underestimated.

Two final points should be made. The first deals with the politicization of Cuban definitions of participation and the new man, the second with what might be called the salvageability of prerevolutionary man. As many authors have noted, it is a common

* In the Cuban case this particular catalogue of virtues is not so much Marxist as it is anti–Latin American middle class. It is in part a reaction against traditional Latin American urban culture, and thus has much of a Cuban version of the "frontier" ethic woven in. For elaboration and some case material on the Cuban use of the rural areas as a forge on which to hammer out new cultural patterns, see Appendix A, "The Cuban Countryside, Spring 1968," pp. 169–79 below.

characteristic of radical regimes to break down the boundaries between different domains of behavior by politicizing as many of them as possible.[23] For instance, economic behavior is seen by the revolutionaries as critical to the performance of the political system—not just in the functional sense (i.e., in the sense that economic disaster spells political disaster), but in the ideological sense (i.e., in the sense that microeconomic behavior is viewed as a form of political behavior). Thus, to underproduce or waste materials is not just uneconomic in the Cuban system; it is unpatriotic and counterrevolutionary. Similarly, almost all participation in revolutionary institutions—whether they be schools, bureaucracies, or citizens' groups—is considered to be fundamentally political. It follows that the new man is, above all, a new citizen. His primary role is that of participant in the transformation of the social order; he must be a new *political* man. Thus, because the lines between what is political and what is not are blurred, the examination of processes of political socialization must become in some measure the examination of attempts to form a new social character, and the study of the transformation of political culture must become in large part the study of the transformation of the entire social order.

The salvageability of pre-revolutionary man is in part a resocialization issue.* Because, as Castro has underlined, the revolutionaries view man as perfectible and see improper behavior as deriving from corrupt institutional settings and social milieus, environmental reform brings with it the possibility of significant changes in adult behavior.[24] Thus considerable energy, attention, and resources have been directed toward Cubans of all ages and social statuses in the general belief that almost no one living in the new environment is without all hope of becoming a revolutionary, or at least useful to the revolution. This doctrine in no way contradicts the youth-orientation of the regime, its emphasis on the children of the revolution as the prime movers and beneficiaries of the new society. Although perhaps only the young—untouched and

* Salvageability as used here refers to redirection and resocialization sufficient to turn the individual into a useful and loyal citizen. It does not imply a profound "conversion" of social character as a concomitant of revolutionary participation.

therefore unsoiled by the old order—may eventually prove capable of becoming "true Communists," the long transitional period of struggle and sacrifice is seen as providing ample opportunity for re-socializing Cubans of all backgrounds and gradations of militancy. Resocialization through participation is thus an element in the overall strategy of cultural transformation. Perfection is not demanded; there is ample work for all who have been sufficiently reoriented and who wish to be considered revolutionaries.

In summary, five main themes have been developed in this chapter:

(1) The transformation of Cuban man into revolutionary man is one of the primary goals of the revolutionary leadership. Both the radicalism and the continuity of the revolution are best understood as deriving from this commitment.

(2) On a national scale, these attempted individual transformations add up to a policy of directed transformation of the political culture of Cuba. Political culture is here understood to include patterns of action as well as states of mind; additionally, the revolutionary movement itself has politicized and thus made relevant to our inquiry previously nonpolitical domains of action.

(3) The primary mechanism for effecting individual and cultural transformation is directed participation in revolutionary institutions. These institutions serve both as instruments for facilitating social change and as testing grounds for changes thought to have already been accomplished.

(4) Not all the participatory activity directed by the revolutionary leadership has as its primary purpose the transformation of social character and political culture. Much of it is more narrowly practical, the mobilizing of citizens' energies to perform specific developmental tasks. It is thought, however, that social character is shaped in a multitude of ways through participatory activity even when cultural transformation is not its primary goal.

(5) The Cuban effort is embedded in and draws meaning from a symbol system in which images of struggle and utopia loom large. By means of the evolving ideology of "the new man" and the part he plays and will play in the transformation of society, the mun-

dane, day-to-day world is linked with visions that are more global, abstract, and lasting.

As has been suggested throughout, these themes—thought of as ways of approaching and understanding the revolution—have not been imposed on the events as extraneous analytical categories. The Cuban leaders themselves view the revolutionary experience as a culture-transforming process, and at times they have been impressively articulate in tying together the several thematic threads listed above. On the sixth anniversary of the founding of the Committees for Defense of the Revolution, for example, the following passage appeared in an editorial in *Granma*, the official newspaper:[24]

> The revolution has advanced in the most extraordinary and diverse ways. All the steps to date, no matter at what moment or in what sector they have taken place, have aided . . . in the fundamental task: the formation of the new man, a man with a profound consciousness of his role in society and of his duties and social responsibilities, a man capable of constructing Communism and living with it.
>
> The construction of Communism demands, as its fundamental element, the struggle for the formation of the new man; and it will not terminate until this job has been completed. All the political, economic, and social tasks entrusted to our mass organizations have to be inspired by this principle.
>
> The struggle to make spiritual and social sentiments predominate over narrow, limited, and individual feelings ought to be at the center of our effort to forge the new man. This battle is acquiring decisive importance in our country.
>
> We see the new man as arising from the huge educational programs that the revolution has started, from the troops that protect our Fatherland against the threats and aggressions of the imperialist enemy, from the heroes of the fight against the counterrevolutionary bandits, from the permanent voluntary laborers, from the women who march off to agriculture, from the efforts undertaken by the labor movement and the Union of Young Communists to incorporate thousands of workers into agricultural jobs. The new man is the one who is truly indignant over the imperialist aggression in Vietnam, and who is ready to swell the ranks of those fighting men who are being cut down in the jungles of that heroic country, in order that it may achieve full and lasting liberation. We see the new man producing in our factories and working in our fields. We see him in the schoolrooms studying and becoming interested in technology, science, and production. We see him in the trenches of our Revolutionary Armed Forces.
>
> This conception obliges the revolution to develop plans involving increased participation by the masses in the execution of diverse tasks. On

the road to Communism, the masses will daily have to increase their participation in societal tasks, paying more attention to the management and direction of these activities.[25]

One need not be receptive to either the polemical or the self-congratulatory aspects of this editorial to appreciate that it strikes very close to our own understanding of what the revolution is all about. The Cuban Revolution involves a massive attempt by the political elite to forge a new social order by forming and reforming men who will worship new images, behave in new ways, and relate to one another in the context of new institutions. Although we cannot yet fully appraise the successes and failures of this experiment, both its audacity and its scope command our attention.

2 The Setting: Some Cautions

TREMULOUS critics and enthusiastic supporters of the Castro regime have at least one thing in common: both see the Cuban Revolution as a model for other Latin American nations seeking to throw off the shackles of backwardness and political dependence. The critics, in their fearfulness, see Castroism as sweeping like brush fire through countries in which a majority of the people lack social justice, opportunities for political participation, and adequate life chances. The supporters, in their enthusiasm, argue that once the masses of these countries understand their own real interests they will heed the call of radical leaders and rise up in armed struggle against the authorities who now oppress them.

The two arguments are badly flawed, even when elaborated in more sophisticated fashion. Both misinterpret the nature of the Cuban experience, overestimate its transfer value, underestimate the stability of Latin American socioeconomic forms, and grossly oversimplify processes of political transformation. This is not to say that we shall see no more attempts at social revolution in Latin America. There were at least two important examples before the Cuban—the Mexican and the Bolivian—and there will be others. Nor is it to say that future movements will not be influenced by the Cuban example. The centuries-old tradition of revolutionary change has been enriched by the Cubans, just as it has been enriched by the French, the Mexicans, the Russians, and the Chinese. But there is no a priori reason to believe that future movements will be triggered by or directly modeled after the Cuban experience. This is particularly apparent when we focus on how the Revolutionary Government has behaved since actually taking power. When examined closely, the revolution in power is too specifically Cuban to serve in detail as an operative blueprint for other movements, either in this hemisphere or abroad. It is this Cubanness that we now wish to examine.

The uniqueness of the Cuban Revolution derives from a set of conditioning factors that serve as a background for the more generic drama of mobilization and cultural change as discussed in Chapter 1. The larger drama, of course, has occurred and will reoccur in other nations. But because the conditioning factors in each case constitute a highly individualized setting, no revolution unfolds as a repeat performance of any other. This is particularly true of the Cuban Revolution, which is not only the most radical historical experiment in the hemisphere but also fundamentally different from what at first glance might seem to be its African and Asian counterparts.

The special characteristics that have shaped the Cuban experience can be grouped under four headings: sociocultural integration, socioeconomic development and potential, leadership characteristics, and particularities of the interaction of Cuban history and world politics. In the following analysis no effort is made to explain why the Cuban Revolution occurred in the first place or why it took such radical form once in power. Our narrower interest is in the cumulative impact on mobilization politics and cultural change of certain features of Cuban society, Cuba's revolutionary leadership, and the world environment. For analytical purposes, we take the revolution and its radicalism as givens and seek to understand the factors that have conditioned the growth and operation of revolutionary institutions *a la Cubana.*

Sociocultural Integration

By almost any comparative standards, Cuba in the middle of the twentieth century was a reasonably homogeneous society. There were, of course, problems of national integration, but they did not approach in magnitude the typical problems of Asian, African, or many Latin American states. Cuba was not rent by what Clifford Geertz has called the "primordial attachments" of language, tribe, race, and geographical separatism that so often condition the politics of development in other nations.[1] In fact, Cuba had no sociocultural cleavages important enough to be considered first-order obstacles to development.

Living on an island without great climatological extremes, with no insurmountable geographical barriers, and with no overpopulation problem on the horizon, the more than seven million Cubans present a striking contrast to countries like Indonesia, or for that matter Mexico. Moreover, in pre-Castro Cuba there was no important history of boundary disputes or geographically based political factionalism, no challenge to the dominance of the Spanish language, and no undigested or semi-digested indigenous population. Again, contrasts with countries like Nigeria, India, and Bolivia are illuminating.

From the outsider's point of view, the most salient sociocultural problem in pre-Castro Cuba might seem to have been racial relations. Members of the sizable Negro minority were everywhere in evidence. Although the 1953 census classified 12.4 percent of the population as Black and 14.5 percent as of mixed race, as many observers of the Cuban scene have pointed out, the census figures underestimated both the cultural and the physical presence of the Negro.[2] African art forms, vocabulary, and blood were diffused through the society to a much greater degree than census statistics indicated. Moreover, because racial relations were of the Latin rather than the Anglo-Saxon variety, mulattoes—like Batista—could be found in top political and upper-middle economic positions, if not in the front ranks of high society.* There was, however, widespread social and economic discrimination based on custom and personal prejudice, and the man of dark skin was in general greatly disadvantaged in pre-revolutionary Cuba. But this racial

* The differences between the Anglo-Saxon and Hispanic varieties of racial relations, and the roots of these differences in the respective systems of slavery, are well explored in Herbert S. Klein, *Slavery in the Americas: A Comparative Study of Cuba and Virginia* (Chicago, 1967).

cleavage was not so complete as to constitute an enduring impediment to mobilization and cultural transformation after Castro came to power. Quite to the contrary, although the legacies of Negro cultural deprivation linger on, the most serious manifestations of discrimination—social exclusion plus lack of equal educational and economic opportunities—were terminated by revolutionary fiat. Whatever undercurrents of personal prejudice remain do not find expression in institutionalized discrimination. Thus the racial problem in Cuba was, if anything, a boon to Castro: the revolutionaries found it extremely useful for discrediting the old social order, and with the "instant liberation" of the Negro tens of thousands of previously disadvantaged Cubans were recruited into the ranks of revolutionary enthusiasts.

In sum, when Castro came to power, Cuba was among the most culturally homogeneous nations in Latin America, Asia, or Africa. As we shall see in the next section, Cuba had its share of social and economic problems, but it was not a fragmented or agglomerate nation. Elite efforts encountered no obdurate tribal minorities, no separatist territorial factions, no language enclaves, no paralyzing racial problems, and no premodern Indian communities. In fact, Batista's Cuba exhibited a greater degree of national integration than did Mexico after fifty years of "integrative revolution." Such was the sociocultural legacy inherited by Castro, and in evaluating the revolutionary system in Cuba it is necessary to keep this legacy in mind.

Socioeconomic Development and Potential

As Theodore Draper and others have shown, Cuba in the 1950's was far from underdeveloped when compared with much of the rest of the world.[3] No major Asian or African nation except Japan enjoyed such an impressive socioeconomic profile; and in Latin America, only Argentina, Chile, Uruguay, and occasionally Venezuela topped Cuba on most indicators. Table 1 shows Cuba's socioeconomic rank relative to other Latin American countries at approximately the time Castro came to power. For additional comparisons, the final column lists European nations ranking close to but below Cuba on the various indexes.

TABLE 1. CUBA IN SOCIOECONOMIC PERSPECTIVE

Index	Rank in Latin America	Comparable European nation
Gross national product per capita	4th (1957)	Rumania
Commercial energy consumption per capita	6th (1955)	Yugoslavia
Percentage of population literate	5th (1950's)	Yugoslavia
Daily newspaper circulation per 1,000 population	4th (1960)	Italy
Radios per 1,000 population	2nd (1960)	Italy
Television sets per 1,000 population	1st (1961)	France
Students in higher education per 1,000 population	7th (1960)	Norway
Physicians per 1,000 population	3rd (1960)	Sweden

Note: Data on gross national product, literacy, newspaper circulation, radios, television, higher education, and physicians are from Bruce M. Russett et al., *World Handbook of Political and Social Indicators* (New Haven, Conn., 1964), tables 44, 64, 31, 35, 37, 62, and 59, respectively. Data on commercial energy consumption are from Norton Ginsburg, *Atlas of Economic Development* (Chicago, 1961), p. 82. For more detail about Cuba in the context of other Latin American countries, see Roger Vekemans and J. L. Segundo, "Essay of a Socio-Economic Typology of the Latin American Countries," in Egbert de Vries and José Medina Echavarría, eds., *Social Aspects of Economic Development in Latin America*, I (Paris: UNESCO, 1963). A wealth of data on Cuban socioeconomic development before Castro can be found in José R. Álvarez Díaz et al., *Un Estudio Sobre Cuba* (Miami, 1963), esp. pp. 781–1277.

Aggregate statistics do not, of course, tell the whole story. Despite the comforting averages and national comparisons, Cuba was characterized by vast inequalities in the distribution of goods, services, and opportunities. True, there was one doctor for every 1,000 inhabitants, a ratio that approached the one doctor for every 760 inhabitants in the United States. True, there were 72 television sets for every 1,000 inhabitants, far more than France's 57. But where *were* the doctors and the television sets, or for that matter the schools, the decent housing, and the well-paying jobs? In Havana, of course, and in a few other large urban centers. The countryside, the *campo*, presented a far less attractive picture: illiteracy, poverty, poor health, and seasonal unemployment were widespread. There were few schools, fewer clinics, bad roads, impure water, and little or no electricity.[4] If not underdeveloped in the overall sense, Cuba was unevenly and inharmoniously developed in the manner characteristic of many other Latin American nations.

Other characteristics of the pre-Castro economy that help to explain Cuba's uneven development are equally well known and well documented. First, the country's substantial resource base was only partially exploited and was frequently under foreign control. Second, Cuba's economy was largely dependent on sugar, and hence was subject to the vagaries of weather and to fluctuations in international prices; moreover, production was concentrated on large plantations using some modern technology and employing a seasonal work force that was underemployed or unemployed for the rest of the year. Third, public utilities were dominated by North American concerns, and American money was important (though not predominant) in railways, sugar, and banking. Fourth, the well-developed urban labor movement, though partially captive and corrupt, assured its strongly organized segments many work benefits and levels of real income that were not enjoyed by rural workers. And, fifth, government intervention in the economy was sporadic, often contaminated by favoritism, and too unplanned and unregulated to cope with the existing problems in agriculture, industry, and trade.[5]

Statistics on the Cuban economy, its social consequences, and its potential are typically used in one of two ways. Opponents of the Castro regime fasten on the aggregate and hemispheric data to bolster their claim that since Cuba was already quite well developed it did not "need" a revolution, or at least not so radical a revolution as Castro's. The revolutionaries, on the other hand, never tire of pointing to the sharp contrasts on the island itself and to the disparities between the Cuba of Batista and the Cuba that "might have been." The coexistence of impressive resources and extensive poverty, of modern cities and rural underdevelopment, has been used from the beginning by the revolutionaries to give bite to their charge that Cuba was "a rich land inhabited by impoverished people."[6]

The statistics, however, can also be used in a third way, less dramatic but ultimately more useful for analysis. Despite disagreement about particulars, three general characteristics of pre-Castro socioeconomic conditions can be agreed on. First, in the urban industrial base, in the economic infrastructure of transportation and communication, and in the manpower pool there could be found many of the human and material resources necessary for a developmental effort of national scope. Second, socioeconomic conditions were severe enough to both trigger and justify such a national effort. Third, the depressed sectors of the society were not sufficiently isolated, either geographically or culturally, from the more advanced sectors to render such an effort impossible. To cite only one example, Mintz notes that "A very substantial part of the Cuban rural labor force was a proletariat, but a rural proletariat: landless, propertyless, wage-earning, and store-buying."[7] Clearly, this rural proletariat, though poor, was already partly "modern" and therefore more available to the planners than an isolated or indigenous subsistence farming peasantry would have been.

Thus, after taking power, the urban-based revolutionaries declared war on conditions in the countryside and on socioeconomic backwardness in general. They controlled enough men, materials, and political support to initiate such a war, and they faced enemies —hunger, disease, illiteracy—real enough and evil enough to make their efforts both self-explanatory and popular. In some ways these efforts may have been strategically and tactically mismanaged, organizationally inept, economically wasteful, and ideologically perverse. In the larger context of Cuban socioeconomic development, however, the decision to declare war was neither unrealistic nor rash. On the contrary, economic and moral criteria argued that the effort could and should be made. The question was, how and by whom? Castro and his lieutenants supplied the will and the plan, but many of the resources and almost all of the problems were a legacy from Batista and his predecessors.[8]

The Castro regime fell heir to socioeconomic problems real enough to anger the egalitarians, challenge the technocrats, and mobilize the citizens. The regime also fell heir to socioeconomic resources substantial enough to inspire real hope of massive accomplishments within one generation. The reformer's pledge, "Our children shall live better than we," had a meaning in Cuba that it could not possibly have in Guinea or Burma or even Guatemala. And the same resource base that gave credibility to open-ended radical promises lent support to specific revolutionary programs. For instance, a massive campaign to eradicate illiteracy and educate citizens in a country already enjoying 75 percent literacy and a highly developed mass media system had a ring of realism about it that is lacking in similar campaigns undertaken in nations still predominantly illiterate and preindustrial.

Leadership Characteristics

For better or for worse, the Cuban Revolution bears the indelible imprint of one man—Fidel Castro. This does not make the last decade of Cuba's history any easier to understand, for Castro himself defies easy interpretation.[9] He is extremely intelligent, energetic, proud, an astute politician, and a gifted orator. He is also the bane of conventional economists, both socialist and non-socialist. He appears to be uninterested in personal material gain and intolerant of self-indulgence in others; yet he is relentless in his pursuit of political power. Though hardly consistent over the years in some of his policies and public pronouncements, he has been extremely consistent in asserting his dominance over the shifting revolutionary power structure. Soon after taking power he moved with vigor and skill against dissidents within his own organization, and later he challenged and defeated the old-line Cuban Communists when they tried to usurp control of his new Marxist-Leninist coalition. And he has certainly not proved an easy man for other world leaders, either Soviet or American, to manage.

With respect to mobilization and cultural transformation efforts in Cuba, Castro's most important characteristic is his charisma. Strictly speaking, this is a characteristic not of the man himself, but rather of his relationship with the Cuban masses.[10] As Weber observed, charisma involves much more than popularity; the charismatic leader is perceived by his followers as endowed with exceptional or even superhuman qualities, and he perceives himself as the instrument of a higher destiny. Castro has been just such a leader. Although time and the exigencies of rule have undoubtedly eroded his charisma to some extent, he still commands an impressive and devoted following. The call to associate oneself with

Fidel and through him with the miracle of the *Granma*, the glories of the Sierra Maestra, the defeat of Batista, the victory at Playa Girón, and the transformation of the social order continues to stir the Cuban masses in a way not easily understood by those who have not lived through the events themselves. For many, the revolution remains incarnate in Fidel: he is the prophet who led his people out of the Batistiano wilderness, turned back the Yankee hordes, and is now constructing a promised land of full employment and social equality. He was a legend before he was 33, and has been the maximum leader ever since. Castro's presence—both physical and symbolic—has been a key element in all revolutionary programs undertaken in the new Cuba.

Partly because of Castro's *personalismo* and charisma and partly because of his political audacity and effectiveness, Cuba's revolutionary progress has not been paralyzed by intra-elite struggles. There has been infighting aplenty—moderates against radicals, Communists against non-Communists, new Marxists against old Marxists, even followers of Peking against followers of Moscow—but nothing serious enough to interrupt the revolution or to threaten the hold of the top leadership has occurred. A decade after the revolutionaries came to power, Castro was still number one, Dorticós was still President, and second-level revolutionaries like Armando Hart and Juan Almeida were still active and faithful. The catalogue of early revolutionaries and second-generation militants who have broken with Castro is also long; but none of them have succeeded in organizing an effective opposition. Those who have tried are now silenced, in exile, in prison, or dead.

The continuity in top leadership has made it easier to carry out revolutionary programs in two ways. First, since 1959 there have been no dramatic interruptions or reversals in the direction of the programs. No new elites have come to power to deny the legitimacy of their predecessors or to challenge Castro's vision of a new Cuba. Second, because of the limited nature of the struggle against Batista and the absence of disruptive civil strife since that time, Cuba's socioeconomic resource base has remained relatively intact. The largest single loss has come from the outpouring of exiles possessing technical and social skills in short supply on the island. But as Castro himself has pointed out on many occasions, the flight of the exiles may in fact be a blessing. The exiles take with them needed skills, but their departure also "purifies" and strengthens the movement by removing those of questionable loyalty.[11]

Although the damage caused by Cuban civil strife in the decade 1953–63 may seem immense to those close to the revolution, one need only compare the Cuban case with the Mexican to achieve some perspective. By 1920, at the end of a decade of internal struggle, Mexico had paid dearly. Hundreds of thousands were dead, including such major figures as Madero, Zapata, and Carranza.* Many farms were untended or in ruins, transportation and communication were disrupted, and industry was barely functioning. Moreover, powerful opposition leaders commanding substantial economic and political resources continued to threaten the government in power. In comparison with this decade of turmoil, the Cuban experience seems mild. The Cuban leadership was able to consolidate and maintain its hold on society with considerable ease, capturing almost intact the socioeconomic resources of the island and subsequently expending little of this patrimony on the suppression of civil strife. The regime's resources were invested almost immediately in the work of social transformation, and this has been the emphasis ever since.

Taken one at a time, none of these characteristics of the Cuban leadership is exceptional. Gandhi was probably as complex as Castro, Nkrumah perhaps as charismatic in the early years, Mao certainly as astute and successful in consolidating power, and Nasser as fortunate in seizing and exercising control over a relatively undamaged society. But the gestalt is uniquely Cuban. As we shall see repeatedly in the following chapters, Castro's stamp is on every

* The scope of the destruction is suggested by the following Mexican census figures. In the decade 1901–10 the total population of Mexico increased by 1.55 million. In the eleven years following, the total population *decreased* by .83 million. In the years 1921–30, the total population increased by 2.2 million, and it has been compounding ever since. Data are from Howard F. Cline, *Mexico, Revolution to Evolution: 1940–1960* (New York, 1963), Table IV, p. 336.

aspect of the Cuban effort and so it has been from the beginning. Fidel dominates the revolution; he is Sidney Hook's "event-making man" par excellence.[12]

Cuban History and World Politics

Unlike continental Spanish America, freed from colonial rule by the creole revolts of the 1820's, Cuba remained under Spanish domination until the very end of the nineteenth century. In the later years of that century, there were protests and rebellions against Spain over the issues of independence and slavery. The Ten Years' War of 1868–78 and the War of 1895 are the two historical and symbolic high-water marks of this period, but anti-Spanish and anti-colonial activity was almost continuous. Today the Cuban leaders of this period, such as Carlos Manuel de Céspedes, the wealthy planter who fought in the Ten Years' War; Máximo Gómez and Antonio Maceo, the two great generals of the epoch; and José Martí, poet, politician, rebel, and military strategist are celebrated as heroes and precursors of the revolution. This relatively recent and intense flowering of Cuba's nationalist sentiment, and the thwarting of Cuba's drive to independence by United States intervention in 1898, form the background for Cuba's mid-twentieth-century drama of nationalism and revolution.[13]

Of perhaps more importance to the Castro revolution is the tangled and passionate history of Cuban–American relations in the first six decades of the twentieth century. It is, of course, difficult to separate the real from the imagined Cuban grievances against the United States. Castro supporters can cite chapter and verse to substantiate their claim that for sixty years the United States controlled the politics, plundered the resources, and humiliated the population of the island. Defenders of United States policy are just as quick to list the many social and economic benefits that accrued to the Cubans because of the American presence. Whatever the truth of these conflicting claims, three general assertions about this period can be made with confidence. First, the degree of American political involvement in Cuba was considerable. The Platt Amendment, in which "Cuba consents that the United States may exercise the right to intervene for the preservation of Cuban independence, the maintenance of a government adequate for the protection of life, property, and individual liberty," was in effect from 1901 to 1934. Second, the degree of American economic involvement in Cuba was even greater.[14] Third, it must have been extremely galling to Cuban nationalists to live for sixty years in the political and economic shadow of the United States.

Since the Spanish-American War, anti-Americanism has been a recurring theme in Cuban politics. The most fully institutionalized pre-Castro expression of anti-Americanism came in the first years of the Party of the Cuban Revolution, popularly known as the Auténticos, which was founded in the 1930's. The 1935 program of the Auténticos was organized around the symbolic triumvirate of "nationalism, socialism, and anti-imperialism."[15] By anti-imperialism was meant disengagement from North American political and economic control. Although this antagonism was not as pervasive in the early part of the century as it was later to become under Castro, there were frequent public expressions of dislike for the "Colossus of the North." For instance, in 1922, after certain unwelcome developments in the sugar trade and the sugar industry, one Havana newspaper printed the following banner headline: HATRED OF NORTH AMERICANS WILL BE THE RELIGION OF CUBANS. "The day will have to arrive," the paper continued, "when we will consider it the most sacred duty of our life to walk along the street and eliminate the first American we encounter."[16] Fidel Castro has seldom used more virulent language.

In 1959, the Castro regime's first year in power, there was a rapid disintegration of Cuban-American relations. By January 1961, the United States had broken diplomatic relations with Cuba, and the invasion followed in April. To explain the course of events leading to this antagonism, apologists for each side point accusing fingers at the other. Referring to 1959 and 1960, the Cubans cite American opposition to the agrarian reform and nationalization laws, attacks by Miami-based exiles, the refusal of American-owned refineries to process Soviet crude oil, the reduction of the United States quota for Cuban sugar, the economic embargo on American goods shipped to Cuba, and espionage and subversion by United States agents. The Americans cite executions, Communist infiltration in government, expropriation without compensation, the destruction of press autonomy, the recognition of Communist China, increasing economic dependence on the Soviet bloc, the abetment of revolution throughout Spanish America, and attacks on United States officials, citizens, and property. It is clear that a vicious circle of threats and counterthreats, retaliations and counter-retaliations, was established between Cuba and the United States in 1959 and 1960. By 1961 the antagonism had congealed, and further moves by both sides—the Bay of Pigs invasion, Castro's embracing of Marxism-Leninism, the missile crisis, United States overflights, and Cuban hemispheric mischief-making—only served to reinforce existing hostility.

In the first chapter it was noted that Cuban efforts at mobilization and cultural change are organized around the intertwining themes of struggle and the millennium. The history of modern Cuba provides the revolutionary elite with ample opportunities for linking these themes to meaningful antecedents. The current struggle is seen as rooted in six decades of exploitation, and the millennial order is seen as involving the total rejection of the United States. In support of this view, the Cubans can selectively mine the historical record for events and statistics of great evocative power and high credibility. It is a rich treasure indeed. In the hemisphere, only Mexico, Panama, and now perhaps the Dominican Republic can lay claim to such a convincing catalogue of anti-American grievances.

For the Cubans to indulge in a revolutionary effort having virulent anti-Americanism as a prime component is a luxury made possible in part by the Cold War. It is obvious that without the economic umbilical cord linking Cuba to the Soviet Union and to much of Eastern Europe, the Castro regime could not have survived its first decade—at least not in anything like its present form. Without Soviet support it certainly could never have moved so radically in its developmental programs. If the elite has violated "laws" of history, geography, and economics and has not been brought to a reckoning, it is because under the special circumstances of the 1960's the old laws do not always apply.

Nowhere is this seen more clearly than in hemispheric political–military relations. Cuba, vulnerable throughout most of the twentieth century to incursions by United States money and Marines, is now well defended. Protected by water, by its own armed forces, perhaps by Soviet power and the norms of nonintervention, the regime is relatively well insulated from threats, border incidents, and attacks. Although close enough to the United States—both geographically and historically—to make Castro's expressed fear of the colossus seem reasonable, Cuba is also distant enough and visible enough internationally to make American interference both difficult and politically costly. Given the circumstances of the Cold War and the nuclear age, Cuba can effectively hold the United States at bay and at the same time profit from the symbolic and integrative consequences of anti-Yankeeism.

In sum, Castro's Cuba is a child both of the times and of the ages—both of the Cold War and of the centuries-old revolutionary tradition. It is a social transformation sufficiently far-reaching to be compared to the French, Mexican, Soviet, and Chinese examples; it is also an indigenous movement sufficiently shaped by Cuban history, geography, economy, culture, and personalities to be considered apart. Both perspectives on the revolution, the broadly comparative and the more narrowly particular, contribute to our understanding. The data and analyses in the case studies that form the bulk of this book serve to interpret the specifics of the Cuban case, but ultimately the revolution can be fully understood only when set in its historical and comparative context.

3 The Campaign Against Illiteracy

DURING 1961, much of the attention of the regime and much of the energies of its citizens were focused on a single national program—the campaign to eradicate illiteracy. The year was also a busy one in other respects, but despite massive changes in Cuban society, not to mention the Bay of Pigs invasion, the campaign dominated public life.* During the first decade no other program of nationwide mobilization and mass participation lasted so long and involved so many Cubans so intimately. Furthermore, the campaign to eradicate illiteracy served as a testing ground for many of the ideas, tactics, and organizational devices later incorporated into the revolutionary style of governance and mass mobilization. Thus, both because of its massiveness and because of its centrality to the development of the revolutionary style, the campaign was an essential step in the transformation of political culture in Cuba.

The Roots of the Campaign

On September 26, 1960, Fidel Castro stood before the General Assembly of the United Nations and announced, "Next year our people propose to launch an all-out offensive against illiteracy, with the ambitious goal of teaching every illiterate person to read

* Although other major educational goals were announced for the "Year of Education," the campaign against illiteracy was, from the outset, both the symbolic and the actual core of the year's activities. Subsequently, the "Year of Education" and the campaign against illiteracy have come to be almost synonymous.

and write. Organizations of teachers, students, and workers—the entire population—are preparing themselves for an intensive campaign; and within a few months Cuba will be the first country in the Americas to be able to claim that it has not a single illiterate inhabitant."[1]

The start of the campaign is usually dated from this speech, but the ideological and organizational roots of the effort go back much further. As early as 1953, when Castro was on trial for leading an attack on the Moncada Army Barracks, he said that a country as blessed with resources as Cuba "could easily provide for a population three times as great as it now has. . . . What is inconceivable is that there are men who go to bed hungry while one square inch of land remains uncultivated. . . . What is inconceivable is that 30 percent of our peasants cannot sign their names and that 99 percent of them know nothing of Cuba's history."[2] A more explicit prophecy of the literacy campaign was contained in the Manifesto of the Sierra Maestra, which was promulgated in the summer of 1957, after Castro had been in the mountains approximately six months. As part of a ten-point program to which a victorious provisional government would be pledged, the Manifesto decreed "the immediate start of an intensive campaign against illiteracy and for civic education, a campaign stressing the citizen's duties and rights with respect to society and the Fatherland."[3]

From the time of the first pronouncements on illiteracy by Castro and his lieutenants, the problem has been seen as one facet of the larger educational issue, which in turn has been viewed as central to the entire developmental process in Cuba. The juxtaposition of uncultivated land, hungry men, and illiterate peasants in Castro's Moncada speech was a foretaste of an argument that came to be elaborated more fully and frequently during the first years of the Revolutionary Government. Basically, the argument held, domestic tyrants and foreign exploiters had imposed on Cuba an educational system that was sharply discriminatory toward the lower classes, oblivious to national needs in terms of curriculum and training, insufficient in both quantity and quality, and culturally and fiscally corrupt. Illiteracy was one of the most serious legacies of this educational system—a system that was itself the legacy of social, economic, and political backwardness and degradation. Thus from the very beginning the attack on illiteracy was viewed by the Cuban leadership as not simply a technical or pedagogical problem. It was seen as a profoundly political effort, one tied intimately to the revolutionary transformation of society and the economy.

The following statement by Castro, though taken from a speech that was given after the campaign was actually under way, is representative of earlier and continuing Cuban pronouncements on the relationship between underdevelopment, educational backwardness, and illiteracy:

> Education is an index of political oppression; that is, the lack of educatiton is the best index of the state of political oppression, social backwardness, and exploitation in which a country finds itself. The indexes of economic exploitation and economic backwardness coincide exactly with the indexes of illiteracy and the lack of schools and universities. The countries that are most exploited economically and most oppressed politically are the countries that have the most illiterates. . . .
>
> Only a revolution is capable of totally changing the educational scene in a country, because it also totally changes the political scene, the economic scene, and the social scene. The levels of ignorance and illiteracy, the numbers of children not attending school, are really frightful in the economically exploited nations. Why? . . . Because in reality there is not the least interest in remedying these conditions.[4]

Only in these terms can one understand the unfolding of the campaign and its importance in the development of the Cuban Revolution.

The statistics of the 1950's testified that Cuban society was in fact in dire need of educational reform. The 1953 census indicated that of all citizens ten years or older, approximately 25 percent had never been to school at all and slightly over 50 percent had dropped out of school before finishing the sixth grade. Thus three out of four Cubans who had "completed" their schooling were either illiterate or at best semieducated.[5] Although the picture might have looked slightly different had there been another census in 1958, the basic deficiencies of 1953 remained essentially untouched when the Rebel Army marched into Havana. Despite an average population growth of over two percent a year between 1950 and 1958, total enrollment in the public primary schools in the same period had increased on the average by only one percent a year.[6] In 1958, perhaps no more than half of all Cuban children between five and fifteen years of age were in school, despite a long series of legal enactments establishing free and compulsory education for this age group.[7] By the time Castro came to power, the system was clearly stagnant. Adult education was all but nonexistent, and no new generation of educated young people was being trained to replace the ignorant or semieducated older generations. In the rural areas the system was bankrupt; in the cities the advantaged youth attended private and church-supported schools, whereas the poorer children went to second-rate public institutions—if in fact they attended school at all. If one adds to this picture the graft and corruption in Batista's Ministry of Education, and the irrelevance and insufficiency of much of the curriculum, it is easy to understand why the Castro Government's emphasis on educational reform and development was widely heralded in Cuba as both necessary and just.[8]

Thus the literacy campaign, as a direct attack on one of the most obvious and widely condemned legacies of the old educational system, enjoyed substantial support from the very outset. On this issue, unlike those of agrarian reform and the nationalization of industries, even Castro's enemies had little to say. The campaign promised clear and immediate payoffs in terms of a more capable and integrated work force; moreover, it was within the range of realistic possibilities. With approximately one quarter of the adult population illiterate, the challenge was large enough to appear heroic without at the same time appearing absolutely impossible.

As we have seen, the revolutionaries viewed educational problems in terms of larger issues of underdevelopment. Thus it is not surprising to find that during the first years of the revolution a new educational philosophy, part critique of the old order and part blueprint for the new, was elaborated and publicized by Cubans both at home and at international forums. We are not concerned here with the details of this philosophy, or with the many programs initiated to put it into practice.[9] For our purposes, it is necessary only to reemphasize that the formation of new citizens was to be an integral and crucial element of all programs developed under the new educational philosophy. As stated succinctly in a Cuban report to UNESCO,

> The aims of education in the new Cuba include instilling in our children and young people an unbounded love of the Fatherland and a feeling of solidarity with the workers and peoples of all lands in their noble struggle for a free and happy life, and teaching them to abhor imperialist wars of plunder and to work steadfastly for peace....
>
> The teaching programs must help to develop a love of country and a love for the workers and peasants—for the people as the creators of labor and the source of all social wealth. They have to indicate what is represented by the struggle against exploitation and misery.... They must encourage a moral sense founded on the struggle against social inequality. They must stress the underlying causes of inequality and its terrible consequences.[10]

As we shall see, the literacy campaign, even though it dealt in the main with adults, partook fully of this philosophy of education. Skill training and civic education were tied together in a program that was intended to bring literacy and political awareness to the disadvantaged while at the same time introducing literacy workers to the hard realities of underdevelopment and backwardness. Both the illiterates and the literacy workers were expected to emerge from the encounter with a deeper understanding of national problems, a new concept of citizenship, and a new willingness to work for the transformation of the old society.

Just as the sociopolitical views that shaped the campaign predated Castro's speech at the United Nations, so did some of its organizational devices. When the Rebel Army was in the Sierra, classes combining literacy training and political education were held both for those soldiers of peasant background who lacked formal education and for *campesinos* who lived close to the guerrilla encampments. This activity was sporadic and informal, even during 1958, when true liberated zones were established in the mountains and the need for constant mobility and tight security was diminished. Though relatively few Cubans were actually taught to read during this period, echoes of this early effort are apparent in the teaching materials, symbolism, and mobilization tactics of 1961.[11]

After the rebels came to power, a Comisión de Alfabetización (Literacy Commission) was established in the Ministry of Education. Beginning in April 1959, the Commission organized literacy centers and recruited teachers, particularly in urban areas. Shortly thereafter, the newly founded National Institute for Agrarian Reform (INRA) began literacy work in less populated areas as part of its larger program of rural development.[12] The Rebel Army also continued its literacy work; and as a direct antecedent to programs that were later to become characteristic of the literacy campaign, brigades of student volunteers, after a period of training in the mountains, were sent to the remotest rural areas as literacy workers and primary school teachers. After their "veritable revolutionary bath in the Sierra Maestra," it was thought that the student volunteers would be able to work under any conditions, no matter how isolated or trying.[13] Although the youth brigades that subsequently taught in the rural areas during the literacy campaign had to take their "revolutionary baths" while actually teaching rather than before beginning, the spirit of the early voluntary programs was carried over into 1961. Thus when planning for the national literacy campaign formally began in the autumn of 1960, there was already considerable organizational and pedagogic experience to draw on. Although the pre-campaign effort had reached fewer than ten percent of the island's illiterates, sufficient work had been done to determine the logistical, motivational, and organizational dimensions of the national problem.[14]

The Campaign Begins

"Death to illiteracy will be the number one goal of 1961," declared the First Congress of the Municipal Councils of Education in October 1960.[15] At that time, the Comisión de Alfabetización was replaced by a new Comisión Nacional de Alfabetización. Despite the similarity of names, the new Comisión Nacional had a quite different structure, incorporating as key members representatives of Cuba's most important governmental, quasi-governmental, and mass organizations and tying in at the municipal level to the councils of education, which in turn had substantial representation from the local branches of the same organizations.[16] With technical, financial, propaganda, and publication departments at the national, provincial, and local levels, the new Commission represented a broadly based national organization for information-gathering, mobilizing, and teaching.*

The National Commission immediately took steps to prepare suitable teaching materials and to organize a census of illiterates. Departing rather sharply from the teaching materials that had been used in 1959 and 1960, a team from the Ministry of Education prepared a new instructor's manual, *Alfabeticemos* (Let's Alphabetize),† and a new primer, *Venceremos* (We Shall Triumph), designed to lead the illiterates step by step through the technicalities of reading and writing. Both were printed in inexpensive format and widely distributed throughout the island.[17] Both, as one might expect, were political in content. The instructor's manual, in particular, was a profoundly political document, consisting primarily of 24 "themes of revolutionary orientation"

* The most important participating organizations, in addition to the Ministry of Education, were the Revolutionary Armed Forces, the Integrated Revolutionary Organizations, the Confederation of Cuban Workers, the National Union of Educational Workers, the National Association of Small Farmers, the Federation of Cuban Women, the Association of Young Rebels, the Committees for Defense of the Revolution, the Federation of University Students, and the National Institute of Agrarian Reform. (Some organizations such as the Committees for Defense of the Revolution were themselves being formed in the autumn of 1960 and thus did not participate fully in the work of the Comisión Nacional until somewhat later.) Among the many reasons for creating the Comisión Nacional was the goal of revitalizing and "making revolutionary" the Municipal Councils of Education, which according to one commentator were ineffectual during the first two years of the revolution because of their "professionalism, technicalism, verbal speculation as opposed to concrete work, and conformism [to the old ways of teaching]." Virgilio Gómez Fuentes, "Los principios sociales aplicados a la organización y desarrollo de la gran campaña nacional de alfabetización," in Ministry of Education, *Alfabetización, nacionalización de la enseñanza* (Havana: Imprenta Nacional de Cuba, 1961), p. 5.

† There is no natural and easy translation of the Spanish verb *alfabetizar* or of the nouns *alfabetizador* and *alfabetización*. In this chapter I have avoided the English cognates "alphabetize," "alphabetizer," and "alphabetization" in favor of the phrases "make literate," "literacy worker," and "literacy work."

on such subjects as nationalization, racial discrimination, and imperialism.[18] By way of example, Theme 1 was called "The Revolution" and was headed by a quotation from Castro: "Revolution means the destruction of privilege, the disappearance of exploitation, and the creation of a just society." The text continued:

> People need revolution in order to develop and advance. When a nation is dominated by another, more powerful nation, only through revolution can it end foreign domination and establish its own government free from such domination.
>
> When the riches of a nation are in the hands of another nation, a revolution is needed to recover those riches.
>
> When the humble men and women of a country are without work, without land to cultivate, without education, they must revolt.
>
> When the work of the humble serves to enrich a small group of exploiters, then the humble must make a revolution so that the wealth produced by labor ceases to enrich the exploiters and remains in the hands of the working people.
>
> That is revolution: liberty, work, land, schooling, and respect for those who struggle and work. And to attain these things it is not enough to take up arms against tyranny; it is also necessary to make all those changes that are now being made in our country.[19]

The special census to locate illiterates was begun in November 1960 and concluded in August of the following year.[20] Using a simple, single-page questionnaire, teachers and voluntary census takers combed the countryside for illiterates. The 1953 national census had found the illiteracy rate to be approximately 42 percent in rural areas and 11 percent in the cities. Thus a special effort to locate illiterates had to be made in precisely those areas in which transportation and communication were most difficult. Furthermore, among those with little or no education—both urban and rural—there was often substantial reluctance to be interviewed. Some were simply embarrassed to display their ignorance; others feared loss of jobs or status once they were discovered to be illiterate. As the national campaign gathered momentum, however, and as the organizational chart of the National Commission became an administrative reality, it became increasingly difficult for illiterates to escape the census takers. By February 412,000 illiterates had been located, by April 546,000, by June 684,000.

At the end of August, when the census was declared completed, the total came to 985,000.

The preliminary plans for the literacy campaign did not include a fully developed program for recruiting and training literacy workers. Prior to January 1961, as we have seen, there were student volunteers in training and actually teaching in the mountains, and others were involved as members of the Rebel Army and INRA. Moreover, some adults in the cities had been working in their spare time to instruct illiterates at special night and weekend classes set up by the Ministry of Education. But when Castro officially opened the "Year of Education" in a New Year's Eve speech to more than ten thousand teachers and dignitaries at Ciudad Libertad in Havana,* the National Literacy Commission certainly had not yet worked out the organizational implications of what the Prime Minister said:

> We are sure we shall be able to proclaim to the entire world [by the end of the year] that in our country there remains not one person who is unable to read and write. And to achieve this goal, we are counting on you [the schoolteachers] in the first instance.... If the number of teachers and other literacy workers proves insufficient, we shall terminate the school year early and mobilize all the students from the sixth grade up; and from the month of May until the 31st of December... we shall organize an army of teachers and send them to every corner of the country, so that, if every last illiterate needs a teacher, we shall give him one![21]

In fact, even the plans for recruiting large numbers of *alfabetizadores populares*—adults who would teach in their spare time either at their place of work or in the evening classes—had not progressed very far. Thus during the first months of 1961 the campaign to eradicate illiteracy consisted largely of recruiting and training literacy workers.

* Ciudad Libertad, the site of the banquet, reception, and speech to the teachers—known as Camp Columbia before Castro came to power—had been the most important military base of the Batista regime. One of the first official acts of the Revolutionary Government was to convert the base into a "school-city" and to make it the national headquarters of the Ministry of Education. The symbolism of "barracks into schools" has been much used by Castro and his followers to emphasize the contrast between the "revolutionary style" and the "Batistiano style."

The decision whether or not to call on students to supplement the adult literacy workers was made well before the first returns of the literacy campaign were in. On January 23, addressing the graduation ceremony of a group of voluntary teachers, Castro announced that a *maestro voluntario* named Conrado Benítez had been assassinated by counterrevolutionaries while teaching under the auspices of INRA in the mountains of Las Villas. According to Castro, Benítez had not been "the son of a landowner, an industrialist, or a businessman. [He] didn't go to Miami or Paris. He was an eighteen-year-old youngster who knew only poverty and sacrifice.... He was poor, he was a Negro, and he was a teacher. There you have three reasons why the agents of imperialism assassinated him."[22]

Five days later, at the inauguration of a school-city in Santa Clara, Castro announced that all secondary and pre-university schools would close on April 15 and that "an army of one hundred thousand literacy workers" would be recruited from those students who had completed at least the sixth grade and were at least thirteen years old. He told the students it would be both a privilege and a duty to serve, to live, work, and learn with the poor and humble of the island. Shortly, he promised, the necessary organizational arrangements would be made, and eligible students throughout Cuba would be able to sign up for the program.[23] Thus was announced the formation of what came to be known as the "Conrado Benítez Brigades," the legions of schoolchildren and young people who eventually taught in the remotest areas of Cuba. Although there were never as many Conrado Benítez *brigadistas* participating in the literacy campaign as there were adult *alfabetizadores populares*, it was the élan, the image, and the exploits of the former that captured national attention and set the entire Year of Education apart from any previous mass mobilization effort, either in Cuba or in the rest of Latin America.

However, as the end of the school year approached, the brigadistas and alfabetizadores still were not in the field in appreciable numbers. Pilot brigades of students were teaching in the Zapata Swamp, and the parents of potential brigadistas were invited to visit the area to allay their fears about what might happen to their sons and daughters if they allowed them to volunteer for the campaign.[24] Intensive literacy work was being done with small groups of fishermen, charcoal burners, and others who for reasons of isolation and mobility presented special logistical and pedagogical problems.[25] By the middle of March, when Minister of Education Armando Hart left for a six-week tour of Eastern Europe, the literacy campaign was considered so important by the leadership that Castro himself took over the Ministry of Education.[26] But only after the smoke had cleared at the Bay of Pigs and the secondary and higher-level schools had been closed for the year did the campaign really begin to assume mass proportions. On the first of May, in a speech that was at the same time a reaffirmation of the Socialist character of the revolution and a post–Bay of Pigs victory celebration, Castro announced that all private schools in the country would shortly be nationalized, and he praised the "hundred thousand young people that already are marching toward the interior of the republic . . . to eradicate illiteracy completely."[27] The speech both sounded the death knell for the pre-revolutionary system of education and marked the symbolic opening of the second stage of the literacy campaign. Although in fact the hundred thousand young people were not *yet* marching toward the interior, the phase of planning, organizing, and experimenting was drawing to a close.

The Campaign Expands

The Conrado Benítez brigadistas were trained at Varadero Beach, once the most elegant and well-known resort area of the island.[28] Living in the hotels, homes, and clubs that a few years earlier had housed the rich and near-rich of Cuba and the United States, the young people received seven days of intensive instruction in the use of *Venceremos* and *Alfabeticemos.* There were special classes on revolutionary politics, personal comportment, rural nutrition, and hygiene. Sports, movies, and beach recreation, as well as a physical examination for almost everyone, were also included in the program.

The first brigadistas to come to Varadero, approximately a thousand boys and a thousand girls, arrived on the eve of the Bay of Pigs invasion. During May, the capacity of the training center was expanded to accommodate first 7,500 young people and then 12,000. At full strength, the center had nine dining rooms staffed by three hundred cooks and helpers, a 125-bed hospital, over sixty private homes and hotels housing the students, approximately one hundred physical education instructors, and over a hundred teachers giving both political and technical instruction. There were also other teachers who went through training with the brigadistas and then moved into the countryside with them. But it was not the physical facilities, the logistics, or even the technical instruction that was of primary importance to the revolutionary leadership. Their main concern was the *ambiente*, or spirit, of the training center and the infusion of this spirit into the brigadistas. The young people were urged to head toward the countryside "fully conscious of their revolutionary obligations, . . . dedicated to the betterment of the peasantry, . . . and ready to overcome all obstacles."* They were to form the "elite corps" of the "army of education," and no effort was spared to consolidate and reinforce this image of specialness and national service during the seven short days at Varadero.†

When the program was terminated at the end of August, some 105,700 young people had been through the training center. As might be expected, most of them were from the cities, and after their week in Varadero they were assigned disproportionately to the most rural provinces, above all to Oriente. As the data presented in Table 2 show, the percentage of eligible students that actually did enlist signifies a substantial mobilization success. This

* On Mother's Day, May 14, 1961, Castro spoke at Varadero to a group of departing brigadistas and their families. His speech, translated in Appendix B below, captures the intended ambiente of Varadero and the Conrado Benítez brigades better than any other single document.

† Each brigadista was given, in addition to his teaching materials, a knapsack, a hammock, and a lantern. And as befits an army of education, the brigadistas were in uniform: each was issued a pair of boots, two pairs of socks, two pairs of pants, two shirts, a shoulder patch, an olive-green beret, and a blanket. Many, both boys and girls, also wore the necklace of beads and dried seeds that had been worn in the Sierra by members of the Rebel Army.

TABLE 2. CHARACTERISTICS OF THE CONRADO BENÍTEZ BRIGADISTAS

Age:		*Race:*	
10 to 14 years	40.0%	White	61.9%
15 to 19	47.5	Negro	19.6
20 to 29	9.1	Mestizo	18.5
30 to 39	1.7	TOTAL	100.0%
40 or older	1.7		
TOTAL	100.0%		

Educational level and participation:

	All brigadistas	Brigadistas among all those eligible
Primary	52.2%	36.3%
Basic secondary	31.6	47.0
Pre-university	4.3	23.9
University	4.5	22.6
Teachers	2.6	—
Others	4.8	—
TOTAL	100.0%	

Residence:

Urban	88.2%
Rural	11.8
TOTAL	100.0%

Movement:

	Province of origin	Province of assignment
Pinar del Río	4.3%	8.0%
Havana	34.7	2.7
Matanzas	4.8	3.3
Las Villas	15.9	13.9
Camagüey	9.4	10.2
Oriente	31.0	62.1
TOTAL	100.1%	100.2%

Note: Approximately 52 percent of the brigadistas were girls. Data on age are from the medical records of 83,500 brigadistas. Data on race are from the medical records of 82,600 brigadistas. Data on educational level and participation and on movement are from the records of all 105,700 brigadistas. Data on residence are from the medical records of 83,300 brigadistas. These data are presented by Richard Jolly, in Dudley Seers, ed., *Cuba: The Economic and Social Revolution* (Chapel Hill, N.C., 1964), pp. 200, 202. The same data are available in Havana at the Ministry of Education and in public display at the Literacy Museum on the grounds of the Ministry at Ciudad Libertad.

is particularly apparent if one considers the nature of the task for which the students volunteered. They were not asked simply to attend a mass meeting or to work for a day or two on some project. Becoming a brigadista promised three to six months of sustained participation in an uncomfortable and often unfamiliar environment.

In addition to being the period during which a hundred thousand Conrado Benítez brigadistas were trained and sent out to teach, May through August was also the time of greatest activity in the mobilization of other kinds of literacy workers. During May and June, the number of adult *alfabetizadores populares* working in urban areas expanded rapidly. After the primary schools closed in May, thousands of teachers joined the campaign, some as leaders of the Conrado Benítez brigades, many as instructors and technical overseers of literacy work at the municipal level. Finally, in the middle of August, Castro called on the Confederation of Cuban Workers (CTC) to mobilize 30,000 *brigadistas obreros* (workers) within the next few days.[29] Unlike the *alfabetizadores populares,* who were spare-time volunteers, and the Conrado Benítez brigadistas, who were paid only a small monthly stipend of ten pesos for personal expenses, the *brigadistas obreros*—like the schoolteachers—were to continue to receive their salaries while doing literacy work on a full-time basis. So that production would not suffer while they were away from their jobs, their fellow workers were expected to put in such overtime and extra effort as might be necessary. The *brigadistas obreros* were conceived of as a backup force for the Conrado Benítez brigades, for even with a hundred thousand young people in the countryside there were fears that the campaign was understaffed. Those workers who actually did leave home to live and work in the rural areas came to be known as *brigadistas obreros "Patria o Muerte"* (Fatherland or death), and were invested with some of the same symbolism of sacrifice and service as the student volunteers.

At the end of August, according to official statistics, there were 308,000 Cubans working as literacy teachers. As can be seen in Table 3, the final official statistics on the campaign, released at

TABLE 3. THE LITERACY FORCE: OFFICIAL STATISTICS FOR AUGUST 1961 AND FOR THE ENTIRE CAMPAIGN

Types of literacy workers	Number
August 30:	
Alfabetizadores populares	178,000
Conrado Benítez brigadistas	100,000
Brigadistas obreros	30,000
TOTAL	308,000
Entire Campaign:	
Alfabetizadores populares	121,000
Schoolteacher brigadistas	35,000
Conrado Benítez brigadistas	100,000
Brigadistas obreros "Patria o Muerte"	15,000
TOTAL	271,000

Note: The August data are from the final report of the Second Congress of the Municipal Councils of Education, held Sept. 2–5, 1961, in Havana. See *Congreso Nacional de Alfabetización* (Havana: Imprenta Nacional de Cuba, 1961), p. 103. The summary data for the entire campaign are from the final report of the National Literacy Commission, *Revolución*, Dec. 23, 1961, p. 4. The final report hinted at a partial reconciliation of the earlier and later totals by pointing out that if technicians, statisticians, and overseers were added to the final total, the figure would swell to "over 300,000." (It would seem that teachers, technicians, overseers, and statisticians were all grouped together and counted as *alfabetizadores populares* in August.) Furthermore, because of the part-time nature of the work of the *alfabetizadores populares*, it was difficult to say just who was or was not participating fully enough to be counted. Some Cuban adults worked only for a week or two in the campaign and then dropped out. The August estimate of the number of *brigadistas obreros* was undoubtedly inflated by revolutionary enthusiasm. Evidently only half of the 30,000 workers who reputedly signed up actually turned out to be "Patria o Muerte" brigadistas.

the end of the year, suggest that the August total was inflated by about 14 percent. But whatever the true figure, it is clear that as the summer of 1961 ended, the "literacy army" was fully mobilized, as well trained and equipped as it was ever going to be, and deployed to launch the final offensive against the "entrenched forces of ignorance."

During the middle four months of the year, one other major development took place in the campaign. Since October 1960, when the National Literacy Commission was organized, there had been a great deal of talk about integrating the revolutionary organizations and "the masses" into the literacy effort. As mentioned earlier, from the outset representatives of all the important organizations had been members of the National Commission. But representation at the top was one thing, and effective participation and use of resources at the grass roots was quite another. Only in the summer of 1961—concurrently with and partly because of the formation of the Integrated Revolutionary Organizations (ORI)—did the system begin to operate as the table of organization had earlier suggested that it should.[30] In short, as increasing amounts of political resources and attention were turned to the campaign, the bureaucratic structures began to respond in the manner originally intended.

As might be expected, the increased attention paid by Castro and his top aides to the overall effort evoked amplified responses all through the associated administrative and support structures. As we have seen, the Confederation of Cuban Workers recruited their quota of brigadistas in a matter of days. The same zeal was shown by the other mass organizations: the Young Rebels formed pilot brigades of literacy workers; the Committees for Defense of the Revolution joined in the census of illiterates; the Federation of Cuban Women canvassed from house to house to convince recalcitrant female illiterates to sign up for instruction; the Association of Small Farmers proselytized in peasant areas that could not effectively be reached by any other group. These and other organizations did everything from taking advertisements in the newspapers to holding street dances and poetry contests in order to raise men, materials, and enthusiasm for the campaign.

Most significant of all was the new life breathed into the Municipal Councils of Education. It was in the community that the resources and information relevant to the campaign had to be brought together. The census of illiterates and the dispatching, provisioning, control, and at times training of the literacy workers were decentralized to the *municipio* level. Thus the Municipal Council of Education—frequently called the Municipal Council of Literacy during this period—became responsible for overseeing and coordinating all aspects of the campaign within its territorial jurisdiction, whether carried on by the mass organizations, the Conrado Benítez brigadistas, or the other teachers and citizen volunteers. In order to handle these diverse tasks, smaller *unidades de alfabetización*, or literacy units, were set up under the direct supervision of the Council. These units ranged in size from no more than a dozen teachers and their students to more than a hundred literacy workers and several hundred illiterates, with each unidad responsible for a designated urban or rural area of the municipio.[31] Ideally, therefore, through the literacy unit, the Municipal Council of Education, and finally the Provincial Council, every illiterate and every literacy worker was linked directly to the National Commission and the national effort. With the renovation of the Municipal Councils, this ideal became at least a partial reality. The system never really worked perfectly—illiterates were still overlooked in the census, literacy teachers still occasionally failed to show up for their evening classes, the mass organizations still duplicated each other's efforts, brigadistas still came to the homes of peasants only to find that their supposed pupils were either unwilling or unable to learn. But taking into account the scope of the national effort, the haste with which the bureaucratic apparatus was put together, and the massive participation of amateurs and volunteers in that apparatus, the plans and programs of the National Commission were carried out very effectively indeed. By the end of August the improvements in the program's organization fully paralleled the increase in manpower that had taken place during the same summer months.

The Final Push

September opened with the National Literacy Congress, a convention held at the ex–Havana Hilton Hotel, renamed the Havana Libre after the triumph of the revolution. For four days, over eight hundred members of the national, provincial, and municipal councils, representatives of the mass organizations, and assorted revolutionary leaders met at the hotel, where they took turns congratulating, criticizing, inventorying, and exhorting each other about the campaign. The opening address was given by Hart, and the closing address by Castro. Sandwiched between the addresses were reports from all the provinces, speeches by lesser dignitaries, and innumerable working sessions.[32]

If it had not been generally appreciated before the Congress, at

TABLE 4. PROGRESS OF THE LITERACY CAMPAIGN, JUNE–DECEMBER 1961

Category	End of June	End of July	End of August	End of October	End of campaign (Dec. 21)
Illiterates located	684,000	822,000	985,000	988,000	979,000
Persons studying	465,000	594,000	776,000	500,000	n.a.
New literates (cumulative total)	22,000	62,000	119,000	354,000	707,000

Note: Data are from Richard Jolly, in Dudley Seers, ed., *Cuba: The Economic and Social Revolution* (Chapel Hill, N.C., 1964), p. 195. The June, July, and August data are available in more detail in Ministry of Education, *Alfabetización, nacionalización de la enseñanza* (Havana: Imprenta Nacional de Cuba, 1961), pp. 9–11. The October data are from *Revolución*, Nov. 14, 1961 (supplement), p. 1. The final campaign data are those of the report of the national Literacy Commission, *Revolución*, Dec. 23, 1961, p. 4. The ongoing statistical control of the campaign was never very exact. For instance, early in December it was announced that 600,000 Cubans had already been made literate, and that 300,000 more would complete their studies by the end of the campaign (*Revolución*, Dec. 6, 1961, p. 1). Yet less than three weeks later, the final official report listed only 707,000 new literates.

least one key aspect of the campaign was perfectly clear by the time the gathering adjourned: a great deal of teaching would have to be crammed into the last three and a half months of the campaign if all that had already been accomplished in terms of organization and mobilization were not to be wasted. As we have seen, nearly all of the teaching force had been recruited by the end of August; and as Table 4 makes clear, the census of illiterates was also completed by then. More striking, however, is how few Cubans had actually learned to read and write during the first eight months of the campaign. Despite the official report that almost half a million Cubans were already studying at the end of June, two months later only 119,000 were listed as having been made literate.

In his address to the Congress, Castro said that at the end of the summer vacation all Cuban schoolteachers would be called on to participate in the final three months of the campaign.[33] Until September such participation had been voluntary, but on the 18th of the month it became mandatory. Every teacher was assigned by his local Council of Education to some literacy task—as instructor, technical assistant, or brigade leader. The incorporation of the regular teaching personnel of the Ministry of Education into the campaign delayed the beginning of the regular school year from its normal September opening date until January 1962. In effect, this meant that most Cuban schools were closed for eight months during 1961, since most had adjourned two months early in the spring, at the time the Conrado Benítez brigades were created. In order to occupy the hundreds of thousands of Cuban children who were out of school during the autumn of 1961, a special "plan of attendance" (*plan asistencial*) was set up whereby parents, members of the Association of Young Rebels, and volunteers of all sorts organized substitute activities. Official suggestions for such activities ranged from planting flowers and learning the national anthem to visiting museums and factories and writing about the experience. There is no way to assess the successes and failures of the plan; undoubtedly many children simply extended their already overextended summer vacations, much to the dismay of their parents. In any case, the revolutionary leadership was so single-mindedly determined to push on with the literacy campaign that the canceling of the first three months of school was not considered too great a sacrifice.

If the attention paid to the campaign by the revolutionary leadership and the mass media is a fair index of the actual level of literacy activity, the months of November and December can only be described as frenzied. Beginning with a mass celebration of the announcement that Melena del Sur was "the first municipio free of illiteracy"—a celebration at which both Hart and Castro spoke —the *reuniones, actos, declaraciones,* and *manifestaciones* of the campaign came by the hundreds.[34] From one end of the island to the other, communities vied with each other to terminate their literacy work and to celebrate their achievements. There were mass "graduations" of the new literates, flags and banners were distributed to areas declared free of illiteracy, and—to spur on the young people—scholarships were promised to the brigadistas who carried out their responsibilities. Full-time "acceleration camps" were set up to aid those illiterates who had fallen behind in their studies, and the newspapers were full of reports both of literacy quotas overfulfilled and of municipios that would have to intensify their efforts in order to meet the December deadline set for the closing of the campaign.

In Cuba, every revolutionary battle either has or finds its martyrs, and the final month of the literacy campaign was no exception. Just as the death of Conrado Benítez at the beginning of the year had been used to motivate tens of thousands of young people to become brigadistas, so the assassination at the end of November of a brigadista, Manuel Ascunce, was used to infuse the final three weeks of the campaign with a special sense of urgency and solidarity. According to Castro's narrative of the events, Ascunce and the father of the peasant family with which he was living and working were taken at gunpoint from the peasant's house by a band of counterrevolutionaries and hanged from a nearby tree. "What could have been the cause, the motive, of that action?" asked Castro.

> The irritation of the enemies of the revolution when they were confronted with the statistics on hundreds of thousands of new literates? What has motivated them? Impotence, irritation, and hate? Or are they trying to block and upset this final push, to sow terror among the tens of thousands of families whose children are doing literacy work, in an effort to weaken and frustrate the tremendous effort of the final stage of the campaign?

Whatever the motives of those who assassinated Ascunce and the peasant, Castro continued, there would be no slackening of the campaign. On the contrary,

> to call back one single young person would be to do exactly what the assassins want.... To recall one single young person would indicate a real lack of solidarity with the family of the assassinated boy; it would indicate a real lack of solidarity with all the other mothers. For we know that the mothers will have courage; we know that they will trust in the vigilance of all the people and in the strength of the revolution to prevent this from happening again, to prevent it... by mobilizing whatever resources might be necessary.[35]

For days afterward, the speeches of the revolutionary leaders rang with exhortations to avenge Ascunce by working harder and contributing more to the final weeks of the literacy campaign.

As the end of the campaign approached, plans were made for a victory celebration. The fiesta was organized around the Conrado Benítez brigadistas, all of whom were invited to come to Havana for a week of sports, recreation, and cultural activities culminating in a massive parade and a speech by Castro in the Plaza de la Revolución.[36] On Friday, December 15, special trains from the provinces packed with brigadistas began to roll into Havana. Those who lived in the immediate metropolitan area went home, and those from the provinces who could not stay with friends and relatives were housed in schools, social clubs, and the homes of *habaneros* who had volunteered to take in the overflow. Dressed in the remnants of their uniforms, often wearing peasant hats and beads, and carrying their knapsacks and lanterns, the brigadistas swarmed into the capital, singing and laughing and exchanging stories of their experiences. The similarities between the joyous return of the literacy army and the triumphal entry of the guerrilla troops only three years earlier were not lost on the population. It was one of the revolution's finest hours, and the parade and mass meeting that closed the campaign were of a scale and spirit befitting the occasion.

The grand finale was held on December 22, under a gray and occasionally rainy sky. The brigadistas were instructed to gather at 6:30 in the morning in specified areas of the city according to where on the island they had taught. The line of march was assembled as it moved through the streets toward the Plaza. First came a gigantic Cuban flag escorted by motorcycle police, then the flags of Socialist and Latin American countries, followed by the red, white, and blue banner of the campaign bearing the legend "Territory Free of Illiteracy." Various dignitaries and officials of the campaign came next, then five hundred literacy workers with lanterns, then a thousand more, each carrying the special banner of the Conrado Benítez brigades. Preceding the brigades came five thousand "soldiers of the literacy army" bearing giant pencils in place of arms; and then came the brigadistas themselves, marching 24 abreast in blocks of 150 rows. They were followed by lesser numbers of "Patria o Muerte" brigadistas arrayed in the same formation. From the time the Cuban flag passed the reviewing stand until the last brigadista marched by, four hours elapsed. Then, after a few relatively brief introductory speeches, Castro came to the microphones. It was clear from his address that he relished the moment.[37] With pride and a great deal of scorn he repeated again and again that this mighty campaign against illiteracy had been waged under the very nose of imperialism, that while the mercenary army had been drawing up battle plans to attack Cuba, the Cubans had been drawing up battle plans to eradicate illiteracy. What, asked Castro, would Señor Kennedy say now about his vaunted Alliance for Progress, a scheme designed to prevent other revolutions like Cuba's? What so-called "representative democracy" in Latin America could fill a plaza with tens of thousands of cheering young people freshly returned from months of literacy work? None, he answered; only Socialism could do it, and only Socialism had done it. Needless to say, no one among the hundreds of thousands gathered in the Plaza raised his voice to argue.

The Campaign as a Mass Movement

It is possible to evaluate the campaign against illiteracy in terms of rather conventional criteria. One can point out that only first-grade levels of skill in reading and writing were officially claimed for the new literates, and that such levels are much too low to be of real and immediate use either at work or at home.[38] Similarly, it is clear that many of the new literates were so located geographically and demographically that even this marginal increment would rapidly slip away from them without intensive follow-up work and practice.[39] Furthermore, as the final statistics of the campaign attest, 272,000, or 28 percent, of the illiterates located in the special census either could not or would not be taught to read and write during the year.* Finally, when the costs, both direct and indirect, of organizing, training, supplying, and at times paying those who participated in the campaign are measured against the tangible results, it is easy to conclude that the campaign was far less than the smashing success the revolutionaries claimed.[40] But such a conclusion, however true in some respects, is in large mea-

* See Table 4. The 272,000 illiterates remaining from among those located in the special census amounted to approximately 3.9 percent of the estimated total population of Cuba at the end of 1961. Thus, beginning in 1962, the Cubans reported their national literacy level to be 96.1 percent, the highest in Latin America.

sure irrelevant to an appreciation of the enduring legacy of the Year of Education. The literacy campaign, if not an overwhelming and unquestionable triumph from the scholastic point of view, was nevertheless seminally important in the evolution of the institutional life and political culture of the revolution.*

In the first place, the campaign represented a mass mobilization of impressive proportions. Out of a total population of approximately seven million Cubans at the end of 1961, one and a quarter million had been drawn actively into the campaign as either students or teachers. Subtracting approximately two million Cubans from the total population as having been too young to be eligible for the campaign in any role whatsoever, we are left with five million, of whom one out of four participated directly in literacy work. If we add to these direct participants the tens of thousands of others who contributed in some fashion through the mass organizations, and the hundreds of thousands who were linked emotionally to the effort because of family and friends, it is probably safe to say that the campaign affected in some real way the lives of most Cubans who by 1961 were old enough to have even minimal political awareness.

Indeed, participation in the campaign went far beyond the bounds of what a manpower specialist might have suggested was necessary to accomplish the goal of wiping out illiteracy. As the campaign progressed, it assumed a scope, duration, and intensity that are rare at any time or place except under conditions of war. It is not surprising, then, that the revolutionaries adopted a military metaphor to characterize both the organization of the movement (the literacy army) and the desired national psychology (crush the enemy). The public rhetoric and the symbolism of the campaign were permeated with the imagery of national emergency, battle, and triumphal march. Illiterates were told that in this, Cuba's hour of need, it was their patriotic duty to become

* Even those who were most cynical about the pedagogical achievements of the campaign would probably admit that the widespread cultural and psychological barriers inhibiting adult education in Cuba were broken during 1961, even if functional literacy was not achieved for very many of the so-called new literates.

literate.[41] When Castro spoke to brigadistas about to depart from Varadero for the rural areas, he reminded them that the army to which they belonged had a longer and harder battle to fight than the Revolutionary Armed Forces themselves.* When brigadistas were sent by the hundreds to the Playa Girón area to work, they arrived by way of a mock invasion of beaches still littered with the residue of battle. While airplanes bombarded the shore with booklets and teaching materials, the brigadistas disembarked from small boats, armed with giant pencils and notebooks.[42] By such means the revolutionary leadership sought to inspire awareness of the campaign, and active participation if possible, throughout the social structure and in every corner of the island.

The literacy campaign was the first of the great revolutionary mobilization efforts designed to involve all Cubans, regardless of age, sex, occupation, education, social class, or place of residence. If you were literate, you could teach; if you were illiterate, you could study; if you were unable to leave your job, you could fill in for a "Patria o Muerte" brigadista who was in the countryside; if you were a housewife, you could help care for the children left without schooling because of the incorporation of teachers into the campaign; if you were a literate agricultural worker, you could agitate among your illiterate *compañeros* to encourage them to enroll in classes. Throughout the year, the Cuban mass media celebrated this theme, largely through the publication of feature articles on the extent and inclusiveness of participation. Much was made of Castro's interview with María de la Cruz Sentmanat, a 106-year-old ex-slave who had been among the first to become literate during the campaign.[43] At the other extreme was eight-year-old Elan Menéndez, the youngest Conrado Benítez brigadista in the country.[44] There were also reports of literacy workers teaching from wheelchairs, a mother teaching in the area where her *miliciano* son had fallen in combat, pretty identical twins

* See Castro's speech to the brigadistas on Mother's Day, translated in Appendix B below. The literacy army, in a fashion reminiscent of other "people's armies," had an international dimension. Not only did the brigadistas carry lanterns from mainland China; there was also an international brigade of non-Cubans, one of whom—a Mexican—spoke at the mass meeting that officially closed the year.

playing tricks on their students, and countless others—young and old, rich and poor, white and black—all working together to make the year a success.

In addition to the human interest stories appearing in the mass media, the Revolutionary Government's entire publicity and organizational apparatus worked at keeping the public involved in the campaign—actively if possible, otherwise psychologically. Auto races, tree-planting expeditions, athletic contests, beauty pageants, dances, songfests, literary events, inspirational talks, radio programs, television shows, symbolic displays, and even Coca-Cola advertisements all carried essentially the same message: "Whoever you are, wherever you are, this is *your* campaign, participate in whatever way you can."* And because the mass organizations offered ready opportunities for translating predispositions to participate into direct involvement, tens of thousands of those Cubans who otherwise might have remained aloof were swept into the effort.

One of the more interesting contributions to the publicity and motivational effort mounted on behalf of the campaign came from the new literates themselves. As part of the final test taken upon completion of the primer, each student was supposed to write a letter to Fidel. The proportion of new literates actually writing these letters was probably quite high, for the letters had to be countersigned by their teachers and then passed through the local education councils. The Literacy Museum† has thousands of such letters to Castro either on display or carefully filed away, and dozens if not hundreds of them were published in Cuban news-

* With what was undoubtedly unintended irony, an advertisement for the soon-to-disappear Coca-Cola Company showed the lily-white and well-manicured hand of the lady of the household (with a Coke bottle nearby) guiding the darker and rougher hand of a domestic servant through the ABC's. The slogan read, "In 1961, the Year of Education, use your 'pause that refreshes' to teach reading and writing to whomever you have near." *Bohemia*, Mar. 5, 1961, back cover.

† It is interesting that the literacy campaign is the only aspect of the revolution that is commemorated by its own museum, geographically and organizationally separate from the national Museum of the Revolution. At certain important revolutionary sites like the Moncada Barracks and Playa Girón there are small collections of relevant artifacts, but these are more properly thought of as national monuments than as true museums.

papers and magazines during the final months of the campaign. The following is typical:[45]

Finca el Naranjal
November 12, 1961
Year of Education

DOCTOR FIDEL CASTRO RUZ
Dear Compañero:

I write this to let you know that now I know how to read and write thanks to our Socialist and democratic Revolution. That's why I'm writing to you, so that you can see with your own eyes. I take leave with a firm Revolutionary and democratic salute.

I used to be illiterate,

FELICIA CARPIO BARCELÓ
Literacy worker, Wilfredo Neyra R.

Fatherland or Death
Doing Literacy Work, We Shall Triumph

The testimonial letters seem to have served at least two purposes. First, they gave a special importance and individuality to the end of the process of becoming literate. Both as a goal and as an actual experience, writing a letter to Fidel must have been richer and more satisfying than passing a standardized test. Second, from the point of view of the general public, the letters and other testimonials—misspelled, unpunctuated, direct, and frequently impassioned—lent variety and gave human meaning to the statistics in the newspapers. For all except the most cynical, these rustic letters—often published alongside touching and ingenuous notes from the brigadistas—must have helped to scale down the mass effort into numbers and images more easily understood.*

* Other publicity devices were used for translating the effort into terms understandable by those who were still illiterate. For instance, one of the love ballads popular at the time had the following words:

How many things I can now tell you
Because I have finally learned to write!
Now I can tell you that I love you,
Yes, now I can tell you.

By the quiet sands of the river,
On the trunk of that flamboyant tree,
I am carving your name and mine,
Enlaced forever together.

I used to read in your eyes
What your heart was telling me.
Now I can read it in your letters.
Now, my love, I am beginning to live.

Now the Fatherland has given me a treasure;
I have learned to read and write.

This and other songs of the period are available in Spanish on a record entitled "Chants de la Révolution Cubaine" (Paris: Le Chant du Monde).

The Campaign as a Socializing and Motivational Experience

As suggested previously, the campaign was seized upon by the revolutionary leadership as a tool for transforming the images, values, and behavior of Cuba's citizens. Not only were those who were teaching and those who were learning supposed to emerge from the experience as better revolutionaries and therefore as better Cubans, but all the others involved—mothers of brigadistas, workers who filled in for the missing "Patria o Muerte" literacy volunteers, and ordinary citizens who had to adjust to having their children out of school for nine months—were expected to learn from the experience. Above all, what was supposed to be experienced was the critical revolutionary lesson of "national fusion." As seen by one perceptive Cuban educator, the literacy effort had the following key consequences:

> Our campaign . . . has put the youth of Cuba in direct contact, on a daily and prolonged basis (for almost a year), with the peasants and mountain folk, the poorest and most isolated people on the island. Almost 100,000 teachers and students, aided by more than 170,000 adult volunteers, have launched a true movement of national fusion. This extensive experience in communal life cannot help greatly increasing understanding among the various classes and strata of the population. But in our view there is something more; [during the campaign] the entire populace could participate in the tasks of the revolution. The revolution no longer was a phenomenon reserved for a small group, zealous and active; it was converted into a true mass movement.[46]

With some aspects of this assessment there can be little disagreement. The opening up of revolutionary participation to almost the entire population and the greatly increased contacts across class and geographical lines have already been discussed at some length. The campaign's more enduring attitudinal and behavioral consequences, however, are not so obvious or easy to evaluate. What the revolutionary leadership wanted and expected to happen was well articulated in the speeches and reportage of the period; what actually happened was at times another matter.[47]

In order to evaluate the campaign as a socializing and motivational experience, we must rely primarily on inferences from the logic of the situation.[48] In the absence of survey data of any kind, we must ask what there was about the experience itself that could have affected the participants' attitudes and behavior, both immediately and in long-run terms, and what the different effects might have been for various types of participants. For simplicity, we shall ignore fine distinctions and differentiate only between illiterates, literacy workers, and those who contributed indirectly either by participating in the related work of the mass organizations or by interacting with family members and friends directly involved in the campaign. Our discussion of the individual consequences of the campaign will be organized around the following five themes: the newness of the experience, the centrality of the experience, the intimacy of the activity, feedback and reinforcement, and identification with the larger revolutionary effort.

The newness of the experience. The vast majority of Cubans connected with the literacy campaign were engaged in activities that were wholly unprecedented for them. Most of the male Conrado Benítez brigadistas had never spent much time with peasants before; certainly they had never lived in the huts of campesinos or shared their daily life. To the girl brigadistas, though they usually did not live in the homes of the peasants they taught, the change of scene was equally remarkable. For girls, most of them from the cities, just to be dealing with the peasantry, to be away from home and out from under the watchful eye of parents and relatives, was a dramatic change. Even for the adult *alfabetizadores populares,* who taught in the urban areas and lived at home, there was much that was new. Almost none had ever taught before, and few had ever performed any kind of service work that crossed class lines, except perhaps for a little holiday charity. As for the illiterates, not only were they students for the first time in their lives, but they were involved in an encounter that directly challenged their experience of isolation and backwardness. Many peasants must have been shocked indeed when some fresh-faced city boy appeared at their door with lantern and knapsack in hand and announced that he was "their literacy worker." Finally, the family and friends of both literacy workers and illiterates underwent experiences that broke sharply with the past. Parents were separated for long periods of time from their brigadista sons and daughters; peasant youngsters lived, played, and worked with city children;

women were given instruction and responsibilities on equal terms with men; and people who only a few years earlier had sedulously avoided political involvement found themselves tied by family and friendship to a massive governmental campaign.

To be sure, the new activities and relationships were not always experienced as positive. Some parents undoubtedly were resentful and bewildered at having their children leave them and go to remote areas as literacy workers; some peasants undoubtedly were frightened and offended by the intrusion of the campaign and the campaigners into their lives; and certain brigadistas undoubtedly felt little but scorn and pity for the rural folk among whom they had to work. But, for reasons that will shortly become clearer, negative responses of this sort were probably a small minority. Whatever the reaction, good or bad, the campaign gave people new experiences that could not easily be brushed aside.

The centrality of the experience. Another reason for the lasting impact of the campaign is that for most of the teachers and their students literacy work was the central fact of their lives during the two to six months or more that they were engaged in it. For the brigadistas, teaching and its associated responsibilities were full-time work, and for the alfabetizadores it was often almost equally demanding. Although peasant illiterates spent only a few hours a day at most with the primer, the constant presence of the brigadista and the continued emphasis on learning affected many of the other rhythms and routines of rural life. To a lesser extent, the same was true in the city. Thus the literacy campaign deeply affected the lives of both teachers and learners.

The intimacy of the activity. A goal of the campaign—as stated during the National Literacy Congress of September 1961—was to have the literacy worker teach only one illiterate at a time. Above all, a classroom atmosphere was to be avoided. The one-to-one ratio was never actually realized, but the values that led to its being proposed were made manifest in other ways during the campaign. At times, persons connected with the effort became absolutely lyrical about the teacher-pupil relationship. One official spoke of the "marriage" of literacy worker and illiterate;[49] and one of the year's most widely circulated poems cast the teaching-learning relationship entirely in the familial metaphor. The peasant father tells the brigadista:

> Here you will not be alone,
> Here you will have a mother,
> Noble brothers and a father....
>
> You will follow me and I will follow you,
> Over the plain and through the mountains;
> And in this brotherhood that enfolds
> The offspring of my Island,
> I will learn from your primer
> And you will learn from the land.[50]

Separated as we are by time, distance, culture, and politics from the literacy campaign, it would be easy to dismiss these characteristics as a simple romanticizing of what in reality was just another job. But, at least for the brigadistas, there is absolutely no evidence to support such a conclusion. For them it was more akin to a revolutionary rite of passage, their first opportunity to prove that they were full-fledged revolutionaries. One can only assume that many brigadistas (and some illiterates also) poured heart and soul into developing intimate and continuing human relationships across lines of class and age.[51] Although the "marriage" of literacy worker and illiterate may never have taken place, some degree of revolutionary fusion undoubtedly did, with concomitant changes in attitudes and behavior.

Feedback and reinforcement. From both the national and the individual point of view, the literacy campaign was rich in feedback and reinforcement. The letters from brigadistas and new literates, the flood of general publicity given to the effort, and the innumerable meetings, celebrations, and graduations all focused public attention on the progress of the campaign. In addition, the campaign was reported in what might be called a self-reinforcing fashion. That is, progress was well enough defined and rapid enough to give month-by-month if not week-by-week evidence to the general population that all the struggle and sacrifice was paying off. Moreover, from the individual point of view—especially for those who participated directly—the campaign was even more self-reinforcing. Compared with more complex skills, literacy at the first-grade level is quickly taught and easily measured. Thus neither literacy workers nor their students were ever long in doubt about how they were doing. This quick and easily measured progress, together with the national emphasis on the importance of the Year of Education, gave teachers and pupils throughout Cuba not only a feeling of individual pride and accomplishment, but a respect for the power and viability of the revolutionary way of doing things. One key way of learning such lessons is to experience personally the small triumphs of which the national triumph is the aggregate.

Identification with the larger revolutionary effort. Just as most citizens and soldiers of a victorious power emerge from a "just" war with a heightened perception of their nation's capabilities and rectitude and a stronger sense of identification with their leaders' goals and values, so we would expect most Cubans to have emerged from the battle against illiteracy not only with heightened self-esteem but also with a stronger sense of revolutionary citizenship and a determination to continue to act in a revolutionary fashion. In a psychological and organizational sense, the campaign was experienced as a war, with the classic tension between the glory and the danger of mortal combat replaced by a lesser but nonetheless vivid interplay between personal discomfort on the one hand and personal and national triumph on the other. As a Uruguayan educator pointed out at the time, years after the brigadistas return from the countryside they will be telling stories about the rivers they crossed, the mountains they climbed, the hardships they suffered, and the peasants they taught, just as old soldiers now recall old battles.[52] It is unnecessary to invest participation in the campaign against illiteracy with the characteristics of true heroism in order to appreciate that for hundreds of thousands of Cubans it was one of the revolution's finest hours as well as one of their own most satisfying, meaningful, and enduring experiences.

The Campaign as a Learning Experience for the Leadership

The Year of Education was also a special year in other respects. To name only three, it was the year of the break in diplomatic relations with the United States, the year of the Bay of Pigs invasion, and the year of Castro's public embrace of Socialism. In addition, 1961 was perhaps the key year in the evolution of the political institutions and style of the Revolutionary Government. As we shall see in the following two chapters, the Committees for Defense of the Revolution and the Schools of Revolutionary Instruction—two of the Castro government's most interesting institutional experiments—first assumed nationwide importance in 1961. And it was also in 1961 that the Integrated Revolutionary Organizations, the precursor of the United Party of the Socialist Revolution and the Communist Party of Cuba, was born. It was a year during which the top leadership was very much in search of institutions and a style of governance that fit their idea of what the revolution should be and do.

Under these conditions of search and experimentation, East European practices were sometimes adopted as the most available and appropriate for a Socialist Cuba.[53] But at the same time there was also an attempt to find a "Cuban way"—if not a full-fledged tropical doctrine of Marxism-Leninism, at least an ideologically acceptable method of revolutionary transformation that would deal directly and effectively with Cuban problems. In this sense the literacy campaign served as a kind of experiment in Cuban revolutionary techniques. Because of the particular historical juncture at which the campaign occurred, the overall importance attached to it, and the considerable pedagogical and political successes it achieved, it was one of the revolutionary leadership's most influential learning experiences during their first years in power.

To be sure, other learning experiences were just as important. The guerrilla struggle in the Sierra profoundly shaped the leadership's views on armed struggle; the missile crisis of 1962 contributed to a reevaluation of the geopolitics of big power–small power relationships; and the economic problems of the mid-sixties led to a reversal of emphasis in investment policy, with much more attention paid to agriculture. What is special about the literacy campaign, however, is the part it played in the forming of the leadership's "operational code" of national development and revolutionary transformation.[54] It should be emphasized that this code was not (and still is not) a tightly woven fabric of beliefs and prescriptions for action. Especially in 1961, it was little more than a loosely linked and changing set of beliefs about how to mobilize and transform men and materials in the service of revolutionary goals. Moreover, because the literacy campaign was only one of a number of events that helped shape the development of this code, any discussion of its effects on the leadership's beliefs is necessarily incomplete.

In the following pages we shall consider the four elements of the belief system that were most affected by the literacy campaign. The beliefs are here stated in propositional form, but it cannot be assumed that Cuba's leaders then or now would articulate them in precisely this manner. The idea is simply to represent as accurately as possible—on the basis of speeches, writings, and political practice—their dominant attitudes toward the process of social renovation and change.

Organization flows from revolutionary activity rather than activity from organization. In retrospect it is obvious that when Castro spoke to the United Nations in September 1960, neither he nor anyone else in Cuba had a clear idea of how the campaign would actually be organized. From the revolutionary point of view, the important thing at that moment was to make a public pledge to eradicate illiteracy. The planning and organizational work would come after, not before, this commitment. This is not, of course, a particularly unusual political and developmental occurrence, but in the Cuban case it has assumed a special meaning and importance. In Cuba, it is not just political bravado, impatience, or inexperience that leads the elite to launch developmental programs before the detailed planning and organizational work that will ultimately be needed to keep them going is begun. Rather, it is the belief that the act of trying, the struggle itself, opens up possibilities that could not have been imagined before the battle was actually joined.

The negative corollary of this belief is that too much thought given in advance to the possible consequences of a program tends to erode revolutionary will and courage. Thus "planning does make cowards of us all" could almost be taken as a motto of the revolutionary leadership. Would the literacy campaign have been undertaken at all if a careful study of its manpower and opportunity costs had been made in advance? Would the Conrado Benítez brigades ever have been formed, the schools closed for nine months, or the workers sent from the factories to teach in the countryside if the need for such measures had been seen from the outset and doubts and cautions been given a full hearing? Would the interplay between problems and solutions have produced so many creative responses if the entire landscape of difficulties had been mapped beforehand and the campaign adjusted accordingly? Of course not, the revolutionaries would answer; moreover, not only did the revolutionary style of problem solving lead to no dire consequences, but the "unimaginable" policies developed during the campaign were central to its success. "The revolution itself is our great teacher," Castro is fond of saying. No event of the years immediately after the guerrilla struggle gave this belief more substantial reinforcement than the literacy campaign.

Revolutionary programs are not limited by lack of human resources so much as by the difficulty of mobilizing and using the population at large and the resources of other organizations. Almost all the characteristics of the campaign emphasized earlier in this chapter bear on this second proposition. The various plans to recruit and train literacy workers, the use of members of the mass organizations for a wide variety of administrative tasks, and the incorporation of the schoolteachers into technical and supervisory positions all attest to the leadership's growing awareness of the need to draw both the public at large and specific groups into the campaign.

Viewing almost the entire population as the potential manpower pool for a developmental effort implies two subsidiary beliefs. The first is that given a bit of initial guidance and a revolutionary orientation toward work, almost anyone can be helpful in one way or another. Thus all children with a sixth-grade education can teach illiterates (although they cannot teach physics), any housewife who can count and write a simple sentence can be a census taker, and any peasant who understands why it is a revolutionary duty to become literate can help in recruiting his compañeros for the campaign. The basic problem is not training the child, the housewife, and the peasant, but locating, recruiting, and motivating them. In the revolutionary view, people grow to fit the responsibilities thrust upon them. The second belief is that at times the manpower pool of one developmental project can expand only at the expense of other programs and institutions. Here the problem is not locating and recruiting new participants, but knowing when to rob one organization for the sake of another. The lesson of the literacy campaign was that few institutions, organizations, or activities need be considered sacred when the momentum of the revolution or the reputation of its leadership is at stake.

Every developmental project is above all a political project. In the Cuban view, the developmental problems faced by the poorer nations cannot be solved by the conventional application of conventional technology. In fact, national development is not in the first instance a technical or even an economic problem. It is a political problem: its causes are political and its solutions must be political. At no time was this view, as applied to and reinforced by the literacy campaign, more clearly articulated than by Armando Hart in his opening address to the National Literacy Congress:

> There is no technical or pedagogical instrumentality capable of launching a campaign like this one; only when technique and pedagogy are subordinated to the revolutionary power of the people and the organization of the masses can they really be of service in a political project like this. . . .
>
> Literacy work requires such energy, such popular effort, that any nation whose population is a half, or a third, or a fourth, or a fifth illiterate will require the participation of its citizenry in this work. There is no school organization, no educational structure, capable of resolving this problem. Only a political structure incorporating the masses can confront it; and only when the illiterates and the literacy workers understand that they are working on a task of great importance for their own political, social, and economic development will they be able to complete the extensive job of eradicating illiteracy.[55]

Not only must developmental projects be seen as political projects if they are going to succeed, but they must provide occasions for the political education of participants, for the forming of citizens. In the literacy campaign, this belief was manifested concretely in the manual *Alfabeticemos,* and more diffusely in the various socialization practices previously described. Thus the literacy effort was seen as having political origins, as taking place under political auspices and direction, and as yielding increments of political learning for all who participated. As a model of how to mount a campaign that was at the same time both developmental and political, it was much emulated by the leadership in subsequent years.

Although developmental resources may be concentrated in the cities, revolutionary values, virtues, and experiences are concentrated in the countryside. As we have seen, one major goal of the movement was to bring the urban and rural sectors of the society together, to enable each to learn something about the other, and especially to give city people some appreciation of the hardships and sacrifices of rural life. But the elite did not see the city and the countryside as simply two different environments whose populations should become acquainted. There was a strong and frequently expressed feeling that the urban environment, when it does not actually corrupt, at least teaches nothing of real revolutionary importance. Organizational and technological resources are found in the cities, but the personal virtues needed by the true revolutionary (selflessness, social consciousness, willingness to sacrifice and work long hours) are found more frequently in the countryside. Moreover—and this is most important to the revolutionary world view—if one is going to learn such things, if one is going to be transformed into a true revolutionary (a new man), this transformation will almost surely involve an extended encounter with the rural environment. This, of course, is the lesson of the Conrado Benítez brigadistas, as earlier it had been one of the most important lessons of the guerrilla struggle against Batista. During the first decade of the revolution, perhaps no other element of the operational code has been as continuously reemphasized and reinterpreted through developmental programs as this belief.[56]

4 The Committees for Defense of the Revolution

ON SEPTEMBER 28, 1960, immediately upon returning to Havana after his appearance before the United Nations, Fidel Castro formally launched the Comités de Defensa de la Revolución (CDR). In a speech from the north balcony of the Presidential Palace to tens of thousands of spectators and hundreds of thousands more on television, the Prime Minister said,

> We're going to set up a system of collective vigilance; we're going to set up a system of revolutionary collective vigilance. And then we shall see how the lackeys of imperialism manage to operate in our midst. Because one thing is sure, we have people in all parts of the city; there's not an apartment building in the city, not a corner, not a block, not a neighborhood, that is not amply represented here [in the audience]. In answer to the imperialist campaigns of aggression, we're going to set up a system of revolutionary collective vigilance so that everybody will know everybody else on his block, what they do, what relationship they had with the tryanny [the Batista government], what they believe in, what people they meet, what activities they participate in. Because if they [the counterrevolutionaries] think they can stand up to the people, they're going to be tremendously disappointed. Because we'll confront them with a committee of revolutionary vigilance on every block.... When the masses are organized there isn't a single imperialist, or a lackey of the imperialists, or anybody who has sold out to the imperialists, who can operate.[1]

As Castro spoke, two bombs exploded near the plaza, lending dramatic counterpoint to his words and evoking cries of "¡Paredón!" (To the execution wall!) and "¡Venceremos!" (We shall triumph!) from his audience.[2]

In some later reports of the events at the Presidential Palace, the announcement of the founding of the CDR was clothed in an aura of spontaneity that undoubtedly was lacking in the speech itself.[3] Castro's plan for Committees for Defense of the Revolution had in fact been in gestation for many months. At least since March 4, 1960, when the French freighter *La Coubre* had mysteriously exploded while unloading ammunition in Havana harbor, there had been discussion of the growing need for some form of urban-based civil defense against sabotage and counterrevolutionary terror.[4] In a mass meeting in support of the Revolutionary Government held on August 13, 1960, the following oath formed part of the document "ratified" by the audience in public assembly: "We swear to increase our revolutionary vigilance at work, at home, and in the streets in order to uncover counterrevolutionary conspirators, saboteurs, and propagandists of imperialism and the counterrevolution, and to silence them or turn them over to the revolutionary authorities."[5] This was only the most public manifestation of a mood that by then was already deeply felt in Cuba, particularly in Havana, where mounting counterrevolutionary activity was most apparent. By the time Castro spoke at the Presidential Palace, the ground had been prepared, at least ideologically, for the first Committees for Defense of the Revolution. The threat to the revolution was real, and Castro did not need the bombs on the night of September 28 to be moved to action.

The first committees began to form almost immediately following Castro's speech, despite the absence of official guidelines for the program. Although some members of a National Directorate of the CDR had probably been appointed, no true bureaucratic structure at the national level yet existed.* Formal power to grant permission to organize committees was lodged with the municipal authorities, but groups of enthusiastic citizens went ahead and formed

* The organization of the CDR will be treated in more detail later. The first Coordinator of the National Directorate was José Matar. In 1965 Matar was named one of the original members of the Central Committee of the (new) Communist Party of Cuba. Andrés Suárez, in *Cuba: Castroism and Communism, 1959–1966* (Cambridge, Mass., 1967), p. 128, suggests that Matar was probably not a member of the Partido Socialista Popular, although the question of his early political affiliation is of limited relevance to our concerns. In 1966, Luis González Marturelos was named National Coordinator of the CDR. In January 1968, at the time of the public exposure and denunciation of the anti-party "microfaction" led by Aníbal Escalante, Matar was implicated and separated from the Central Committee. See *Granma*, Jan. 28, 1968.

their own committees without much attention to procedural niceties. Like so many other institutions of the early years of the revolution, the first CDR displayed more energy than order, more enthusiasm than discipline.

In Castro's original reference to a system of revolutionary vigilance, it was implied that the CDR were to be organized along geographical lines; that is, they were to be block or neighborhood committees that would draw their membership from and exercise surveillance over given residential areas. Most of the new committees were in fact of this type. With anywhere from five to twenty or more members, block committees were set up first in Havana and then almost immediately in other cities throughout the island. But neighborhoods were not the only basis of organization. Because there was much to be kept under surveillance, CDR were also formed in factories, stores, administrative offices, and schools. In fact, some Cubans belonged to two committees, one at work and one at home, a practice that came to be discouraged as the national organization matured and the Directorate tried to impose some semblance of order on the system.

Although the primary and original purpose of the CDR, as stated by Castro, was to discover and denounce counterrevolutionary behavior, to defend the revolution from "the enemy within," the leadership soon came to see vigilance as only one of their many possible functions. By the beginning of 1961, various lists of the committees' purposes and responsibilities were being circulated. The following is representative:

> The Committee for Defense of the Revolution will be an instrument for promoting the unity and cohesion of the people, taking into its ranks all citizens disposed to defend the Fatherland.
>
> By mobilizing itself it will prevent all types of counterrevolutionary activities by the agents of imperialism and by those who plot against the Fatherland.
>
> It will observe the movements of all counterrevolutionary elements in order to prevent any attempt to return to the past, denouncing such elements to the appropriate authorities.
>
> It will cooperate voluntarily in all operations and necessary steps of the productive process.
>
> It will organize discussion groups to publicize the work of the revolution and to increase the political and civic capacity of all its members.

During the Year of Education it will work to make sure that not one illiterate remains within its radius of action.

In case of aggression by the imperialists and their lackeys it will organize civil defense and give first aid, etc.

It will organize public audiences when the leaders of the revolution speak to the people, taking radios, television sets, and amplifiers out into the street.[6]

The Bay of Pigs and Its Aftermath

Despite increasing pressure from other responsibilities, vigilance remained the CDR's main task during the anxious early months of 1961, an emphasis fully vindicated by the events of April. Even before the break in United States–Cuban diplomatic relations on January 3, 1961, there was a growing official, well-publicized feeling in Havana that the island was going to be invaded.[7] After the first of the year, hardly a day passed without some newspaper story on the impending invasion or on the necessity of keeping on the alert against counterrevolutionary activities. In March, the National Directorate issued a special call for the formation of committees in places of work, saying, "We are going to show the counterrevolution that the people are ready; we are going to form defense committees factory by factory, shop by shop, cooperative by cooperative, store by store, to smash all counterrevolutionary elements by means of vigilance and public denunciation."[8] At the end of the month, the National Directorate issued another proclamation, this one calling for night and day watchfulness both at home and at work: "The worms are waiting, hidden in the shadows, to do their ruinous work of destruction and terror, paid for by the Yankee gold to which they have sold their hearts and consciences. ... The National Directorate of the Committees for Defense of the Revolution calls on the people to be on the alert 24 hours a day in order to oppose any aggressive move our enemies attempt."[9] Less than three weeks later, as the first bombs were dropped and the first shots were fired at Playa Girón, the CDR had ample opportunity to exercise their twin responsibilities of vigilance and public denunciation under conditions of true national emergency.

On April 17 Fidel Castro declared the country to be in a state of alert and ordered the CDR to redouble their vigilance efforts and to uncover and denounce counterrevolutionaries.[10] The historic three-day struggle had begun. While the Revolutionary Armed Forces and the Militia were engaging the exile troops on the beaches and in the swamps near the Bay of Pigs, the committees, in a frenzy of activity in the cities and towns, were reporting and rounding up persons suspected of counterrevolutionary sentiments and behavior. These suspects were detained in schools, churches, theaters, public buildings, and whatever other structures could be pressed into service and made fairly secure. "Women, old people, and children participated in the task; some armed with frying pans, others with clubs, and a few with side arms, they rounded up suspects for detention."[11] By April 19, tens of thousands of Cubans had been detained, the invading forces had been defeated, and the "counterrevolution in the cities and towns"—what there was of it—had been smashed.[12]

It seems safe to say that relatively few of the detainees were actually active counterrevolutionaries. Members of the CDR moved rapidly and often indiscriminately against neighbors whom they regarded as insufficiently revolutionary in outlook, or whom they simply disliked. The spirit of the moment was not conducive to moderation, fine distinctions, or charity, as Castro conceded a few days later in reviewing the situation for a national television audience:

> In addition to the action of the military forces, the Committees for Defense of the Revolution also participated. It was felt necessary to arrest all those persons who for one reason or another might be active [in the counterrevolution], or who could be active, or who might possibly give aid to the counterrevolution. Under these conditions, naturally, some injustices are always committed; such a result is inevitable. The nation, at such a dangerous juncture, faced with an attack of this kind, had to take every possible measure to defend herself. And for that reason the Committees for Defense of the Revolution arrested all those persons who in some fashion or other might have threatened the nation. I repeat, there might have been cases of injustice, even some revolutionaries arrested by mistake. But any revolutionary will understand that.[13]

As it became apparent that the immediate threat to the revolution had passed, most of those detained were released. Others charged with actual or suspected counterrevolutionary activities were transferred to regular prisons.

Despite the number of persons detained and the seemingly impressive job of vigilance done by the committees, it is not at all certain that the CDR "smashed the urban counterrevolution" at the time of the Bay of Pigs, as both friends and foes of the revolution frequently claim. It was later widely admitted on both sides of the Florida Straits that urban opposition to Castro was sparse, poorly organized, and ideologically fragmented at the time of the invasion. Thus there was probably not much of a threat in any event. Moreover, the CDR system itself was only just beginning to assume some scope and coherence; at the time of the invasion, there were only about 8,000 committees with a total of 70,000 members on the entire island.[14] Had a well-organized and massive internal threat to the revolution actually existed, the CDR would probably have been hard put to cope with it.

Although the centrality of the work of the CDR to the total defense effort at the time of the invasion can be questioned, the importance of those same events to the growth and development of the organization itself is beyond a doubt. The civil defense effort of April 17–19 was the high point of the first months of the CDR, and when the National Directorate met immediately after the invasion, there was not only a great deal of self-congratulation but also ambitious planning for the future.* An immediate goal of 100,000 committees and 500,000 new members was set. In addition to individual proselytizing, the existing CDR, other mass organizations, and local officials sponsored mass meetings for the membership drive. All supporters of the revolution were expected to attend, and as many new committees were formed on the spot as were needed to enroll all those in attendance.[15]

Throughout May and especially during June and July thousands

* See "La lucha en la retaguardia," *Verde Olivo,* Año II, No. 20 (May 21, 1961), pp. 12–15. As might be expected, stories of the glorious behavior of the masses during this national emergency were circulated both by word of mouth and in the mass media after the victory at Playa Girón. The following is typical: "Jacoba Morales, a 77-year-old lady, a resident of San Antonio de los Baños and the mother of a committee president, on hearing the airplanes rend the air with the roar of their engines, became so enraged that with clenched fists she shouted at them from the middle of the street: 'Mercenaries, worms, cowards! ... Give me a rifle, a firearm....' And when no one gave her anything, she bent over, picked up two rocks, and threw them into the air, trying to reach the criminal machines." *Ibid.*, p. 14.

of meetings were held, countless speeches made, hundreds of articles printed in the newspapers, and numerous programs produced on radio and television, all to further the expansion of the CDR system. Lest the masses let down their guard, they were constantly reminded that the battle against the counterrevolution was still being fought, both in the Escambray Mountains, where organized counterrevolutionary bands clashed with the Militia and the Revolutionary Armed Forces, and in the cities, where there were still sporadic incidents of sabotage and terrorism. In August the goal was reached: the National Directorate announced, with surprisingly little fanfare, that there were now 100,000 CDR on the island.[16] Nothing was said, however, about the state of organization or disorganization of this massive system that had in three short months grown out of the original 8,000 committees, or about the problems caused by this extraordinary expansion.

The Organization, Reorganization, and Subsequent Growth of the CDR

The CDR celebrated their first anniversary in a massive meeting held in the Plaza of the Revolution. Committee members came from all over the Province of Havana to participate in the festivities and to listen to Castro give the anniversary address. In a speech laced with pride, humor, scorn, and irony, he discussed the genesis of the CDR, their philosophy, their membership, their revolutionary work, and the new society's brave departure from the Batistiano social order of the past.* He said that there were 107,000 CDR, each with at least ten members and some with as many as a hundred. If these figures are accurate, within one year a mass organization of well over one million members had been created in a country of only seven million inhabitants. As suggested above, however, the rapid growth of the CDR had been anything but orderly and careful. Much of the membership was more nominal than

* *Revolución*, Sept. 30, 1961, pp. 12–14. Castro has made a major speech on each of the eight anniversaries of the CDR to date (1968). His first such speech was the one most centrally concerned with the CDR itself (the others have covered a wide variety of topics). Major sections of the first anniversary speech are presented in Appendix C.

real; the system was hurriedly put together; it was more an agglomeration of separate committees than a fully functioning and well-articulated organization. The system lacked boundaries, criteria for membership, intermediate structures, and effective mechanisms of communication and control. In 1962 the leadership moved to correct this situation.

One of the first organizational reforms of the second year was to create a classical pyramid of command. In addition to the National Directorate of the CDR, six provincial (state) directorates were established. Below them district directorates were created (the districts corresponding rather closely to municipalities), and at a lower level sectional directorates, to which the individual committees were attached. At each level of this hierarchy, including the committee level, individual staff or committee members were assigned responsibility for the various *frentes*, or activities, to which the energies of the CDR were directed.* Furthermore, each of the committees was headed by a chairman, and each of the organizations at higher levels by a coordinator or director. By the second anniversary of the CDR, the full system was in view, and the intermediate levels of command had expanded to include more than 150 district directorates and 1,360 sectional directorates in addition to the six provincial directorates.[17]

Data on the total membership, the number of committees, and the number of intermediate structures during the first four years of the CDR are presented in Table 5. Notice that according to official claims the number of individual committees fell somewhat after the first anniversary of the program, whereas the overall membership and the number of intermediate structures continued to grow during the entire four-year period.

The aggregate statistics on the growth and reorganization of the

* In September 1962, José Matar listed the following thirteen frentes: organization, vigilance and maintaining public order, propaganda, provisioning (distribution of scarce goods), sports, urban reform, revolutionary instruction, public health, popular defense, education, voluntary work, popular inspection, and international solidarity and peace. *Revolución*, Sept. 27, 1962, p. 4. In 1963 the frentes were reorganized.

TABLE 5. GROWTH AND DEVELOPMENT OF THE CDR SYSTEM, 1961–64

Month	Total membership	Number of committees	Number of sectional directorates	Number of district directorates
April 1961	70,000	8,000	—	—
Sept. 1961	1,000,000+	107,000	—	—
Sept. 1962	1,500,000	100,000	1,360	150
Sept. 1963	1,545,000	103,700	3,820	155
Sept. 1964	2,000,000	110,000 (est.)	4,300	197

Note: All figures are approximate. In addition to the sectional and district directorates, there were six provincial directorates.

Sources: For the April 1961 figures, *Revolución*, Sept. 27, 1965, p. 2. For the Sept. 1961 figures, Castro's speech on the first anniversary of the CDR, *Revolución*, Sept. 30, 1961, p. 12. For the Sept. 1962 total membership, José Matar, "Dos años de experiencia de los Comités de Defensa de la Revolución," *Cuba Socialista*, No. 15 (Nov. 1962), p. 36; for the other Sept. 1962 figures, *Revolución*, Sept. 28, 1962, p. 4. For the Sept. 1963 figures, data reported in "Tercer chequeo nacional de la emulación de los CDR," *Con la Guardia en Alto*, Oct. 1963, p. 40. For the Sept. 1964 figures, *Revolución*, Sept. 29, 1964, p. 2. The estimate is mine. The total membership in September 1965 was reported as 2,200,000 in *Revolución*, Sept. 22, 1965, p. 2.

CDR tend to mask or at least fail to indicate clearly what was actually happening in the system during the early years. The critical problems brought about by the mass membership drive could not be solved simply by establishing a chain of command with sectional and district directorates. The individual committees themselves had to be redefined, reorganized, inventoried, "purified," and fully integrated into the national system. At the same time, the various higher directorates had to be staffed to some minimal level of competence.

Efforts to accomplish these immediate goals began in 1962 with meetings of the individual committees for the purpose of self-examination. Each meeting was attended by a representative of the sectional directorate or some other cadre, and nonmembers living or working in the area were also invited. At these meetings, open season was declared on those suspected of joining the committees for the "wrong reasons" (personal advantage or counter-revolution). In September 1962 the National Directorate announced that 73,700 committees had met in sessions of self-examination. "These meetings have enabled us, the CDR and the masses together, to purge our ranks of the unhealthy elements that have slipped in, to wipe out incorrect methods of work, to overcome weaknesses and errors in organization, to strengthen our ties to the people, to reorganize and fortify the Committees for Defense of the Revolution."[18] By the end of the year, over 86,000 committees had been purged and reorganized by means of public assemblies, over 400,000 new members had been brought into the system, and approximately 50,000 men and women had been selected for administrative positions at the sectional and district levels.[19] Even if we admit that the official evaluation of these activities was bound to be optimistic, we must also recognize that a tremendous effort was made during 1962–63 to purify and reorganize the CDR, and that considerable success was achieved.

A number of other practices were also begun in 1962 and 1963 in order to define the membership of the CDR more clearly, continue the process of purification, facilitate organizational bookkeeping, and improve vertical control and communication. Membership cards, first issued at the end of 1962, were one such device. Open meetings were again held, and votes were taken to determine who would and who would not be given cards.[20] By the end of 1963, the card system had been revised, old cards were to be exchanged for new ones, and membership fees were to be levied on a nationwide basis starting in 1964.[21] It was hoped that these fees would reduce the costs borne by the National Directorate and at the same time involve the members more directly in the overall CDR program. As the National Coordinator said,

> We shall now have one more means for maintaining contact with every member of the organization, not to mention the enormous advantage that will accrue in the political and organizational sense as a result of our efforts to make sure every member is paid up. If 1963 saw a jump in the quality of the organizational structure of the CDR, this was due above all to the distribution of membership cards. We are sure that in 1964, because of the fees added to the membership cards, another notable jump in the political and organizational quality of the CDR will be forthcoming.[22]

Perhaps the most important of all the management devices used in the CDR system is what the Cubans call *emulación*, best translated as competition.* Some form of emulación is used in almost every revolutionary institution in order to enlist support, increase productivity, establish and evaluate performance criteria, or intensify organizational identification. The first nationwide emulación in the CDR program lasted from the beginning of March until the end of September 1963. Each committee competed with all the other committees in its section in a competition based on a 35-point checklist of responsibilities and accomplishments covering everything from attendance at meetings to neighborhood cleanliness.[23] Every month each sectional directorate awarded recognition to an "exemplary committee." The sections within each district also competed with each other every month. Furthermore, there was a competition among the districts of each province,[24] and, at the national level, one of the six provinces was chosen as having contributed most to the program. In September, trophies were awarded to the best committee in each section, the best section in each district, the best district in each province, and—by Castro himself at the third anniversary celebration—the best province on the island. Thus intergroup comparison was added to pressure, praise, and publicity in a continuing attempt to heighten the responsiveness of the CDR and improve the performance of the entire system.

It is impossible to say how much management devices like self-criticism, membership cards and fees, and emulación contributed to the effectiveness of the CDR. It is clear, however, that as these devices were put to use, the most serious problems of control, communication, and organization were met. By 1964, for example, the National Directorate could say fairly accurately how many sub-

* The Cubans have gone to some length to differentiate between *competencia* (competition) and *emulación*, associating the former with capitalism and the latter with socialism. For instance, in discussing this terminology with respect to the productive process, the following distinction was made at the outset of the first nationwide CDR emulación: "Capitalist competition is based on the law of the jungle: Devour the others before they devour you. Increased production in large factories is accompanied by reduced production and disaster in small factories. Socialist emulation is based on the principle of elevating the production of all factories. The more backward industries struggle to achieve the performance level of the more advanced. And the factories in the vanguard struggle to achieve even greater successes." *Revolución*, Apr. 5, 1963, p. 8.

directorates, committees, and individual members were in the system and who their members were, and the National Coordinator could issue a directive with some confidence that it would filter down intact to the grass roots. The organization and functioning of the CDR had improved significantly since September 1961, when Castro had spoken of 107,000 committees with over 1,000,000 members, many of whom undoubtedly had been unaware as Castro spoke that they belonged to any such revolutionary organization.

The Functions of the CDR

As we have seen, almost from the outset the CDR have organized their work into a number of frentes, or areas of responsibility. Although the list changes slightly whenever new tasks are added to the program, the fourteen frentes of 1963 show the kinds of day-to-day activities in which the CDR engage: coordination, organization, administration of finances, revolutionary instruction, vigilance, popular defense, education, public health administration, urban reform, provisioning (distribution of scarce goods), voluntary work, propaganda and cultural instruction, sports and recreation, and the furtherance of international peace.[25] The first four frentes are primarily concerned with intraorganizational maintenance, and the other ten in one fashion or another with services the CDR perform for the neighborhood, various bureaucracies, and the revolution in general.

However, instead of viewing the responsibilities of the CDR in terms of specific activities and accomplishments—how many children have been enrolled in school, how many peace pamphlets have been distributed, or how many new members have joined since the last report—we shall address ourselves to the more general question: what higher-order tasks are the CDR expected to perform in support of the Revolutionary Government and its programs? In answer we would say that the CDR are expected to integrate, socialize, and mobilize the masses, to implement revolutionary policies and programs, and to protect both the material and the social resources of the revolution. The day-to-day activities of the various frentes listed above can be seen as contributing to one or more—usually more—of these five intended functions.* Note that the higher-order responsibilities are central to the larger revolutionary enterprise. Viewed this way, the purpose of the CDR is not so much accomplishment in specific frentes as it is to contribute to the maintenance of the revolution itself.

The CDR as integrator. During the first anniversary celebration, no theme received more attention than what one commentator had earlier called the role of the CDR as *centros de aglutinamiento popular.*[26] By this was meant that nearly all the diverse types of people living and working in revolutionary Cuba could and should come together in the committees. In contrast to other mass organizations, in which membership was limited by occupational or demographic criteria, the CDR were designed to incorporate all Cubans fifteen or older who were disposed to work for the revolution. As Castro emphasized in his first anniversary speech, anyone can belong—the young and the old, men and women, students and housewives, workers and pensioners, intellectuals and peasants. "It is the organization that permits those citizens who cannot belong to any other organization to work for the revolution. . . . There are even cases of persons who cannot do physical work; there are cases of compañeros who are invalids but who nevertheless work actively in a Committee for Defense of the Revolution."[27]

Open membership, however, did not mean uncontrolled membership. Even before the reorganizations and purifications of the second year of the CDR, some restrictions were established. In the same first anniversary speech, Castro made it very clear that precisely because the revolution was "the grand union of all honorable persons, of all useful persons, of all studious persons, of all worthy persons, of all persons who produce for the populace," there was no room in the organization for "enemies of the people, enemies

* These have been called "intended functions" to suggest that they might not actually have been performed well or completely, if at all. In the case of the CDR, however, sufficient integration, socialization, mobilization, implementation, and protection do take place, so that we are describing not only the system's goals and ideology, but also—under the same set of headings—its operation and its functional importance within the larger revolutionary context. Some of the CDR system's problems and dysfunctions will be treated in the concluding section of this chapter.

of the masses, parasites, exploiters, slackers, those who don't work, those who live off the work of others."*

This basic goal of bringing into the CDR all Cubans willing to work for the revolution has taken the organization to the most remote and at times unlikely corners of the island: to the mountains of Oriente, to ships at sea, and even into the prisons.[28] Because the criteria for belonging to the CDR are based on attitude and behavior rather than on demography, growth in membership is taken as an index of the overall success of the integrative efforts of the Revolutionary Government. The larger the membership of the CDR and the closer it comes to being a true cross section of the Cuban population, the more successful the integrative effort is adjudged to be.[29] Because of this emphasis on continued expansion, reasons for denying membership in the CDR are kept to a minimum. Of course antirevolutionary activists must be excluded, but the leadership recognizes as unrealistic any requirement that all members be true militants. To be eligible to join, one has only to be favorably disposed toward the revolution. For the leadership to insist on more would result in a dramatic shrinkage of the total membership, an outcome directly contrary to the notion of the CDR as *centros de aglutinamiento popular*.

By the end of the third year of the program, enough information had been gathered by means of membership cards and other forms of organizational bookkeeping for the leadership to publish detailed demographic data on the membership of the CDR. Data on the occupational composition of both the membership and the cadres of the CDR are presented in Table 6. The third anniversary celebration was a propitious time to publish such data, for the system was by then fully established in the larger cities where the committees had first been formed, and it had reached almost all the smaller towns and villages and much of the countryside as well.

* *Revolución*, Sept. 30, 1961, p. 12. A more formal list was published on the third anniversary of the CDR: "The licentious and lumpen, the criminals, procurers, and prostitutes, the old political bosses, the vagrants and parasites, and all those who had close relationships with the bloody tyranny of Batista, as well as those who place themselves actively against the revolution, cannot be members of the CDR." *Revolución*, Sept. 27, 1963, p. 2.

The CDR were all over the island by 1963, and the leadership could point with pride to both the number and the diversity of citizens who had been brought into this most inclusive of revolutionary organizations. Specifically, it was announced that the more than one and a half million members of the CDR represented approximately one third of the total adult population of Cuba (those fifteen or older). Of this membership, about one out of three was between fifteen and twenty-five years old, and 44 percent were women. It was also announced that 34 percent of the adult urban population and 30 percent of the adult rural population belonged to the CDR, although the basis for differentiating urban from rural populations was not made clear.[30] As Table 6 shows, however, the peasant sector made up only a small part of the total CDR membership, despite organizational efforts in the countryside.

TABLE 6. THE OCCUPATIONAL COMPOSITION OF THE CDR MEMBERSHIP AND CADRES IN SEPTEMBER 1963

Occupation	Percent of total membership (*N* = approx. 1,540,000)	Percent of all cadres (*N* = approx. 50,000)
Workers (industrial and agricultural wage earners)	30.2%	49.8%
Housewives	26.4	17.1
White-collar employees (*empleados*)	20.1	16.1
Peasants (small landowners)	6.8	10.0
Students	5.6	6.5 (Students through Small businessmen combined)
Self-employed persons	3.8	
Unemployed persons	2.9	
Professionals	2.1	
Retired persons	1.5	
Small businessmen	.6	
TOTALS	100.0%	99.5%

Note: Cadres are defined as those who hold positions in the provincial, district, or sectional directorates. The approximate total membership in the CDR is taken from "Tercer chequeo nacional de la emulación de los CDR," *Con la Guardia en Alto*, Oct. 1963, p. 40. The approximate total number of cadres is taken from Radamés Mancebo, "El trabajo de organización en los CDR," *Con la Guardia en Alto*, Sept. 1963, pp. 16–18. All other data are from *Revolución*, Sept. 27, 1963, p. 2. After 1963, it was not again possible to find such complete statistics on the membership of the CDR. It is unlikely, however, that growth from 1964 to 1968 altered the demographic profile of the organization dramatically.

As will be shown later, any evaluation of the CDR as integrator cannot be made exclusively on the basis of the size and diversity of the total membership. The committees are, after all, predominantly neighborhood organizations. Because their immediate concern is with neighborhood activity, the final proof of their integrative capacity depends not only on aggregate accomplishments but also on local impact. And because of the nature of the CDR, its role as an integrator of citizens at the local level is a difficult one: the presence of a committee in any neighborhood or place of work, no matter what new opportunities it affords for local solidarity and action, automatically brings at least some divisive consequences. Even when committee members do not engage in vigilance and public denunciation of their neighbors, the fact that some citizens are "in" and others are "out" establishes a new and highly political basis for differentiation in the community. With the formation of the local committees, the last refuge for the apolitical citizen or the quietly antirevolutionary citizen has been torn down, the last set of excuses stripped away. No longer can anyone get away with saying that he does not participate in revolutionary activities because there are no opportunities close at hand, because he is too busy, because he is too old, because he has no needed skills, or because he cannot leave his children. Nonparticipation has tended to become, in the community's eyes, tantamount to failure to want to participate, which, in revolutionary Cuba, is a serious failure indeed.

The CDR as socializer. As we have emphasized throughout this study, almost all participation in revolutionary organizations is seen by the leadership as conducive to the political socialization of the populace. This is especially true of participation in the CDR, the most inclusive and extensive of all the mass organizations. In the very broadest sense, education for citizenship underlies and justifies all the many activities with which CDR members are supposed to busy themselves. These activities are of course recognized as important in and of themselves; every neighborhood improvement project completed, every child enrolled in school, and every round of vigilance walked contributes directly to the success of

Above. May Day parade of literacy workers, May 1, 1961. *Below*. One of the oldest brigadistas goes off to teach, September 1961.

All photographs courtesy of *Bohemia* with the exception of the last three, which were taken by the author.

Above. A nine-year-old literacy worker in a Comité Infantil of the CDR, November 1961.
Below. A brigadista teaching in a peasant hut, 1961.

Above. A brigadista bids good-bye to the rural family with which she has worked, December 1961.
Below. The line of march of the brigadistas, December 1961.

Above. Returned brigadistas salute with their giant pencils, December 1961.
Right. A peasant woman working on her lessons, 1961.

Above. Fidel reads from the *Diario de la Marina* during the first anniversary speech of the CDR.
Below. The first anniversary speech of the CDR, September 28, 1961.

Above. Children's tricycle parade for the CDR, 1964.
Below. Street manifestation of the CDR in celebration of the Revolutionary Offensive, March 1968.

Above. Personnel of the Ministry of Industries working in the Cordón around Havana, April 1968.
Below. Boys in a camp for *reformación* on the Isle of Youth, April 1968.

the revolution. But equally if not more important is the contribution such activities make to the forming of a new type of citizen with a new set of sociopolitical values. The relationship of instrumental activities to education in citizenship was underlined quite forcefully in a newspaper editorial written to honor the sixth anniversary of the CDR:

> This extraordinary working force [the CDR], oriented and directed toward accomplishing tasks—in local administration, recreation, social service, mass education, and public health—no doubt constitutes a form of organization that not only will be useful for doing pressing and immediate jobs, but also will aid decisively in the formation of a new collective conscience concerning the acceptance of social responsibilities.[31]

The part played by the CDR in educating their members for citizenship is related to the program's integrative role at both the local and the national levels. Ideally, the local committee brings together all those who are willing to work for the revolution and provides them with an immediate opportunity for service to the local community. The area served by the local committee is purposely kept small, so that personal acquaintance with all of its residents is possible. The committee member's first identification is thus with his own community, and this community is in turn identified as a vital subunit of the regional and national communities to which it belongs. Local service is thus seen as contributing directly to the higher goal of service to the nation. The airy abstractions of patriotism and civic responsibility are translated at the local level into a prescribed set of everyday activities. Whatever its shortcomings, this translation leaves little doubt how the average citizen can contribute to and be included in the national effort in revolutionary Cuba.* Thus José Matar emphasized in 1963 that the fundamental responsibility of the CDR was to be

* One of the more bizarre manifestations of what might be called the urge to socialize was the formation of a number of children's CDR, in which "with all seriousness" the youngsters engaged in the same activities as their elders. See *Revolución*, Oct. 26, 1961, p. 14. Whether participating in the CDR *infantiles* gave any children a strong feeling of identification with the state is not reported, but some benefits were undoubtedly derived, if not by the children or by the state, at least by the parents. As one mother said, "The Children's Defense Committee has been a very good idea for improving the behavior of the

the great "teacher" of the Cuban people. It is a mistake to think of the CDR system as an administrative appendage of the government, he said; it is, above all, a political and social (politicizing and socializing) organization: "The CDR are inculcating in hundreds of thousands of their members a feeling of civic responsibility, a sense of responsibility toward the Fatherland, a feeling that the apparatus of the state is not abstract and distant, but close and respected, because it is *their* state."[32]

In addition to this broadly conceived responsibility of education for citizenship permeating almost all CDR activities, the committees and the sections to which they belong are also directly involved in an extensive, more narrowly defined program of political education. Political education in this instance refers to formal or semiformal classroom instruction in the basics of Marxist-Leninist thought and the ideological underpinnings of revolutionary policies. Although this instruction is intended to enrich and support the more general efforts of education for citizenship, it has its own set of immediate goals as well as its own specialized teaching arrangements.

Revolutionary instruction, as it is officially called, dates from the very beginnings of the CDR. At first it took the form of weekly neighborhood meetings or seminars in which key speeches of the revolutionary leaders were discussed, governmental programs and policies were explained, and the civic training manual of the Rebel Army was studied.[33] By 1962 the program was operating on two levels.[34] The seminars had evolved into study circles (*Círculos de Estudios*), which still met about once a week. These study circles were led by local committee members who usually had little or no training either in pedagogy or in Marxism-Leninism. At the section level, there were more intensive seminars called circles of revolutionary instruction (*Círculos de Instrucción Revolucion-*

kids. For example, that boy of mine is very restless. Before, there never was a day when he was quiet. Of course he still gets into mischief, but since the kids were organized he has been much more tranquil and occupied with other things." Vicente H. Blanco, "En un pequeño mundo de estudio, alegría y trabajo," *Con la Guardia en Alto*, Sept. 1964, pp. 15–17; the quoted passage is from p. 17.

aria). These met three evenings a week for three months under the guidance of members who had a bit more intellectual sophistication and background than the others, or, in the early months, by cadres temporarily loaned to the CDR by the ORI and other mass organizations.

From the outset, the CDR had great difficulty finding men and women even minimally qualified to lead classes of revolutionary instruction. Furthermore, the demand for instructors increased rapidly as the number of Círculos grew. In September 1962 there were 945 circles of revolutionary instruction, enrolling about 16,000 committee members. Two years later there were 2,373 CIR. Most of them were located in the sections as before, but there were also some in work centers and on *granjas*, or people's farms. The total number studying at this level had more than tripled during the two years. In the much less demanding and less well-organized study circles, growth was even more rapid. In September 1962 there were approximately 7,000 committees with study circles, and the total enrollment was just under 70,000. Within one year these figures had more than tripled. To meet the demand for instructors who could stay at least one lesson ahead of their students, the better "graduates" of the circles of revolutionary instruction were recruited as teachers for the subsequent cycles. In addition, to upgrade the entire program, many of those who taught three nights a week in the CIR were themselves attending classes at the district level on the other two nights.* The study circles at the committee level were led by less outstanding graduates of the circles of revolutionary instruction or by any committee member who showed a bit of talent and motivation for such work.

* In Havana in 1963 the core materials in these district-level classes were two translated Soviet manuals, *Marxism-Leninism* and *Political Economy*. For the complete lesson plan, see "Como de las propias masas se extrajeron 1,000 orientadores de los C.I.R. en la Habana," *Con la Guardia en Alto*, May 1963, p. 23. The lesson plan did not differ greatly from what was then being used in certain of the ORI-sponsored Schools of Revolutionary Instruction (EIR). In 1962, members of the CDR began to attend the EIR in significant numbers (almost 3,000 in 1963). Most of those who received such schooling, however, then went on to assume organizational responsibilities at the sectional and district levels of the CDR rather than to assume teaching responsibilities. The structure, growth, and goals of the EIR are described in detail in Chapter 5.

The political education that goes on in the CDR is too minimal and too short to give its participants any profound feeling for the intricacies of Marxism-Leninism or much more than a superficial ability to handle the relevant vocabulary. But significant learning of another sort probably does take place. We may imagine, for example, that the various círculos perform rather effectively as centers for explaining and legitimating the revolution. At both the sectional and the committee levels there is a continuing need among the membership to know what the revolution is all about. The vocabulary, the symbolism, the policies, and the programs of the Revolutionary Government have undergone rapid and sometimes bewildering development and change. How is the average man to understand what is going on? How is he to appreciate what "Communism" means in Cuba, what "imperialism" signifies, why armed struggle is the proper way to achieve national liberation, how moral and material incentives differ, or why food must be rationed? Fidel and other leaders have of course spoken in detail on such subjects, and the mass media constantly carry discussions and explanations. But despite the volume of direct elite-mass communication, the small face-to-face group is viewed by the Cubans as the basic weapon in the struggle to build revolutionary consensus and legitimacy. Thus thousands of such groups, devoted specifically to "revolutionary orientation," are found throughout the institutional framework of the revolution. The program of instruction in the CDR is a key part of this larger effort.

The CDR as mobilizer. Mobilization means getting the people to participate, enlisting their energies in tasks that clearly contribute to government or community programs. CDR members are mobilized to stand guard, to enroll children in school, to distribute ration books, to collect scrap metal, and to perform the many tasks that will be discussed in the following sections on the CDR as implementor and as protector.

But mobilization in revolutionary Cuba does not only refer to enlisting the masses for various instrumental or productive tasks. It also involves boosting participation in symbolic and ceremonial activities with no immediate and obvious financial or administrative payoffs. Of course it is not always easy to distinguish between instrumental and ceremonial activities. The voluntary cutting of sugar cane, for example, can be considered instrumental because cane gets harvested that otherwise would rot on the stalk or cost the government a good deal of money to save. But the ceremonial and symbolic aspects of voluntary cane cutting are just as important. The sight of cabinet ministers and bank clerks swinging machetes alongside campesinos contributes more to the revolution than conventional accounting methods could possibly capture.

Mobilization of this sort is most interesting when it is predominantly symbolic and ceremonial, when it has no instrumental or productive function. The occasion on which this happens most dramatically and extensively is the annual anniversary celebration of the CDR. On each of the eight anniversaries to date (1968), there has been a gigantic mass meeting in Havana, a major address by Castro, and innumerable lesser speeches and celebrations throughout the island. The anniversary of the CDR is one of the three or four most important revolutionary birthday parties; it is a solidarity rite, a time for organizational stocktaking, and a public fiesta all rolled into one.* The amount of time and energy spent on these nationwide birthday parties is impressive. In 1963, for example, the week before September 28 was filled with activities commemorating the founding of the CDR. There were poetry readings, games, dances, beauty contests, street entertainment, a children's day, decorating of homes and neighborhoods, meetings to discuss the programs and problems of the CDR, and finally the climactic mass rally and speech in the Plaza of the Revolution. For those unable to attend this rally, television and radio receivers were moved into streets and public places so that everyone had an opportunity to participate in the final rite, if only indirectly.

Most of the preliminary activity for these birthday parties, al-

* The other major revolutionary birthdays are January 1 (the date on which the revolution took power in 1959), and July 26 (the date of the abortive attack on the Moncada Army Barracks in 1953). January 1 and July 26 are much more important to the revolution than September 28, both symbolically and historically, but September 28 rivals the other two in terms of the time and attention paid to the celebration and the duration of the festivities.

though suggested by the National Directorate, is organized and run by the local committees and sections. It is purposely decentralized not only because of the impossibility of directing so much activity from a single center, but also because of the integrative and socializing benefits to be gained from having each neighborhood work together as a team. Thus the activities take on the coloration of the local communities that plan and stage them; certain committees or sections are good at decorating the streets, others better at organizing popular entertainment, and still others talented at exploiting the spirit of the moment for getting needed community improvements under way. The National Directorate assumes responsibility for communicating general instructions and reports to the sections and committees, apportioning major speakers to Havana and outlying areas, and organizing the final mass meeting in Havana. It also works with the relevant ministries to arrange transportation, sanitary, and other facilities for the tens of thousands who make the pilgrimage to the Plaza to hear Fidel.

In addition to their own anniversaries, the CDR are responsible for generating popular support for the celebration of the 26th of July and other revolutionary holidays as well. Moreover, the same kinds of symbolic and ceremonial activities can be triggered by the visit of a dignitary, the ratification of an important treaty or document, or a domestic or international incident. Hundreds of thousands of citizens have been mobilized by the CDR to attend the funeral procession of a revolutionary martyr or the welcoming parade for a foreign dignitary; in the same manner, millions of signatures have been gathered in ratification of documents like the First and Second Declaration of Havana; hundreds of thousands of meetings have been held to express solidarity with revolutionary and international causes; and everything from composing poetry to donating blood has been done in symbolic support of anti-imperialist movements around the world. Because the extent of the CDR system exceeds that of any other mass organization, the CDR have been given continuing responsibility for mass mobilization on these ceremonial and symbolic occasions.

The CDR as implementor. As the Revolutionary Government

launched program after program in the early 1960's, the gulf between the formulation of ideas and the elaboration and effective administration of these ideas became glaringly evident. The kinds of programs undertaken by the Castro regime very often necessitated extensive bureaucratic organization in both the planning and the implementation stages. And although the organizations grew and multiplied like spring mushrooms, effective administration did not multiply proportionately. The necessary skills and information were either in very short supply or in some cases simply nonexistent. Moreover, the rapid expansion of national programs took place when the traditional structures of local administration had been almost completely destroyed and the party organization was just beginning to be built. Thus, in addition to the burdens imposed by the assumption of a wealth of new programs, the Revolutionary Government also labored under the disadvantage of not being able to use existing political-administrative structures at the local level for aid in implementing national plans. In areas like agrarian and economic policy these problems usually did not lead to involving the CDR directly; but in programs of welfare, public health, housing, education, savings, and the distribution of supplies, the committees took on a substantial role, involving almost the entire population of Cuba in some fashion. Thus, because of its capillary organization throughout the nation, the CDR system appeared almost from its inception to be an administrative arm of the state. Indeed, by the end of 1961 the leadership's most effective way of reaching quickly into every corner of the island for administrative purposes was through the CDR. Imperfect as the system was in terms of its own internal organization, it seemed the logical vehicle—and in fact it was frequently the only vehicle—for carrying out certain kinds of programs.

We have already noted that even the earliest lists of tasks delegated to the CDR included instrumental or administrative activities designed to aid the government in certain programs of national scope. The first truly nationwide attempt to use the CDR in this fashion came in July 1961, when, because of the economic blockade, it was considered necessary by the leadership to begin rationing cooking oils and fats. Castro himself made the announcement, explaining and justifying the policy. The CDR were then charged with making a "census of consumers" for the Ministry of Internal Trade. The official forms were to be filled out in quintuplicate and sworn to by the consumer so that the Ministry would have the information necessary to make plans for distribution, and so the head of each household would know how much of the product he was entitled to and where he could purchase it.[35] The committees subsequently took on much of the early administrative responsibility for the rationing of other commodities, and soon a separate frente of *abastecimientos* (provisions) was set up within the CDR for overseeing the distribution of scarce goods. Censuses were taken and a complicated system of lists and control booklets was established, first in greater Havana and then throughout the rest of the island.[36]

In addition to the distribution of scarce goods, the CDR have also been active in such programs as urban reform, education, and public health.[37] The work of the CDR in such areas usually involves gathering information about the people involved, contacting these people and urging them to comply with the laws or policies, and following up these contacts to ensure compliance. The specific goals are as diverse as getting parents to send their children to school, getting young men to register for compulsory military service, making sure all children receive polio vaccine, and encouraging all members of one's own organization to open savings accounts.* But the style and methods used by the CDR in the implementation process remain relatively constant: the committees depend on legwork, doorbell ringing, the distribution and display of printed materials, neighborhood meetings, and at times bringing social and political pressures to bear on those who remain recalcitrant.

* The scale of some of these projects is impressive. For instance, in 1964 it was reported that with the help of the CDR the first dose of polio vaccine was given to 2,250,000 children within 72 hours and the second dose was given to almost 2,400,000 children within 24 hours. *Revolución*, Sept. 29, 1964, p. 2. (Although they may be subject to some "revolutionary" exaggeration, figures in such areas as public health tend to be reasonably accurate.)

The role of implementor often involves the CDR in far more than the routine, nationwide administrative tasks mentioned so far. The CDR are viewed by the leadership as existing to serve the revolutionary movement, and what constitutes service varies from place to place and from one historical moment to another. When a hurricane struck in the autumn of 1963, the CDR were called upon to supply an emergency work and disaster force.[38] When it was thought that too much water was being wasted in Havana, the CDR were mobilized in a campaign dubbed "operation leak" to discover and repair faulty plumbing.* Beginning in 1967, an attempt was made to institutionalize such service at the community level. Much attention was given to linking the individual sections and committees more closely to local government so that the implementation of programs could be decentralized and made more responsive to local needs. In a television interview at the end of August 1967, a national organizer for the CDR and the national coordinator for local administration discussed how the CDR might best be used to benefit the local community:

CDR organizer: We have a saying that all tasks of local administration are also tasks of the CDR.... We believe that the structure of the CDR system makes it the ideal organization for working with the local administrations. Local administrations have to have eyes and ears among the people to learn of situations that might affect the masses or of the problems that may arise in a community.

Local administration coordinator: [For example] we believe that many CDR members can participate by cleaning streets in each town, by cleaning up the blocks on which they live.... There are many other tasks in which the masses can participate. We are encouraging the masses to help us in the tasks of construction and repairs. In some sections of Havana the CDR are helping us in the job of repairs and in housing maintenance. They are also helping us put social clubs into operation.[39]

One of the most critical tests of the CDR's capacity as implementor and as administrative arm of the state came in the spring of

* See *Hoy*, July 16, 1964, p. 4. At times revolutionary fervor seems to get the best of those who organize such campaigns. For instance, in a meeting in the CDR section of the provincial city Holguín, called to discuss ways of saving electricity, one participant concluded by declaring "war to the death on hotplates from six to ten in the evening." As reported in *Sierra Maestra* (Santiago de Cuba), Sept. 21, 1963, p. 2.

1968. In a speech on March 13 from the steps of the University of Havana, and in a second speech two days later, Castro announced the "Revolutionary Offensive," a massive national rededication to the building of Communism in Cuba, a rededication that would have as one of its first official acts the nationalization of all remaining private businesses on the island.[40] Within a few weeks, over 55,000 stores, restaurants, service centers, and small manufacturing plants had passed into the hands of the government. Overseeing the entire newly nationalized sector were thousands of "people's administrators" (*administradores populares*) chosen from the local CDR and assigned to neighborhood establishments to ensure that those former "nests of parasites, hotbeds of corruption, illegal trading, and counterrevolutionary conspiracy" were now turned to the service of the people and the revolution.[41] Because problems of supply, distribution, and service were generally so acute in Cuba at that time, it is difficult to judge the success of the first months of this experiment. But the fact that the leadership turned immediately to the committees for the implementation of this task shows how central the CDR were to the administrative process in Cuba.

The CDR system has been so useful to the leadership as implementor that it has often been necessary to remind the membership that this is not, in the revolutionary view, its main task. As was emphasized frequently during the Revolutionary Offensive, the system is seen as being primarily political; although the CDR's work does contribute to the implementation of administrative programs, this work should always have a "learning" component. That is, the administrative duties must help make members more aware of the problems and progress of the revolution. To simply turn the CDR into an administrative or bureaucratic appendage of the government would be, say its leaders, to sap the system of its true meaning and importance.[42]

The CDR as protector. The CDR have been engaged in vigilance activities ever since the first committees were formed in the wake of Castro's speech on September 28, 1960. At first, the clear and present danger was to lives, property, and the momentum of the revolution. Security was the dominant concern of those first few months. Under the slogan "sweep the *gusanos* from the cities," the denunciations, detentions, and imprisonments of the early months were carried out. During this phase of sporadic violence, destruction or threat of destruction of physical facilities, and denunciation and detention of those suspected of being counterrevolutionaries, the CDR worked side by side with the other security organizations, the Rebel Army, the Militia, and the Department of Public Order.

Before long, however, security became less of a problem. This was only partially due to the efforts of the CDR. It derived more directly from the failure of the Bay of Pigs invasion, the defeat of the counterrevolutionary forces in the Escambray Mountains, and the growth and improvement of the professional security corps attached to the Revolutionary Armed Forces and the Ministry of the Interior. Overt and violent counterrevolutionary activity had been almost completely wiped out or driven underground by the end of 1962. Gusanos of the old-fashioned sort, plotting physical or organizational sabotage against the Revolutionary Government, were not easy to find. Thus it was no longer possible for the CDR to derive much collective satisfaction from security activities; the classic counterrevolutionary challenge of the early months no longer existed.[43]

The waning of the security challenge and the efforts related to it did not, however, mark the end or even a decrease of vigilance activities in the committees. The notion of the CDR as watchdog was and continues to be inclusive enough to embrace a wide variety of other types of vigilance. Most generally, the CDR are seen and used as a bulwark against the return of the old order. For the leaders continue to see the revolution as threatened in many ways, even if there is no longer an immediate threat of a fifth column intent on violence and destruction.

One example of how the CDR have been used to protect the revolution was the vigilance exercised over the distribution of scarce goods. The imposition of rationing created numerous opportunities and even incentives for cheating, illegal transactions, and personal gain. These kinds of behavior were labeled vestiges of the old order. Clearly no true revolutionary would attempt to profit from the exigencies of the moment, and the CDR were made responsible for cracking down on those who did. The Cuban view of the relationship between those enemies of the revolution who would take advantage of the distributive system and the role of the CDR in protecting against such counterrevolutionaries is set forth in the following statement:

> In the area of distribution, the struggle of the people and the revolution to defeat the plans of the enemy has been long and hard. The enemy has tried and is trying to take advantage of the difficulties and the scarcities of the moment to cause serious problems and disturbances for the revolution. Along with the Ministry of Internal Trade, the CDR fight a daily and tenacious battle to achieve a more just and equitable distribution of products. They do battle against speculators, hoarders, black marketeers, and egoists.[44]

This battle took much the same form as the earlier campaigns against suspected counterrevolutionaries. There was neighborhood surveillance, and there were threats, exposures, and denunciations. Beginning in 1963 and lasting until the nationalizations of 1968, inspectors (*fiscalizadores*) were appointed from the ranks of the CDR and were given the responsibility of actually being present in commercial establishments to oversee all transactions. This work may not have been as exciting as guarding against sabotage and threats during the early months, but the committee members were constantly reminded that it was no less important. In the revolutionary view, the specific enemies and the threats that these enemies pose may change, but the larger threat continues to exist. The safety of the revolution depends on eternal vigilance. Watchdogs will be necessary for a very long time to come, and in this effort the CDR have a crucial part to play.[45]

Performance, Costs, and Problems

In evaluating the success of the CDR we should ask three related questions. First, how successful have the CDR been in accomplishing the many immediate tasks given to them? Here we ask if, when charged with some security, administrative, distributive, or educational responsibility, the committees actually do get the job done. Do the suspects get reported, the children vaccinated, the consumers counted, the evening classes taught? Second, how successful have the CDR been in fulfilling their more general, long-range responsibilities of mobilizing, integrating, and socializing the citizenry? Is there evidence that substantial progress in these directions has been made over the first eight years of the system? Third, what have been the costs and problems associated with both the immediate and the long-range performances of the CDR? These costs and problems do not derive only from failures to reach projected goals; nor are they due simply to shortcomings like imperfect communication or the apathy of members. Both the failures and the shortcomings exist, and there are costs and problems associated with each; but we are more interested in other kinds of costs, those incurred intentionally or unintentionally in the quest for organizational successes. Achievements are tempered, turned bittersweet, and at times undercut or invalidated by such costs and by new problems created en route.

Revolutionary enthusiasm and the public rhetoric that goes with it complicate the problem of evaluating the short-range performance of the CDR. The public record is so full of self-congratulation on goals reached and quotas fulfilled that it is hard for the outsider to judge which tasks of the CDR have been more and which have been less successfully accomplished. In general, however, it can be assumed that the committees' success in any short-range project is inversely related to that project's potential for generating political controversy among the participants. The available published materials and informal interviews suggest, for example, that the CDR have been more successful in getting members to open savings accounts than in controlling the distribution of scarce goods. Similarly, the committees have been more effective in overseeing polio vaccinations than in encouraging participation in labor mobilizations. Another assumption we can make is that compliance tends to be inversely related to the scope and complexity of the behavior demanded. This relationship is common in cases of administered change, and there is no reason why it should not also be found in revolutionary Cuba. Thus the "community development" phase of CDR activity, which demands complex and extensive participation, cannot hope to have the same kind of support given to programs of public health and education, even though building community facilities and beautifying the neighborhood may be no more controversial than encouraging vaccinations or registering children for school.

The cautions just expressed should not be taken as denying the immediate achievements of the CDR system. Quite to the contrary, there seems to be substantial truth in the self-congratulatory revolutionary rhetoric. That is, despite evidence of disorganization and incompetence, in the main the suspects do get reported, the children do get vaccinated, the consumers do get counted, and the evening classes do get taught. It is difficult to imagine that any of these tasks would be handled nearly as well without the CDR.

The long-range performance of the CDR involves their successes and failures in integrating, mobilizing, and socializing the citizenry, while at the same time protecting the institutions and the physical resources of the revolution. As we have seen, certain contradictions arise from this structure of goals. For example, the attempt to integrate the community by incorporating all "good" citizens into the local committees while purging or excluding all "bad" citizens creates new bases of political cleavage. In fact, the entire notion of eternal vigilance as the price of revolution tends to erode the integrative activities of the CDR system. Likewise, the excessive attention given to the mobilization of committee members for symbolic and ceremonial purposes cuts into the organizational time and energy available for other tasks.

Another problem affecting the achievement of long-range goals is the weakness of the committees' personnel in terms of needed skills and desirable patterns of behavior. For instance, within the larger socialization effort, programs of political instruction have been handicapped by lack of cadres with even minimal levels of ideological and teaching competence. More generally, the efforts of the committees to evoke from their members behavior commensurate with public service and good citizenship have run up against the consequences of the lack of such a service tradition in pre-revolutionary Cuba. The socialization task faced by the system is not simply one of transferring loyalty from one set of institutions to another. It is one of creating an essentially new set of orientations toward self and society, orientations that involve both specific and more general behavior. Teaching the citizen not to throw garbage into the street is perhaps more difficult than getting him to identify with the Revolutionary Government. Teaching him that love of the revolution *implies* not throwing garbage into the street is perhaps most difficult of all.

By definition, long-range performance can never be fully evaluated until enough time can be said to have elapsed. Except in cases of failure, however, it is always difficult to determine when this moment has come, especially when the performance must be judged on quality rather than on the attainment of specific goals. Yet despite these vague criteria of time and quality, there do exist historical junctures when it seems safe to judge the performance of some system. Almost all observers of the Soviet Union, for example, would probably agree that by the late 1950's, after the revelations of the Twentieth Party Congress had been assimilated, the capacity of the Soviet political system to adjust peacefully to change had been demonstrated to the extent that such demonstrations have meaning in the sweep of historical time. Such a moment, however, is not yet at hand in Cuba, and the long-range performance of the CDR must be viewed with this in mind. This is not to say that the emerging Cuban system is exclusively or even directly dependent on the performance of the CDR. But the integrative, mobilizing, socializing, and vigilance activities of the CDR can be considered part of a larger effort that has not yet had time to prove itself as a completed stage in the revolutionary development of the nation. Our evaluation, therefore, must depend on evidence of substantial progress toward fulfilling the long-range and continuing responsibilities given to the system. One has only to compare the situation in 1960 with the situation eight years later to be convinced that the CDR have contributed very significantly to protecting the institutions and property of the revolution, to teaching citizens what is expected of them in the new Cuba, to mobilizing the population for participation in revolutionary activities, and to bringing together under a common organizational umbrella persons of the most diverse political and social characteristics.

Among the problems associated with the performance of the CDR, one stands out above all others: the cost to the legitimacy of the revolution. The committees have been plagued from the beginning by various forms of arbitrary, officious, self-serving, and corrupt behavior on the part of some of their members, behavior that has cost the revolution dearly in the coin of support and thus of legitimacy. Many citizens' most direct and frequent contact with any revolutionary institution is with the local committee; and when committee members are arbitrary, uninformed, opportunistic, or corrupt, the popular image of the revolutionary movement suffers accordingly. Castro has discussed publicly and at length both the behavior of committee members and the consequences of such behavior for the legitimacy of the revolution:

> Who denies that the Committees for Defense of the Revolution are necessary? Who denies that they do great service for the revolution? Who denies that many good citizens are members? And yet only a few days ago I was talking with a group of compañeras in a children's center, and many of them had complaints about the Committees for Defense of the Revolution. These were girls from the masses, very worthy girls from the masses. They weren't counterrevolutionaries; no, they were extremely humble girls from the masses and supporters of the revolution. And every one of them had a complaint about a committee.
>
> Why? Because the committee members make mistakes, because they commit errors, because there is no revolutionary vigilance, because they bungle things, because at times they act in a privileged fashion, assuming privileges or setting something aside in the warehouse for someone. And of course the people who see all this are distressed. Our people are very sensitive to all injustices; our people are very sensitive to anything that is badly done. And because a revolution needs the support of all the people, all the people working for it or defending it, it is a disgrace when there are also many others making mistakes. Thousands and thousands of persons suffer the consequences of the mistakes of thousands and thousands of others.
>
> It is because of this that a revolution has such a great need to struggle against those mistakes: so that we do not weaken the revolution, cause damages, injure anyone, or disgust anyone without reason or without justification.[46]

Castro's speech was given in March 1962, and many variations on the same theme were heard during the next few years. In 1963, for instance, José Matar took stock of the problems that had been encountered in the distribution of scarce goods. He attacked those *responsables* of the CDR who, he said, are unable to resolve problems, who insult anyone coming to the committees for help, who are too lazy even to seek information about why the distributive process is not running well. After encounters with such persons, he warned, citizens leave "irritated with the revolution and irritated with the Committees for Defense of the Revolution."[47] In 1964 Matar spoke of a kind of "cold war" between certain committees and the neighborhoods in which they operated,[48] and later in the year he spoke openly of the hatred incurred by the CDR among certain segments of the population.[49] Similar criticisms were being voiced as recently as the fall of 1967. In one particularly acerbic radio broadcast from Havana, the commentator attacked paper revolutionaries and do-nothings in the following terms:

> There are those who are more Fidelista than Fidel, more Marxist than Marx. When they are asked about the organizations they belong to, they answer, "To the CDR," and to prove it they immediately whip out their stamps and say, "And look, I am paid up to date." In this manner they think they are covered. They do nothing. They say nothing. They paint nothing. But they pay, and they paste in their little stamps.[50]

This sort of damage to the legitimacy of the revolutionary movement is, to a considerable extent, unavoidable, owing to the nature of the organization, of the responsibilities assigned to it, and of the setting in which it operates. The concept of a mass organization rapidly incorporating into its ranks as many citizens as possible clearly conflicts with the concept of an exemplary organization, one in which every member behaves with devotion, restraint, self-sacrifice, and creativity. In their drive for mass participation, and in the necessary but rapid elevation of persons of little skill and experience to positions of organizational importance, the committees have sacrificed a great deal of popular support.

Moreover, as we have seen, certain responsibilities of the CDR allow and even encourage the public expression of personal and social hostilities, antagonisms, and vendettas. Turning the watchdog responsibilities over to groups of citizens has made possible and even inevitable the use of public power for personal advantage, revenge, and catharsis. However necessary the vigilance may have seemed to the revolutionary leadership, the mixture of personal and institutional surveillance and sanctions was sure to affect many citizens very negatively. Exiles from the Castro government called the CDR "the spy committees," and they criticized no other revolutionary institution as frequently or as passionately.[51] And from the statements of Castro, Matar, and others, there is also reason to believe that such feelings were not unknown among those who remained in Cuba.

Finally, the expansiveness of the general revolutionary setting in which the CDR operated, particularly in the early years, was conducive to arbitrary, authoritarian, self-serving, and corrupt behavior. Old institutions were being thoroughly and rapidly dismantled and new ones constructed in their place. These conditions offered innumerable opportunities for advancement, self-aggrandizement, and role definition by the people involved. If the first years of the Mexican Revolution were, as Octavio Paz has said, "a fiesta of bullets," the early years of the Cuban Revolution were a fiesta of opportunities. And perhaps no new institution of the revolutionary system provided as many opportunities as the CDR. Within the loose organizational boundaries of the Committees for Defense of the Revolution, one could play or try to play at being an administrator, teacher, policeman, public servant, proselytizer, prosecuting attorney, or any number of other things.[52] The setting did not encourage self-restraint, institutional checks and balances, respect for clientele, or careful consideration of the consequences of organizational style and programs.

The CDR system, like so many other revolutionary institutions, was built piecemeal and by trial and error. As Castro said on the seventh anniversary of the CDR,

> Never, not in any classical book of revolutionary theories, has such an institution been mentioned. In what program, in what manifesto, in what pronouncement has there ever been anything said about an institution like this one?
>
> We learn from the revolutionary process; and the revolutionary process itself, with its infinite variety of new things, with its infinite number of

possibilities, must always be the great teacher of the people, the great teacher of all revolutionaries. The best book, our true textbook in matters of revolution, will be the revolutionary process itself.[53]

In the process of "learning from the revolution," a great many persons have been advantaged and a great many others have been hurt. The history of the CDR is, in microcosm, a history of this process with all that it implies in terms of costs and problems.

5 The Schools of Revolutionary Instruction

LIKE THE campaign against illiteracy and the Committees for Defense of the Revolution, the Schools of Revolutionary Instruction were founded in the latter half of 1960.[1] Unlike the other two, however, the Escuelas de Instrucción Revolucionaria (EIR) were born in secrecy. On December 2, 1960,* Fidel Castro, Blas Roca, Emilio Aragonés, Lionel Soto, other directors of the Partido Socialista Popular (PSP) and the 26th of July Movement, and the nineteen cadres chosen to teach in the first schools met, ironically, in the luxurious home of a departed North American. There they sketched out the final plans for the formal opening of the schools in January 1961.[2] The negotiations, planning, and maneuvering that must have preceded this first national meeting of the Schools of Revolutionary Instruction have never been discussed publicly by the principals; but considerable activity must have taken place

* December 2, 1960, was the fourth anniversary of the landing of Castro's expeditionary force from the *Granma* (the converted yacht that brought the guerillas from Mexico). At the time of the founding of the EIR, Blas Roca was Secretary General of the PSP and Emilio Aragonés was coordinator of the 26th of July Movement. In 1965, both were named to the Central Committee of the Communist Party. The home at which the meeting was held became the site for the Ñico López National School of Revolutionary Instruction, the most advanced of the schools. Antonio López Fernández ("Ñico") was one of the survivors of the attack on the Moncada Barracks in 1953. He was killed in the landing from the *Granma* in December 1956. Throughout their existence, the schools generated few of the symbolic and emotional displays associated with the literacy campaign and the CDR. For one of the very few revolutionary poems inspired by the EIR, see Luis Suardíaz, "Despedida: A mis compañeros del 4° curso de la EIR 'Mártires de Pino 3,'" in *Cuban Poetry: 1959–1966* (Havana: Book Institute, 1967), pp. 668–71 (in Spanish and English).

in the fall of 1960, because the sites of the schools and the initial corps of instructors had already been chosen.

The secrecy surrounding the founding of the schools is understandable, considering the difficulties that must have been encountered. It should be remembered that the PSP, the 26th of July Movement, and the Revolutionary Directorate had not yet joined to form the Organizaciones Revolucionarias Integradas (ORI), and that the PSP and the 26th of July Movement were by no means altogether compatible during the first years of the revolution. Personal animosities, ideological rivalries, generational conflicts, and the clash of ambitions drove the two organizations apart at many points. Moreover, neither the 26th of July Movement nor the PSP could speak with a single voice, for each contained differences of opinion within its own ranks. Thus, as Lionel Soto, the program's director, pointed out, the Schools of Revolutionary Instruction represented the first attempt to bring together under one roof the several organizations and factions that were central to the revolution at the end of 1960.[3] Only the sponsorship of Fidel Castro enabled the EIR to be born of such mixed parentage at this particular moment in Cuban history. And despite Castro's prestige and power, the early years were, as Soto later admitted, no "bed of roses."[4]

The EIR, from their founding in 1960 to their termination late in 1967, had a single purpose: "The task of the schools, the fundamental task of the schools, is the ideological formation of revolutionaries, and then, by means of the revolutionaries, the ideological formation of the rest of the people."* As we shall see, at different

* Fidel Castro, speaking at the sixth national meeting of the Schools of Revolutionary Instruction, December 20, 1961; as quoted in Lionel Soto, "Las Escuelas de Instrucción Revolucionaria en una nueva fase," *Cuba Socialista*, No. 30 (Feb. 1964), p. 63. What has here been translated as "formation" is the Spanish *formación*. The more literal and usual translation of *formación* is "training," but in the context of the EIR, the phrase "ideological formation" conveys more forcefully what is intended than the more literal "ideological training." In the period from December 1960 to December 1961, six national meetings of the EIR were held. In 1962, 1963, and 1964, there were two national meetings each year. In 1965 and 1966 there was only one national meeting each year. The first national meeting to receive what might be considered "normal" publicity in the Cuban press was the seventh, held June 27–28, 1962. For reasons that will be explained below, this was a critically important meeting.

stages in the development of the schools, the notion of what constituted correct ideological formation underwent quite striking changes in both theory and practice. Despite these changes, however, the ideological formation of cadres was always the primary goal, and two key aspects of the operation of the schools remained unchanged from the beginning. First, ideological formation in the EIR always meant training under the philosophical umbrella of Marxism-Leninism as that doctrine was understood by the Cuban leadership. Second, the schools were never "public" or open. By one method or another, a person was chosen or appointed to attend the EIR. The bases of selection changed from time to time, and serious controversies arose concerning the proper way of selecting promising young (and sometimes not so young) men and women to be students. But it was never legitimate for the prospective student to seek out or promote his own candidacy. Selection was in the hands of the leadership, and criteria for membership were intended to be those that would benefit the revolution, not the individual.

It should be remembered that the schools began to operate in January 1961, a few months before Castro's first public announcement that his was a Socialist revolution, and nearly a year before his famous "I am a Marxist-Leninist" speech of December 1, 1961. The Marxist-Leninist content of the formation in the EIR, and for that matter the institutionalization of this formation in special schools, represented something very new and potentially very divisive for Cuba. Thus in January the program was not yet considered appropriate material for public consumption.

The notion of ideological formation, however, was far from new. As early as 1953, during his imprisonment on the Isle of Pines, Castro had organized a school for the study of history and philosophy in order to give the other prisoners his understanding of political, social, and economic realities in Cuba.[5] During the fight against Batista, this tradition was continued in orientation classes given to the Rebel Army, both in the Sierra Maestra and in the mountains of Las Villas. After Castro took power in January 1959, ideological formation became an established part of the programs of public education given in almost all sectors of revolutionary organizational life, although the most developed programs continued to be those offered through the Department of Instruction of the Ministry of the Armed Forces. Throughout this period, however, these programs continued to be public and nonselective. Classes were on a part-time or after-hours basis, and the very broadest mass attendance was sought, if not required. Moreover, the subject matter, though it may have been nationalistic, anti-imperialist, and anti-American, was not overtly Marxist.[6] After the founding of the EIR, mass programs of this sort continued, with Marxist-Leninist doctrine forming more and more of their content. But the EIR should not be understood as merely a continuation or extension of this tradition. Rather, they were an organizational response to a need created by the revolution in power. The need was not just for an expanded program of ideological training, but for the educating of Marxist-Leninists in a revolution going Marxist with neither a party to supply the cadres nor a rich indigenous Marxist tradition to draw on.

The schools began modestly. In January 1961, twelve provincial schools were opened in the six provinces, and the national Ñico López School was opened in Havana.[7] All were full-time boarding schools. More than seven hundred students—approximately sixty in each school—were enrolled in the first courses, which lasted three months in the provincial schools and six months in the national school. Approximately half of the original students came from the ranks of the PSP, and half came from the 26th of July Movement; there were also a few students from the membership of the Revolutionary Directorate. Organizationally, the schools were under the 26th of July Movement, but the first nineteen full-time instructors and the others who taught on a part-time basis were recruited almost exclusively from the PSP, which was the only available pool of "trained" Marxists.[8] The first course of study, at both the provincial and the national levels, consisted of Marxist-Leninist theory, political economy, and dialectical materialism, although precisely what sort of written materials were used in this first cycle has never been made clear. What is evident is that the first courses were put together hurriedly, that they were largely experimental, that the instructional staff was woefully inadequate, and that the familiarity of the first graduates with Marxism-Leninism was rudimentary at best. In what can charitably be called an understatement, Soto characterized the content of the first course as "rather imperfect."[9]

The problems of the first courses in the EIR, however, were not simply the product of the haste with which the schools were organized and staffed. The issues were more basic, and they were related to certain characteristics of the revolution at that time and to other more enduring aspects of Cuban society; as such, some of them continued to plague the schools in later years. These problems will be introduced in more detail at an appropriate point, but a preliminary list would include the following. First, the educational level of the students attending the schools was necessarily low, reflecting the educational profile of Cuba in general. In the provincial schools in 1963, for example, only 21 percent of the students had finished the sixth grade.[10] There is little reason to believe that the educational level was any more impressive in 1961. Second, the teaching cadres in the schools were only slightly better prepared than the students. Particularly with the very rapid expansion of the system in 1961 and 1962, hundreds of new instructors, most of whom were recent graduates of the schools, were called on to teach what Castro called "the most complex science." Third, as suggested above, the materials from which one might teach Marxism-Leninism, especially to a poorly educated student body, were in very short supply. With the exception of certain speeches by Castro, *The Fundamentals of Socialism in Cuba* by Blas Roca,[11] clippings and special articles from the newspapers, and some of the materials prepared earlier for study sessions in the armed forces, there was little in Spanish appropriate for use in the EIR. Even as Soviet classics were translated and published in new editions, there was still the problem of finding texts suited theoretically, substantively, and pedagogically to indigenous conditions. Fourth, at the outset it was clearer what the schools were for than whom they were for. Errors of "inadequate selection" of students plagued the EIR during their first cycle and were not really brought under control until the second half of 1962. Those with appointive power sometimes kept their best cadres from attending the schools for fear of losing them to other organizations after graduation, and careerists of various stripes actively promoted themselves as students in the hope of subsequent advancement. Three months of reading books and listening to lectures followed by the possibility of a promotion did not always lead a student to consider the needs of the revolution first. Fifth, before the founding of the ORI and throughout the early life of that organization, the pattern of authority covering the operation of the EIR was unclear or at least unsatisfactory from the point of view of Castro and his colleagues. Only when the Partido Unido de la Revolución Socialista de Cuba (PURSC) was finally launched in 1963 could it be said that the EIR were integrated into a larger organizational plan befitting schools for the ideological formation of revolutionaries in a nation by then officially embarked on the road to Socialism and Communism.

The problems just mentioned, however, did not make the first graduates of the schools any less important to the revolution. From this first generation were recruited the cadres who not only staffed the expanding system of the EIR, but also figured prominently in the organization of the provincial structures of the ORI. Although the graduates were not very familiar with the classics of Marxism, and although they had not all been chosen "correctly," many of them were nevertheless given impressive responsibilities in the burgeoning political apparatus of the revolution. They became instant cadres, examples of a career pattern that (as it subsequently became necessary to point out) could not be followed by later graduates of the schools.

The System Expands

On April 26, 1961, just ten days after the Bay of Pigs invasion, the third national meeting of the EIR was held. The most important announcement to issue from that meeting concerned the decision to launch a national system of Escuelas Básicas de Instrucción Revolucionaria (EBIR). Unlike the provincial and national schools, there were to be many basic schools, and their students were to be drawn from school-associated work centers rather than from entire geographical units. Thus when the first basic schools opened on May 15, they were tied to large factories, sugar centrals, people's farms, cooperatives, and administrative offices. The school was not always located at the particular organization to which it was attached, but as a rule the students who attended any given school all worked for the same organization. At the outset, the EBIR were either full-time boarding schools (*internas*), or part-time boarding schools (*semi-internas*) where the students spent eight hours during the afternoon and evening after working in the morning at their regular jobs. The course of study lasted 45 days at the full-time schools, 60 days at the part-time schools.

The system of basic schools spread rapidly across the nation. By the fourth national meeting of the EIR on June 21, 1961, there were already 169 EBIR in operation. By September of the same year, the number of schools had risen to 263, enrolling almost 9,500 students.[12] Naturally, the basic schools were far more diverse in their size and operation than the provincial schools. The EBIR assumed the social, intellectual, and even political coloration of the work centers to which they were attached. Some were smaller, some larger (the average size during 1961 was about 36 students); some had students who were barely literate, whereas others could count on a higher level of educational skills; some were attached to centers whose managements viewed the schools as disruptive if not threatening, whereas other schools received full managerial cooperation; some schools lasted for only one course, and others were sustained for years. The common thread tying all of the schools together was a curriculum composed essentially of Castro's *History Will Absolve Me* and Blas Roca's *The Fundamentals of Socialism in Cuba*. Beyond these common readings, there was little except their problems that the EBIR shared during the early months. The difficulties that plagued the provincial and national schools also plagued the basic schools in greater or lesser degree. It is evident that because of the scarcity of intellectual, financial, and organizational resources in Cuba during the early 1960's, the EBIR were run at best by passionate amateurs and at worst by self-serving incompetents.[13]

But, as in the case of the provincial schools, it would be a mistake to dismiss the first stages of the EBIR as unimportant simply because the system was imperfect and haphazard. During 1961 about eight Cubans attended a basic school for every one that attended a provincial or national school. And during the years that followed, the graduates of the basic schools continued to outnumber the graduates of all other schools in almost the same proportion.* By sheer numbers, if not organizationally, the EBIR from the beginning were the most significant part of the system of revolutionary instruction. Discounting the affected rhetoric, we can take at face value Soto's characterization of the origin and purpose of the EBIR.

> The proclamation of the Socialist character of our revolution on April 16, 1961—on the eve of the imperialist-mercenary landing and our glorious victory at the Bay of Pigs—ushered in a new political situation in the country. The revolution had to disseminate the ideas of scientific Socialism.... The ideological battle had to be waged not only against the enemy, but also on the home ground of the revolution itself, where it was necessary to combat anti-Communist prejudice.... It was necessary to equip the masses with theoretical weapons, and it was necessary to convert many good revolutionaries to the ideas of Marxism-Leninism.[14]

It is probable that in waging this ideological battle, even the meager fare offered in the first basic schools was effective. The schools' primary purpose was to legitimate and reinforce the new Socialist order among those who were already most militant in support of the revolution. Success in this task clearly did not depend on the impossible job of making trained Marxists out of workers and peasants in 60 days.

The expansion of the EIR during 1961 and part of 1962 was not limited to the introduction of the basic schools and the addition of a few provincial schools. In the autumn of 1961, the first students entered the newly created Rubén Bravo Escuela Nacional for teachers. Unlike the national Ñico López School, which was linked with the provincial and basic schools below it, the Rubén Bravo School stood more or less alone as a training center. It was not for political cadres selected from the Party or the government at large, but rather for schoolteachers and administrators selected

* Appendix E below brings together data on the total number of graduates of the EIR for each year and from each type of school. Appendix E also contains a chronology of organizational events in the EIR from 1960 through 1967.

from within the Ministry of Education. Thus the Rubén Bravo School was the first of a series of national schools designed to give Marxist-Leninist instruction to those already holding key positions in the work force or active in certain mass organizations.

The following new national schools were opened during the first few months of 1962: the Carlos Rodríguez Careaga School for national and provincial directors of the Confederación de Trabajadores de Cuba-Revolucionaria (Labor Federation of Revolutionary Cuba); the Julio Antonio Mella School for sectional directors of the CTCR; the Andrés González Lines School for fishermen; the Sierra Maestra School for *granjeros del pueblo* (workers on the people's farms); the Fe del Valle School for members of the Federación de Mujeres Cubanas (Federation of Cuban Women); the Juan Ronda School for members of the CDR; and the Niceto Pérez School for members of the Asociación Nacional de Agricultores Pequeños (National Association of Small [noncollectivized] Farmers).[15]

The national EIR, all of which were boarding schools, differed from each other in size, duration of courses, and levels of instruction. As might be expected, the centers for agricultural workers and fishermen had few scholarly pretensions, offering a course characterized as "amplified basic." The CTC-R schools, on the other hand, whose students came with higher levels of education, introduced more advanced materials.[16] In the Ñico López School, the most demanding of all, the curriculum included such works as *The Manual of Political Economy* and *Fundamentals of Marxist Philosophy* of the Academy of Sciences of the Soviet Union, selections from Marx's *Capital*, Lenin's *Imperialism, the Highest Stage of Capitalism*, Mao's *On the Correct Handling of Contradictions*, other Marxist-Leninist classics, and materials generated by the Cuban Revolution itself.[17]

Despite the differences in curriculum, size, and duration, the group of new national schools was unified in purpose. All the schools were expected to introduce key cadres from important sectors of the economy, from the mass organizations, and from the bureaucracy to the fundamentals of the new official ideology. In this sense, they were quite similar to the basic schools, although their audience was more select. The purpose of both systems was to make sure that good revolutionaries—in fact the best and most critically located revolutionaries—were taught the fundamentals of Marxism-Leninism. The schools therefore tried not only to protect key revolutionary organizations from the consequences of anti-Communist prejudice, but also to co-opt the most vigorous and capable cadres into the new faith. If the new schools were diverse, it was precisely because the target groups themselves were diverse in their characteristics, responsibilities, and potential for helping (and for hurting) the revolution.

By the end of 1962, the system of revolutionary instruction had expanded as fully as it ever was to expand in terms of numbers of students graduated.[18] In two years the EIR had grown from a program involving one national school, a dozen provincial schools, nineteen instructors, and seven hundred students to a program with nine national schools, a consolidated system of seven provincial schools, more than two hundred basic schools, more than five hundred instructors, and approximately ten thousand students.[19] Table 7 contains data from the official 1962 year-end report for the EIR, showing the types of programs offered and the total number of graduates during 1962.

In line with what has been standard revolutionary practice in Cuba, the early growth of the EIR was rapid and haphazard; little thought was given to what might or might not be "possible" in conventional terms. As we shall see in the following section, this was also a time of tumultuous political change in Cuba, and the tumult naturally affected the schools' operation. But the slowdown in the growth of the system was not due directly to political conditions, nor was it because the leadership suddenly became cautious. Rather, it was mainly because as the institution gained national scope, increased quality became more important than size. The skeletal structure of the system had been fully formed in the first 24 months; attention then shifted to consolidating, refining, and improving the program. In fact, however, the drive for quality and consolidation was not marked by methods or by an organizational style any less experimental or any less ambitious than those evident during the drive for coverage. If changes in the EIR in the mid-1960's appear more orderly and incremental than those of

TABLE 7. SCHOOLS, COURSES, AND GRADUATES FROM THE EIR SYSTEM IN 1962

Type of school	Type of course offered	Graduates during the year	
Basic schools (both boarding and nonboarding)	Some courses 2 months, some courses 3 months, usually offered 3 times		31,070
Provincial schools (all boarding)	All courses 5 months, offered twice		1,661
National schools (all boarding)	Ñico López School 8 months, offered once	64	
	Agricultural workers $3\frac{1}{2}$ months, offered 3 times	2,356	
	CTC-R, national/provincial 5 months, offered twice	105	
	CTC-R, sectional, 3 months, offered 3 times	576	
	Noncollectivized farmers 3 months, offered once	89	
	Federation of Cuban Women 3 months, offered once	99	
	Defense Committees (CDR) 3 months, offered once	210	
	Teachers 5 months, offered twice	124	
	Fishermen 3 months, offered 3 times	133	
	TOTAL		3,756
	GRAND TOTAL		36,487

Note: Data from Lionel Soto, "Dos años de instrucción revolucionaria," *Cuba Socialista*, No. 18 (Feb. 1963), p. 33. Only one course was offered in the national schools for noncollectivized farmers, the Federation of Cuban Women, and the CDR because these schools were not opened until the second half of 1962.

1961–62, this is largely because rapid expansion is noisier and more dramatic than most other sorts of innovation. But the history of important changes in the schools by no means ends with the passing of 1962.

The Critique of June 1962

On June 27, 1962, at the seventh national meeting of the EIR, Castro delivered a stinging criticism of the system, exposing "certain errors" and "mistaken conceptions" that had been allowed to influence the operation of the schools.* Actually, this speech was only the public announcement of a reevaluation that had been in process for some time. Insiders had already received a circular from the National Directorate of the EIR, countersigned by Castro and dated June 12, describing guidelines for the reorganization of the system.[20] But the problems were not aired publicly until Castro spoke to the cadres of the EIR on June 27 and the Cuban newspapers carried the entire speech three days later.[21]

Castro's attack can be understood only in terms of the larger political crisis that gripped Cuba in the spring and early summer of 1962. The problems of the EIR were serious, so serious, in fact, that Soto later admitted that there had been talk of temporarily closing the schools.[22] But these problems did not originate with the schools; they derived mainly from the full-scale struggle that was going on within the ORI. Because the EIR were, in the main, Party schools by the beginning of 1962, they were intimately affected by both the "errors" and the subsequent purge of the ORI.†

* An abridged version of this key speech will be found in Appendix D below.

† In the summer of 1961, when the ORI was formed, the National Directorate of the EIR passed from the supervision of the 26th of July Movement to become a financially autonomous body attached to the National Directorate of the ORI. For the next year, the national schools were run by the National Directorate of the EIR and the provincial and basic schools were run by the provincial directors of the ORI. Although budgets and "general orientations" for the provincial and basic schools came from the National Directorate of the EIR, the provincial directors of the ORI and their subordinates managed, directed, and staffed these schools in quite autonomous fashion. See Lionel Soto, "Las Escuelas de Instrucción Revolucionaria y la formación de cuadros," *Cuba Socialista,* No. 3 (Nov. 1961), pp. 31–32; and Lionel Soto, "Nuevo desarrollo de la instrucción revolucionaria," *Cuba Socialista,* No. 12 (Aug. 1962), p. 37.

During the latter part of 1961 and the first months of 1962, the basic organizational work within the ORI went on at a rapid pace. Basically, this work involved selecting certain militants from the ranks of the PSP, the 26th of July Movement, the Revolutionary Directorate, and the masses. These recruits were organized into cells that were supposed to coordinate and orient the entire revolutionary effort. Because of the disparate organizations, personalities, aims, and ambitions gathered under the umbrella of the ORI, the processes by which selection, organization, and functioning were to take place were unclear. What past best qualified one for candidacy? By what standards should candidates be evaluated, and how should members be chosen and ratified? Once a revolutionary cell had been organized, what in fact were its duties, responsibilities, and powers? How much local autonomy should exist within the Party itself? Although there had been much general talk about "a Party of the masses" and a "truly revolutionary Party," firm guidelines had never been set down. The ORI was expanding in a very special and very disorganized fashion, largely under the day-to-day supervision of cadres from the PSP, the cadres with the most organizational skill, the most conventional political know-how, and, in many cases, the most personal ambition.

In three speeches during March 1962, Castro tore the lid off the operation of the ORI. The first was on March 13 at the University of Havana, the second was on March 16 to instructresses from the Conrado Benítez School, and the third and most important was his famous radio and television speech of March 26.[23] Before these three speeches, there had been some official acknowledgment that all was not well in the political life of the revolution, but only in March did Castro move publicly against existing conditions and the men he held responsible for them. At that time, Castro characterized the ORI as a garbage heap, a hotbed of sectarianism, a nest of privilege, a haven for opportunists, a center of arbitrariness and distrust of the masses, and a bureaucracy packed with power seekers. He said that "a veritable chaos, a veritable anarchy" was being introduced into the nation.[24] As an example of what had happened, Castro cited the case of Fidel Pompa, who was Secretary of the Sectional Committee of the ORI in Bayamo, Oriente. Pompa, evidently a member of the PSP, had publicly questioned the right of Emilio Aragonés (whom he had called "this filthy fat man"), Sergio del Valle, Guillermo García, and Haydée Santamaría to be named to the National Directorate of the ORI.* Castro asked what right had Pompa, "who hid under a bed" while others had died in the Sierra, to comment now, like a "Nazi *Gauleiter*," about the leaders of the revolution? "What true Communist can have a mind like that—ridiculous, vain, immoral, grotesquely absurd?" Similarly, he cited the case of Sr. Garrucho, a functionary of the National Institute of Sports and Recreation (INDER). Garrucho had been a member of a Batista party, had later entered the PSP, and then had become a member of the seven-man cell of the ORI in INDER. Castro noted that this seven-man cell consisted of Garrucho, two girls he had brought with him from his previous work, the Director of INDER, the Director's secretary, and two old-time members of the PSP. At that very moment, Castro charged, Garrucho was maneuvering to substitute his cousin for one of the two PSP militants. "That was the cell; that was our contact with the masses, our secret contact with a mass consisting of 400 employees. Would you call *that* a political apparatus?"

But the primary target of Castro's ad hominem attack was not lower-level functionaries like Pompa and Garrucho. Rather, he focused on Aníbal Escalante, who, along with Blas Roca and Carlos Rafael Rodríguez, had been considered one of the most important men in the PSP. When the ORI was formed, Escalante was given the job of Secretary in Charge of Organization. Using this position to great personal advantage, Castro said, Escalante turned the ORI into an instrument of personal power, a tyranny, packing its ranks with PSP members, who in turn treated other revolutionaries with disdain and the masses with contempt. Moreover,

> Aníbal Escalante's actions in these matters were not the result of oversight, nor were they unconscious. Rather, they were deliberate and conscious. He simply allowed himself to be blinded by personal ambition. And because of this, he created a series of problems; in a word, he created chaos in the nation.[25]

---

* At that time, all were prominent members of the 26th of July Movement. In 1965, all were named to the Central Committee of the Communist Party of Cuba.

The chaos, whether or not it was entirely Escalante's fault, was everywhere. The ORI, unpopular, arbitrary, and often incompetent, had its nose in everybody's business; it was constantly giving orders, hiring and firing administrators, threatening, punishing, and pushing people around. The newly formed secret or semisecret cells, Castro said,

> decided and governed on all levels. When members of a ministry were faced with a problem, instead of solving it themselves, they would refer it to the ORI. For that matter, if a cat gave birth to a litter of four kittens, it was necessary to refer the case to the ORI, so that they might rule on it.[26]

The situation was seen as so bad that during the next few months the original ORI was almost completely purged; selection to the new ORI, and subsequently to the PURSC, was based thereafter on a system of local elections held in open assemblies at work centers—the so-called method of the masses. During this period Escalante was on an extended "vacation" in Eastern Europe, and the organizational power and remaining political prestige of the PSP were irreparably destroyed.

As Castro made clear in his censure of the EIR on June 27, the problems of the ORI had been felt very directly in the schools. The leadership of the schools, however, was never criticized by Castro in the way Escalante and other ORI cadres were; in fact, Castro was enthusiastic in his praise of the men who had created in the EIR "so much from so little." The problems in the schools were, in the main, treated as deriving from the problems in the ORI rather than as originating in the schools themselves. Because the ORI was such a mess, and because its cadres interfered so arbitrarily and incorrectly in the operation of the schools, the EIR had been deformed and diverted from their original purposes. But the schools could be salvaged; moreover, they could also be called upon to supply much of the human resources and know-how needed for the restructuring of the ORI.[27]

Nevertheless, criticism was the order of the day and the purpose of Castro's speech. Specifically, he pointed out three ways the system of revolutionary instruction had malfunctioned. First, just as with the ORI, many "wrong" people had been selected to attend the schools. Because the selection of students for the provincial and basic schools was largely in the hands of provincial and sectional cells of the ORI, the schools had been damaged by favoritism exercised by corrupt party cadres. The ideal conception of the schools as training centers for those who, by their actions and behavior, had already shown themselves to be the best revolutionaries had been undermined, and the schools had become plums awarded to those with the best connections. A school for revolutionary instruction was not, Castro reminded his audience, "an amusement park for elders, a kindergarten for problem children, or a body shop for the politically damaged."[28] Second, ORI interference in the operation and staffing of the schools had created waste and chaos. Revolutionary instructors, Castro said, must not be appointed to or transferred out of the EIR at the whim of political bureaucrats, nor should they be seen as subordinates of the cells, bound to obey the dictates and fancies of the local ORI personnel. The schools had been raided for administrative and political talent "in a policy that tended to produce permanent anemia, depriving all the organizations of their best cadres." Third, many students and others involved in the EIR used the schools solely for personal advancement. Graduation from the EIR, Castro said, did not entitle one to special privileges. One was not promoted simply because one had attended a school, nor did the schools transform students into "instant cadres." Of course the particular problem to which Castro was referring was not only a consequence of the careerism and opportunism that had spilled over from the ORI; it also stemmed from public knowledge of the career patterns of those who had attended the first sessions of the provincial schools. Many of the first graduates of these schools had been elevated to positions of leadership in both the EIR and other political and administrative bureaucracies. This pattern of rapid advancement had established a precedent and a set of expectations that now interfered with the easy reincorporation of EIR graduates into the work force.

As we have seen, by the time Castro delivered his speech on June 27, action had already been taken to remedy the problems faced by the schools. Among the most important organizational and administrative changes were the following.[29] (1) Responsibility for staffing, administering, and overseeing the entire system of revolutionary instruction was centralized in the National Directorate of the EIR, and the National Directorate of the EIR was made responsible solely to the National Directorate of the ORI. (Later it was made responsible to the PURSC and the PCC.) This reorganization was designed to keep local units of the ORI from interfering directly with the operation of provincial and basic schools. (2) Henceforth, students to attend the basic schools would be nominated by the local revolutionary cells from among the best workers in each work center. Those so nominated would have to be ratified in an open assembly of all workers before they could actually attend the basic schools. (3) Students to attend the provincial schools would be selected in the main (80 percent) from among the best students in the basic schools.[30] The newly constituted provincial ORI organizations would select the remaining 20 percent from among their own cadres. (4) The students of the national Ñico López School would be selected in the main (80 percent) from among the best students in the provincial schools. The National Directorate of the ORI would select the remaining 20 percent from among the party cadres. Attendance at the other national schools would be based on selection of the most dedicated and active revolutionaries from within the relevant organizations. Such selection would be guided by the ORI. (5) Only schools officially under the administration of the National Directorate of the EIR would have the right to call themselves Schools of Revolutionary Instruction. The part-time special schools run by the CDR and other mass organizations must be called Círculos de Instrucción Revolucionaria (Centers of Revolutionary Instruction). (6) The system would be made uniform and manageable: the school calendar would be regularized as much as possible; the provincial schools would be combined until there was only one in each province; the basic schools in the cities would almost all become evening schools (thus only the rural EBIR would continue as boarding operations at the basic level). The rural basic schools would be for peasants and agricultural workers only.*

It should be emphasized that the purpose of the reforms of 1962 was not to divorce the EIR from the political apparatus of the revolution. Quite to the contrary, a system of revolutionary instruction not integrated into and under the control of the political apparatus was and is inconceivable in revolutionary Cuba. The reforms were designed to insulate the day-to-day operation of the EIR from political interference, but certainly not from political control in the larger sense. What was sought was a workable division of labor and viable mechanisms of coordination between the Party and the EIR. Certainly divorce was not intended when the National Directorate of the EIR was made directly responsible to the national leadership of the Party. It should be remembered that the overwhelming majority of Party functionaries were themselves graduates of one or more EIR; moreover, the local cells, sectional committees, and provincial committees of the Party were intimately involved in the selection of students.

After the purge of the ORI and the subsequent formation of the PURSC and the PCC, there was no indication that really serious tension arose again between Party functionaries and those who worked in the EIR. This is not to say that all the problems to which Castro directed his attention on June 27 were solved. Careerists and opportunists undoubtedly still promoted their own candidacy to the schools. Admission was probably not as impersonal and open to all "revolutionary talents" as the official literature would lead us to believe. But there is little doubt that the purge of the ORI and the reforms in the EIR did effectively end the worst examples of selfishness, favoritism, political interference, and disorganization.†

* The boarding aspect of the basic schools was increasingly perceived as very uneconomical. No budgetary figures for the schools have ever been made public, but the costs must have been substantial. Not only did students at the boarding schools receive all room, board, books, and uniforms, but they continued to receive their regular salaries if they had families dependent on their wages. Additionally, of course, when they entered the schools they were taken out of the productive process, although some continued to contribute voluntary labor.

† The related problems of privilege and careerism are difficult to assess. My

After 1962 the problems faced by the schools were of a different order, involving the cultural level of both students and instructors, the curriculum, and the role that the schools should play in meeting the non-Marxist educational needs of the revolution. These problems will be discussed in more detail below.

The Technical Revolution

After the criticism levied in June 1962, a year and a half passed before the EIR were once again given a new charge and an enlarged set of responsibilities.[31] At the tenth national meeting of the Schools of Revolutionary Instruction, held from November 28 to December 1, 1963, it was announced that the courses of the basic schools would be extended from three to five months, the provincial school courses would be extended from five to nine months, and the national Ñico López School course would be extended from ten and a half months to a year and a half. Courses at the other national schools would all last five months.[32] The primary purpose of the expanded course schedule was to allow the schools to enter, in a preliminary way, into what later came to be called the "political-technical cycle."

Just as 1962 had been—unofficially of course—"the year of the great political crisis," so 1963 was "the year of the great economic rethinking." This reevaluation of economic possibilities and prob-

---

own impression, based on observation and talks with party functionaries and graduates of the EIR in Cuba in 1966, is that expectations of privilege were under control by that time, but that the practice of privilege was still in evidence. That is, the majority of party and political functionaries to whom I spoke did seem to approach their work with a service ethic rather than with an ethic of personal gain and advancement. However, owing to the scarcity of goods and services in Cuba, being associated with the political apparatus ipso facto brought certain advantages, even though these were not actively sought or reflected in salaries. The Party and other official organizations had vehicles, guest houses, freedom of movement, decisional power, and access to a range of values and experiences that were largely denied to the general public. Although these resources did not in the main seem to be cynically and corruptly exploited, they did constitute an operative base of privilege. Given this state of affairs, to be a political cadre or government functionary in Cuba at that moment must certainly have been attractive; thus it is likely that some did not wait to be "tapped" by the masses or by their superiors, but rather schemed and manipulated to get into the EIR or any other channel that might lead to eventual membership in the new elite.

abilities in Cuba involved a movement away from industrial visions of the immediate future and toward visions of the Cuban economy in the 1970's as being dominated by a diversified and modern agricultural sector based primarily on sugar, cattle, poultry, citrus fruits, and fishing. Agricultural development was seen as the key to Cuba's immediate economic future; increased productivity by means of technology was in turn the key to agricultural development. Not surprisingly, this change in thinking led in 1963 to the announcement of a "technical revolution" as the critical battlefront in the struggle for economic development, and this announcement was reflected almost immediately in the plans and programs of the EIR.

It had not been determined by December 1963, however, just what the long-term role of the EIR in the technical revolution would be. Like so many other aspects of the system, the political-technical aspect was not formally structured at the outset. Rather, it was worked out in practice over a number of years. According to official sources, the expanded program announced at the tenth national meeting would allow students time to study "the regional and provincial developmental plans of the Party . . . and as much material as possible on the Cuban economy" in addition to the usual Marxist-Leninist texts.[33] The schools, said Soto, must contribute to a "*consciousness of the technical revolution*" and "open the eyes of thousands of Party militants and advanced workers to the 'royal road' of the technical sciences."[34] An introduction to Marxism-Leninism, it was suggested, would henceforth form only part of the militant's training experience. An understanding of Cuban economic realities, the elements of technology, and the application of this technology to the productive process would also be required. Students not only would study printed materials on the relevant technology, but would also put theory into practice by participating in appropriate and hopefully profitable agricultural and in some cases industrial labor. No attempt was made to convert any of the schools into centers graduating technically competent cadres. Rather, the graduates were expected to be Marxist-Leninists sensitized to the potentialities of technology. The guiding philosophy of the first year of the political-technical cycle was summed up by Castro in September 1964 as the necessity of relating Marxism-Leninism to the economic realities of Cuba.

> In the first stage of the revolution, ... what we can call a theoretical consciousness of the problems of the revolution began to be acquired; ... the necessity and inevitability of social change began to be understood; political doctrines and philosophies began to be studied in depth; the international situation and the position of each country in that international situation began to be understood.
>
> That is, we began to acquire a theoretical preparation for the revolution, and the Schools of Revolutionary Instruction began to function—*the study of Marxism-Leninism began.* Thousands, tens of thousands, hundreds of thousands began to understand theoretically the problem of history, the dialectical conception of history; the phenomenon of societies divided into classes from the earliest times began to be understood. Hundreds of thousands began to understand these phenomena theoretically....
>
> We have fortified ourselves a great deal from the theoretical point of view, but now we also have to fortify ourselves from the practical point of view. *Our Schools of Revolutionary Instruction have filled a great ideological gap by contributing to the ideological formation of tens, of hundreds of thousands of citizens.* And now in the Schools of Revolutionary Instruction, in addition to theory, questions related to techniques of production are being included. That is, *elements of technological education* are being introduced into the Schools of Revolutionary Instruction.[35]

Castro was saying that since one could not eat Marxism, the EIR's new critical responsibility was to contribute to the technological modernization, and therefore to the productivity, of the Cuban economy.

By the beginning of 1965, the role of the EIR in the technical revolution had been somewhat clarified. Once again most of the school cycles were extended to allow more detailed instruction in the elements of technology. Additionally, guidelines were established for the proportions of political and technical education that would be offered in the various types of schools. Beginning in January 1965, the provincial schools of the Party, with their school year extended to ten and a half months, and the Ñico López School, with a two-year course, would offer instruction predominantly in Marxism, with elements of technology offered as a secondary academic subject. The other national schools, the provincial schools of the Union of Communist Youth (UJC), and the basic night schools would offer a balanced curriculum of Marxist, technical, and cultural education. The national schools and the provincial schools of the UJC would have a ten-and-a-half-month school year, and the basic night schools would continue to offer two five-month courses annually. The 30 existing basic boarding schools, all located in rural areas, would offer a ten-and-a-half-month course consisting predominantly of technical and cultural education; Marxist theory would make up only about 30 percent of their program. These basic boarding schools would actually offer courses of a vocational sort, focused on the cultivation of sugar cane or on the raising of cattle, depending on the location of the particular school. Land, technical facilities, and agricultural instructors would be attached to the schools so that learning could be based on field work as well as on classroom instruction.[36]

Thus during 1965 the EIR moved openly into technological education in the service of agricultural development. No longer was the political-technical cycle limited to "winning the consciousness" of the militants to the importance of technology. The vocational training of agricultural cadres became an integral part of the EIR program. The Sierra Maestra School for agricultural workers was converted into a technological institute, and it ceased to be called a national school. The basic rural boarding schools were converted into agricultural training centers for peasants but were formally retained in the EIR system. Later in the year, the bulk of the national program of technical education in agriculture was placed administratively under the National Directorate of the EIR. This program, concentrating at first on the preparation of technicians in soils, fertilizers, and cattle, envisaged the graduation of forty thousand young Cubans by 1974.[37] In 1965 the first seven training centers were opened in the province of Havana; and in 1966 several other institutes, including the Camilo Cienfuegos School City in Oriente, were converted into technological training schools.*

* The technological institutes were organized under the Council of the Plan for Technological Education in Soils, Fertilizers, and Cattle (*Consejo del Plan*

These new centers for agricultural education were not officially considered Schools of Revolutionary Instruction, although administratively they did come under the EIR. They were fundamentally technological schools dedicated to the formation of agricultural specialists, albeit specialists with a high level of revolutionary consciousness. The Cubans felt that not just agronomists but *revolutionary* agronomists must be formed. Soto stated this philosophy of training most emphatically:

> The system of technological institutes of the Council of the Plan is not only a strategic solution to questions related to our agriculture.... The Institutes are also centers for the political, intellectual, moral, aesthetic, and physical formation of those who are being educated. We consider the technological institutes, at the same time, to be shapers of Communist militants, institutions with a high political level, and producers of really revolutionary technicians who will also serve as the frontline military reserve of the Commander in Chief.[38]

It is indicative of the political importance of the agricultural question—and perhaps also of the high regard in which Soto and

---

de la Enseñanza Tecnológica de Suelos, Fertilizantes y Ganadería). For a list of the institutes under the plan at the end of 1966, see Lionel Soto, "Lo importante es que desarrollemos nuestro camino," *Cuba Socialista*, No. 65 (Jan. 1967), p. 55. After a visit in September 1966 to the Camilo Cienfuegos School City, the largest of the institutes, I wrote the following in my journal: "This school center *(Ciudad Escolar Camilo Cienfuegos*) was originally designed as a live-in educational facility for children from the Sierra, but with the development of other plans and programs for rural education, it was changed in 1965 to a school for the agrotechnical education of young campesinos and workers. Now 4,500 future agricultural technicians live at the school, serving their military obligation while they study. Discipline is paramilitary, studies range from accelerated primary school, through intensive basic secondary, to a two-year postsecondary course of technical instruction. Eventually 20,000 boys and young men will be in residence. Those who have families outside receive monthly support stipends based on the number of their dependents.

"Architecturally, the school is interesting because in its original form it is the child of the most romantic-utopian phase of the revolution. The school was begun soon after the triumph of the Rebel Army. Much of the original labor force was, in fact, composed of rebel troops. Nothing, it was felt, would be too good for the children of the Sierra, those neglected offspring of the most neglected group in pre-Castro Cuba. As a result, the first residential units and classrooms built were almost luxurious. Provided with ample recreational facilities and lovely rooms and bathrooms, and surrounded by trees and extensive lawns, they were a child's dream and an economist's nightmare. Recent construction is more spartan and more compact. The students themselves are used as a work force for construction when they are not attending classes, studying, taking military instruction, or playing sports."

his lieutenants were held—that this massive program was initially placed under the direction of the EIR. "As goes agriculture, so goes the revolution" might well have been the motto of those who managed the enterprise. As Soto, paraphrasing Castro, has said, it is necessary "to prove that Socialism and Communism can triumph fully in the field of agriculture—until now the weak point in Socialist experience."[39] When viewed this way, it is not surprising that the system of revolutionary instruction was initially called upon to oversee the formation of technological cadres.

Higher Studies and Research

Early in 1963, the first public mention was made of the possibility of founding, within a year or two, an Institute of Higher Studies of Marxism-Leninism dedicated both to the examination of key theoretical issues and to research into "our history, our present realities, and our future solutions."[40] As of 1967, when the EIR were closed, the Institute of Higher Studies was still not founded. The promised research program, however, was in full flower.[41]

The program began modestly in 1964 with a study of the Cuban labor movement and an investigation into the economics of the sugar industry.[42] From the outset this program in the EIR had three primary purposes. First, it would produce the sort of written materials considered essential for continued training and for diffusion of "revolutionary knowledge," both inside and outside the EIR system. It was felt that there were not enough basic studies of the Cuban economy, polity, and society; moreover, most of those that did exist were rendered almost worthless—if not absolutely dangerous—by their capitalistic, bourgeois bias. Second, it would supply basic knowledge and data on current conditions in Cuba. This information would help in the planning and implementing of policy. Thus, in addition to the didactic and orienting payoffs, it was expected that the research program would also yield direct, instrumental, administrative benefits. Third, it would provide, for those who participated in the program, a healthy and necessary corrective for formalism, dogmatism, and the mechanical application of theory among both cadres and students. Whether or not this pragmatic and empirical philosophy of research was able to flourish in an atmosphere of considerable ideological rigidity is another question, but certainly a great deal of lip service was paid to the value of fresh investigation. Typical of the official research philosophy is the following statement by Soto:

> The National Directorate of the EIR of the Communist Party of Cuba has decided to enter into social research without any particular scheme in mind, without dogmatism, with an audacious, revolutionary spirit, open to the objective study of situations, and in the spirit of always finding the Cuban forms that the universal principles of Marxism-Leninism take.[43]

Although it was not so clearly articulated from the beginning, the emphasis and resources funneled into research in the EIR grew out of a more general conviction that uncritical borrowing from Soviet and Eastern European practice would not answer Cuba's political and developmental needs. This position reflected not only a certain disenchantment with the level and type of political and economic support offered by the Soviet Union and Eastern European countries, but also a profound feeling that conditions in Cuba were so different from those in Europe that little direct institutional transfer was possible. This general conviction was reflected in the motto of the fourteenth national meeting of the EIR, "What is most important is that we develop our own way," a phrase taken from one of Castro's speeches.[44] In reporting on that meeting, Soto quoted liberally from Castro to the effect that through study, research, and the creative use of experience, the revolution must find its own theoretical and operational style:

> We believe that regarding all these problems of Socialism and Communism it is necessary to meditate, to reflect, to study, to analyze, to do a great deal of research. . . . Thought that stagnates is thought that rots. . . . We should admit that our revolution, in its early phases, had various imitative, mechanistic tendencies. . . . To copy in life, or to copy in the revolution, is like copying on an examination. And nobody can graduate as a revolutionary by copying.[45]

The EIR, as the most important locus of political education in the country, was made responsible for conducting research relevant to finding "the Cuban way."

Although the first research under the auspices of the EIR was conducted in 1964, it was not until early 1965 that a permanent organizational infrastructure was raised. At that time, the Comisión Nacional de Investigaciones y Estudios Sociales de las EIR del PURSC (later of the PCC) was established.[46] By 1966, the Commission had created separate national subcommissions devoted to research on economics, history, methodology (instructional techniques), sociology, and philosophy. There were also separate provincial committees coordinating work in each of these fields. In the entire nation, at the end of 1966, approximately 150 cadres of the EIR were working on the various research projects. Of these, about half devoted all their time to research and the other half combined their research work with administrative responsibilities in the schools. Of course, many students in the schools were also brought into the research projects as data gatherers, assistants, and semiskilled workers of various types.

The scope of the research effort in 1966 is suggested by the following partial list of projects then under way. (1) Under the Commission of Sociological Research: a replication and elaboration in twelve rural zones of some aspects of Lowry Nelson's study and other studies of rural life,[47] and a contribution to a UNESCO international study of recreation and the uses of leisure time.[48] (2) Under the Commission of Historical Research: a history of the Communist movement in Cuba, a history of the labor movement in Cuba, a history of the 26th of July Movement, and a chronology of the revolutionary movement from 1952 to 1965. (3) Under the Commission of Economic Research: a general study of the economics of the sugar industry, and a general study of the economics of the cattle and dairy industries.[49]

It would be misleading to assume that research projects such as these were attempted with only the internal resources of the EIR. On the contrary, many of the project directors, although they might have been members of the national EIR subcommissions on research, were not actually cadres of the system of revolutionary instruction, but were recruited from the universities, various ministries, and special governmental organizations like the Junta Central de Planificación. Nevertheless, despite the resources and support lent by other organizations, the research projects bore the unmistakable stamp of their sponsorship by the EIR. What was being conducted was revolutionary research, research intended to strengthen, clarify, and direct the revolutionary movement. By some standards, the ideological bases of the effort, the minimal sophistication of many of the participating cadres, and the applied or instrumental character of most of the work would serve to disqualify the entire program from the select company of scholarship. But to apply such standards to the research program in the EIR would be to misunderstand its avowed purposes. The EIR were charged with conducting research relevant to finding the Cuban way, and the standards for the effort were established by the revolutionary leadership itself, not by a national or international community of scholars. How fully the studies conducted actually fed back into the policy-making process as a corrective for dogmatism and the self-fulfilling characteristics of closed information systems is difficult to say. In any case, although the scholarship may not have been of the highest and most impartial order, much of it was empirical self-investigation of the sort not usually engaged in by revolutionary regimes during their formative years.

Students, Cadres, and Curriculum

One of the least talked about but perhaps most important characteristics of the Schools of Revolutionary Instruction was the low educational level of their students. In 1963, for example, only about one out of five students in the provincial and basic schools had as much as a sixth-grade education;[50] and at the national level, only the Ñico López School required a sixth-grade certificate for admission.* Teaching "the most complex science" to students who were barely literate must have been a difficult and at times an un-

* In 1964 the only official scholastic requirement for entering any of the EIR (with the exception of the Ñico López School) was that the student know how to read and write correctly. It was also expected that those entering provincial schools would have completed or have adequate knowledge of the basic program, and that those entering the Ñico López School would have completed or have adequate knowledge of the provincial program. For most schools, the minimum age was set at sixteen years; for the Ñico López School it was set at eighteen years. See *Hoy*, Dec. 10, 1963, p. 2. Similar standards were in force during 1965. See *Hoy*, Nov. 24, 1964, p. 3.

rewarding task, particularly when using translations of Soviet materials designed for more sophisticated audiences and Marxist-Leninist classics that could not readily be applied to Cuban reality.

To overcome the problems created by the low educational level of their students, the EIR tried, whenever possible, to include courses in cultural improvement in the curriculum. Especially after the inauguration of the political-technical cycle, nonpolitical subjects formed a significant part of the course of study in the lower schools. But throughout their seven years the EIR continued to receive many students who could barely read and write and for whom even the most basic works in Marxist-Leninist thought must have remained unintelligible except as a source of slogans.

One reason the cultural level of incoming EIR students remained low despite the rise in the educational level of the overall Cuban population was that students were selected according to a policy that consciously favored those of lower social origin. How this policy was enforced in practice is not completely clear, but after Castro's public criticism of June 1962—in which he said that the schools were not drawing enough of their students from the working masses and were depending too heavily on self-serving bureaucrats, old political hacks, and the offspring of the urban middle class—the national leadership of the EIR went to some lengths to increase and to publicize the representation of the working class in the schools. This official emphasis on the working class probably means that official statistics on class origin are not altogether accurate; nevertheless, Table 8 does give an idea of the representation of occupational sectors among students in the EIR.

Notice that in both the provincial and the basic schools the percentage of students from the working class was much higher in 1966 than in 1962. Furthermore, if we could subtract the 2,356 agricultural workers of the Sierra Maestra School from the 1962 national totals, we would find that the same relationship held at the national school level as well. Thus the EIR were successful in increasing their percentage of lower-class students. But beyond this success, there was obviously some point at which the policy of selecting students from the most disadvantaged strata ran up against Cuban social and political realities. The schools found it difficult

TABLE 8. OCCUPATIONAL ORIGINS OF STUDENTS IN THE EIR, 1962 AND 1966

Type of school and year	Total number of graduates	Percentage of industrial workers	Percentage of agricultural workers	Percentage of peasants	Total percentage of working-class students
National schools, 1962	3,756	13.6%	66.0%	2.3%	81.9%
National schools, 1966	609	55.6%[a]		18.7%	74.3%
Provincial schools, 1962	1,661	24.1%	9.8%	3.4%	37.3%
Provincial schools, 1966	779	65.8%[a]		9.1%	74.9%
Basic schools, 1962	31,070	28.6%	14.9%	4.6%	48.1%
Basic boarding schools, 1966	2,640	27.1%	52.5%	14.5%	94.1%
Basic night schools, 1966	13,636	52.1%[a]		6.6%	58.7%

Note: The 1962 data are from Lionel Soto, "Dos años de instrucción revolucionaria," *Cuba Socialista*, No. 18 (Feb. 1963), pp. 33–34. The 1966 data are from Lionel Soto, "Lo importante es que desarrollemos nuestro camino," *Cuba Socialista*, No. 65 (Jan. 1967) pp. 39, 41. Occupational origin refers to the family background in those cases when a student came to the school directly from another training center rather than from the work force. The percentage of agricultural workers (and hence of working-class students) in the national schools in 1962 is inflated by the existence of the Sierra Maestra School for agricultural workers, which accounted for more than 60 percent of all graduates from the national schools that year.

[a] Percentages of industrial and agricultural workers combined.

to recruit a significant minority of students from the peasantry, and there were always more industrial and agricultural workers—taken separately or combined—than peasants. Moreover, except in certain schools specifically organized to handle agricultural workers and make allowances for their cultural shortcomings, the industrial workers, who had the advantages of a better education and an urban life-style, continued to make up most of the lower-class students in the EIR.[51]

The inexperience and the relatively low educational level of the administrators and instructors in the EIR affected the operation of the schools even more profoundly than the low cultural level of the students.[52] From January 1961, when the nineteen original cadres assumed their responsibilities in the schools, to the end of 1966, when 573 men and women were working as full-time directors and political instructors, the EIR leadership consistently emphasized political rather than academic criteria in the selection of cadres. This policy was clearly articulated by Soto. After noting that the overwhelming majority of cadres were recent graduates of the schools, and that intellectual potential rather than intellectual accomplishment was sought in the new instructors, he continued,

> We have interpreted the political bases of selection as follows: *absolute fidelity to the revolution, class spirit, and practical action in support of the revolution.* That is, in forming the apparatus of the EIR, we have been guided primarily by *political criteria,* . . . because we have established the fact that if we have political fitness we can do anything. And we have proven that fact fully in our brief history. The primary thing that we demand is a revolutionary feeling toward life, a revolutionary consciousness in the cadres that we select.[53]

It was a policy designed, above all, to make sure that the schools were staffed with loyal and enthusiastic young revolutionaries. Table 9 presents a demographic and political profile of the cadres associated with the EIR at the end of 1966 as a result of this recruitment policy.

Because the schools were staffed with enthusiastic but untutored revolutionaries, many of those teaching Marxism-Leninism had only recently been introduced to the subject matter themselves. Moreover, they were so lacking in general education that they were in no position to learn the classics by studying on their own, and their chances for rapid self-improvement became even more remote when extra instructional and intellectual burdens were imposed on them by the political-technical cycle. In an attempt to overcome these problems, to raise the cultural level of the cadres and give them needed skills, the leaders of the EIR instituted a number of programs: special year-end courses, study circles, the Marx-Engels-Lenin School specifically for cadres of the EIR, and various programs associated with the universities. But, as the authorities themselves admitted, the path leading to appropriate levels of educational achievement and specialization is long and rough: "We are advancing and winning ground; we are on the road [to cultural

TABLE 9. SOME DEMOGRAPHIC AND POLITICAL CHARACTERISTICS OF 573 EIR DIRECTORS AND POLITICAL INSTRUCTORS AT THE END OF 1966

Characteristic	Percentage of all cadres
Age:	
25 or younger	39.4%
26 to 30	30.0%
31 to 35	15.5%
36 to 45	11.6%
46 or older	3.5%
TOTAL	100.0%
Sex:	
Masculine	84.5%
Feminine	15.5%
TOTAL	100.0%
Occupational origins:	
Intellectuals (students and teachers)	13.4%
Service and commercial workers	34.6%
Industrial and agricultural workers	45.5%
Peasants	6.5%
TOTAL	100.0%
Political origins in the revolution:	
26th of July Movement	19.0%
Popular Socialist Party	4.7%
Revolutionary Directorate	1.0%
Socialist Youth	2.3%
Unattached (when the revolution triumphed)	73.0%
TOTAL	100.0%
Political militancy in 1966:	
Militants of the Party	82.7%
Militants of the Communist Youth	8.4%
Not yet militants	8.9%
TOTAL	100.0%

Note: Data are from Lionel Soto, "Lo importante es que desarrollemos nuestro camino," *Cuba Socialista*, No. 65 (Jan. 1967), pp. 42–43.

improvement]; and we shall continue to be on it for five to ten years more, at least."[54] As we shall see, however, the schools were closed long before the journey could be completed.

Related to the difficulties raised by the low cultural levels of both cadres and students were the problems deriving from inappropriate and inadequate teaching materials. As noted previously, the difficulty of introducing the unlettered to complex classics of the faith was compounded by the lack of Marxist-Leninist materials based on and related to the Cuban experience. In fact, until the first studies prepared by the various research commissions of the EIR were made available in 1965 and 1966, virtually the only indigenous Marxist materials were Blas Roca's *Fundamentals of Socialism* and Castro's speeches, hardly an impressive body of Socialist literature despite its political importance and persuasive power. Caught between the inability of most students to study the classics directly and the lack of a Cuban Marxist literature, the EIR had to depend heavily on translated Soviet manuals as basic texts for the study of Marxism-Leninism in all but the most advanced schools. This practice was constantly criticized by many government leaders, school cadres, and students, who evidently found the Soviet texts wooden and inappropriate. In almost every discussion of teaching methods in the EIR, the problem of rote-learning and *manualismo*, or excessive reliance on digests and résumés, was brought up. Moreover, the Cuban use of Soviet manuals was considered particularly inappropriate at a time when political relations between the two countries were deteriorating. On the other hand, the use of these manuals was defended by those who pointed out not only that it was impossible to introduce workers and peasants directly to the Marxist classics, but also that in the not too distant future the texts used in all political education would be predominantly of Cuban origin, written by revolutionaries, based on revolutionary experiences, and cast in terms that any true son of the revolution would be able to understand.[55]

In the autumn of 1967, however, the debate about the problems and shortcomings of the EIR was ended. Following a decision that must have been confirmed if not made by Castro himself, the entire

EIR system was gradually phased out. By February 1968, with as little fanfare and publicity as had attended their creation, the Schools of Revolutionary Instruction had been closed.*

The reasons for the closing of the schools can be inferred in part from the nature of the criticism to which they had been subjected during the mid-1960's. The sterility of manualismo, the inappropriateness of Soviet teaching materials, the problems encountered in staffing the schools, and the basic difficulty of forming true revolutionaries in the classroom all contributed to the demise of the EIR. Castro drew these several threads together in the same speech of March 1968 in which he launched the Revolutionary Offensive. Although he referred primarily to manualismo, he also showed his more general dissatisfaction with the notion that one can learn to act in a correct and truly revolutionary fashion simply by studying Marxism-Leninism:

> Ignorance leads to the idea that everything is easy, to the oversimplification of problems, and to the thought that everything, no matter how complicated, has an easy and immediate solution right around the corner. The tendency to speak without sufficient grounds and to analyze things facilely and superficially is greater than the tendency to analyze in depth. We have always been prone to produce a great many street-corner philosophers. This is a tendency that has hung on from the past, as if the revolution hadn't taught us anything about the profundity of these processes.
>
> It must be remarked that one certain factor has contributed much to the lack of sufficient political instruction, and that factor has been not so much the use as the abuse of the manuals of Marxism-Leninism. It must be said that many revolutionary militants went through the schools known as Schools of Revolutionary Instruction—schools that did, in fact, have the aim of giving revolutionary instruction—and philosophical questions were studied, including the elements and fundamentals of Marxism.
>
> Naturally, all this is as useful as it is necessary and convenient; but there's something else the revolution itself has taught us—because after all, the revolution is the greatest teacher of revolutionaries—and that is that an enormous gap sometimes exists between general concepts and practice, between philosophy and reality. And, above all, it has taught us how far the manuals have gradually become outdated and anachronistic. In many instances, they don't say one word about the problems the masses should understand. Often the manuals are nothing but a series of abstract generalities, vague and devoid of content, so that just when you think you

* This discussion of the closing of the EIR is based on informal interviews held in Havana in March 1968.

have a truly developed revolutionary, you find that what you have is a militant who does not understand many of the most serious problems of the contemporary world.

We must also acknowledge that the manuals contain a large number of clichés and stereotyped phrases and even some falsehoods. . . . This factor unquestionably has been instrumental in that weakness of formation, of instruction, from which our people are still suffering.[56]

In short, by the end of 1967 the leadership had come to perceive the EIR as preventing rather than helping the Cubans to find their own way. Therefore, with little hesitation and no ceremony, the schools were closed. It was an action quite in keeping with their earlier history, for, as we have seen, the schools had always developed and changed in response to the top leadership's idea of the revolution's needs. When the masses needed an introduction to Marxism-Leninism, the basic EIR were founded. When the technical revolution became the focus of attention, the EIR were given responsibilities in the field of technical education. When social research was needed, the EIR formed special commissions for research. Thus the system of revolutionary instruction was used as a flexible instrument to attack a series of problems cast up both by the revolution itself and by the changing views of Castro and his lieutenants. But the institutional format, tied as it was to the classroom, did not prove flexible enough to warrant its own indefinite continuation. Certainly what came to be called the new Cuban man was not being created in the EIR; nor, in the Cuban view, was there any possibility that the schools could be redesigned as appropriate settings for the formation of a new generation of true Communists.* The schools had been useful for training cadres during a certain historical phase of the revolution, but that moment had passed. It was now felt that other organizations could better perform the few remaining functions of the Schools of Revolutionary Instruction.[57]

* Schools for the training of Party and other cadres did not, however, disappear with the closing of the EIR. For a report on the situation in mid-1969, see "La formación de cuadros y la educación interna del Partido," *Granma*, July 11, 1969, p. 2.

6 Conclusion

THE DESCRIPTIONS, if not the interpretations, contained in a book of this sort are inevitably overtaken by events. The Year of Education has passed into revolutionary history and mythology, its youthful brigadistas now grown to adulthood. Although the Committees for Defense of the Revolution continue to operate on a nationwide scale, their role as administrative and vigilance organizations now clearly overshadows their role as innovative and experimental settings for the transformation of political culture. And the Schools of Revolutionary Instruction, once heralded as the training ground for an entire generation of revolutionary cadres, are now closed, their students scattered throughout the island.

This does not mean, of course, that the institutions and events discussed in the preceding three chapters are no longer relevant to the study of mobilization and the transformation of political culture in Cuba. Quite the contrary, if only because they represent key aspects of the growth of the revolutionary style of governance and national development during the first decade, they inevitably inform much that is currently going on and much that will be attempted in the future. But the focus of attention is no longer on these particular settings. Thus, in order to achieve some closure in our discussion of a system that is still in *plena revolución,* it is necessary to sketch briefly the current Castroite theory and practice as they relate to the formation of the new Cuban man.

Cuban thinking about individual formación and the transformation of political culture after a decade of revolutionary experience can be considered in terms of the following five themes: Communism and the interrelation of abundance and consciousness, technology as the motor of abundance and a component of the new man, money as a "bitter and transitory instrument" of exchange and distribution, the promise and importance of youth, and the burden of the past. As noted earlier, these themes have been talked about in one fashion or another since the beginning of 1959. It has only been since about 1965, however, that Castro and others have woven them together into a relatively clear and consistent developmental doctrine.

Communism and the interrelation of abundance and consciousness. In a speech given on July 26, 1968, the fifteenth anniversary of the attack on the Moncada Barracks, Castro outlined in detail what had come to be his basic views on the content and construction of Communism in Cuba. So many key elements of the revolutionary doctrine were brought together in this speech that it is worth quoting at length:

> No human society has yet reached Communism. The paths by which one arrives at a superior form of society are very difficult. A Communist society is one in which man will have reached the highest degree of social awareness ever achieved. In a Communist society, man will have succeeded in achieving just as much understanding, closeness, and brotherhood as he has on occasion achieved within the narrow circle of his own family. To live in a Communist society is to live without selfishness, to live among the people and with the people, as if every one of our fellow citizens were really our dearest brother....
>
> At the very core of Marx's thought [is the idea that] Socialist society and Communist society must be based on a complete mastery of technology, on a complete development of the productive forces, so that man will be able to create enough material goods to satisfy everyone's needs. It is unquestionable that medieval society, with its minimal development of the forces of production, could not have aspired to live under Communism. It is also clear that the old [Cuban] society, with even poorer and more backward forces of production, could have aspired even less to live under Communism....
>
> People aspiring to live under Communism must do what we are doing. They must emerge from underdevelopment; they must develop their forces of production; they must master technology in order to turn man's efforts and man's sweat into the miracle of producing practically unlimited quantities of material goods. If we do not master technology, if we do not develop our forces of production, we shall deserve to be called dreamers for aspiring to live in a Communist society.

> The problem from our point of view [however] is that Communist consciousness must be developed at the same rate as the forces of production. An advance in the consciousness of the revolutionaries, in the consciousness of the people, must accompany every step forward in the development of the forces of production....
>
> [And above all] we should not use money or wealth to create consciousness. We must use consciousness to create wealth. To offer a man more to do a bit more than is expected is to buy his consciousness with money. ... As we said before, Communism certainly cannot be established if we do not create abundant wealth. But the way to do this, in our opinion, is not by creating consciousness through money or wealth but by creating wealth through consciousness.[1]

The several strains of the doctrine are here brought together as a set of linked propositions. (1) The ideal Communist society is defined as a cultural system in which every man acts as a true brother to every other man. (2) It is not possible to achieve such a cultural system until abundance replaces want as the collective situation of the citizenry. (3) The very process of creating abundance, however, can easily destroy the potential of the abundant society for being a truly Communist society. (4) Thus a society must strive to achieve abundance by creating and nourishing those values and motivations—shared feelings about collective responsibility and gain, and an ethic of societal service—that will one day become internalized as the general character structure of Communist man. Above all, abundance achieved by appealing to individual aggrandizement, by rewarding *egoismo* (self-centeredness), leads inexorably not to Communism but to increased exploitation of man by man, increased individual alienation, and rising levels of social disorganization.*

Thus the Cuban insistence on the correctness of moral incentives and social consciousness as the mainsprings of the productive

* Although Castro has never publicly criticized Soviet and East European societies in detail, he has often suggested that the bureaucratized, materialistic, elitist, and essentially conservative and nationalistic way of life of Socialist Europe does not even begin to approximate his vision of what a Communist society ought to be. See, for instance, his speech on the Soviet invasion of Czechoslovakia, *Granma*, Weekly Review, Aug. 25, 1968, pp. 1–4. The only Socialist system that receives unqualified and continuous public approbation from the Cuban leaders is North Vietnam. Vietnamese sacrifices, courage, and skill in resisting the Yankees are the qualities most often praised, but Cuban leaders also express admiration for the country's social and economic equalitarianism.

process should not be understood simply as a cynical attempt to keep the workers at the lathes and the peasants in the fields at the lowest possible cost in wages. It is, rather, an integral part of a thought system in which the way men are motivated to create wealth is considered inseparable from the way they will relate to each other in the more abundant society of the future. It is the Cuban variant of a line of thinking that links Castro to radicals otherwise as diverse as Mao and Tito.[2]

Technology as the motor of abundance and a component of the new man. As suggested by Castro's explication of the relationship between Communism and abundance, modern science and technology are seen as playing a very special role in the process of creating wealth. In the most material sense, this is little more than a recognition that in order to develop and compete in the second half of the twentieth century, a nation must draw on, modify, and apply the scientific and technological skills and resources available in the world community. Thus revolutionary leadership is firmly convinced that there can be no dramatic growth in any sector of the Cuban economy unless the productive process in that sector is modernized.[3] This commitment to bringing technology to bear on production is manifested in the sugar industry as an attempt to move toward mechanized planting and harvesting cycles, in the dairy industry as an attempt to introduce controlled breeding and artificial insemination, and in various other sectors of the economy as a series of programs designed to increase productivity by borrowing, modifying, or developing an appropriate scientific style of labor.

The most interesting aspect of this emphasis on technology, however, is how it affects the formación of the work force. Since the mid-1960's, when a curriculum thought appropriate to the technological revolution was introduced into the Schools of Revolutionary Instruction, much attention has been paid to making a scientific attitude part of the equipment of every Cuban. More narrowly conceived, this is seen as a kind of vocational training, the teaching of skills needed to run a more modern and dynamic economy. But more broadly understood, the scientific attitude implies an appreciation for the part science and technology play in the entire developmental process.* "What place can the scientifically illiterate man, the technologically illiterate man, possibly have in the community of the future?" Castro has asked on many occasions.[4] The man of the future, the Communist man, will be not only his brother's keeper, but a trained and scientifically sensitive man as well.

This notion of Communist man as a technologically trained and sensitive man is increasingly being linked with the earlier concern for moral incentives. The idea of what constitutes a moral incentive has undergone revision and enlargement. Thus, when speaking at the University of Havana on March 13, 1969, Castro emphasized that work need not inevitably be viewed as duty and sacrifice—that moral incentives need not derive their motive power exclusively from the individual's sense of duty to the collective. Quite the contrary, he continued, whenever technology and science are needed in the performance of a task, there arises the possibility that the work will be done not "with a sense of duty and necessity alone, but rather with pleasure. The work itself will excite enormous interest, and become one of man's most pleasant activities."† Cutting sugarcane or pulling weeds is not work of this

* Appreciation for science and technology implies respect for the nuts and bolts as well: "Today machinery arrives and, because of ignorance, it is often put into the hands of persons who haven't the slightest notion of what machinery is. They don't know how to take care of it, or what kind of maintenance, fuel, and oil it needs. They know nothing of its countless parts or of all the details that must be attended to. There are those who use machinery, and if a bolt drops out, they put it next to the seat; if a cap falls off, they put that next to the seat; the accelerator is soon no longer an accelerator but instead a wire to be pulled. If a valve gets lost, a makeshift connection is made. And by the time we see it, a new machine that cost twenty or twenty-five thousand in foreign exchange has become a piece of junk." Castro, speaking to graduates of the University of Oriente, *Granma,* Weekly Review, Dec. 15, 1968, p. 3.

† The speech continued: "And if we want all men to work some day with such spirit, it will not suffice just to have a sense of duty. [That kind of] moral motivation will not be enough. It will be necessary for the marvelous nature of the work itself, work directed by man's intelligence, to be one of the basic motivations." *Granma,* Weekly Review, Mar. 16, 1969, p. 3.

Although Castro seldom if ever uses the word, he is actually discussing the concept of alienation in the Marxist sense. Unlike many other Marxists, however, he views the nature of the task performed as more central to ameliorating alienation than to the prior (and larger) issue of controlling the means of pro-

sort, but scientific and technological pursuits are. Thus, in the more modern society of the future, the opportunities for integrating work with life, for deriving personal satisfaction from confronting problems and bringing knowledge to bear on their solutions, will multiply. The distinctions between manual and intellectual work will increasingly blur, and both for individuals and for society in general the separation between education and production will be bridged as the former becomes a continuing process without which growth in the latter is impossible. In sum, in the emerging revolutionary vision, technology not only makes possible the advent of abundance, but also contributes importantly to ending alienation by enabling more men to work at callings instead of at jobs.[5]

*Money as a bitter and transitory instrument of exchange and distribution.** It follows from Castro's attack on material incentives that in the new revolutionary culture increments of cash income should not be used to reward those who contribute most to the productive process or to the construction of Communism. But the feeling against the role of money in society extends well beyond a simple rejection of extra pay for extra work. What is called into question by Castro and his followers is nothing less than the exchange and distributive functions of the monetary system. That is, in the Castroite vision of Communist society, as in much early Marxist thinking, transactions involving the exchange and distribution of most goods and services are not mediated or controlled by concomitant exchanges of cash or credit. Notice that the manipulation of prices in favor of the poorer sectors is not an element

---

duction. Furthermore, as one deeply engaged in struggling against backwardness, he attaches positive value to the technicalization of the productive process at a time when others see it as a prime causative factor in the alienation of contemporary man in the more developed societies, both Socialist and non-Socialist.

* The characterization of money as a "bitter and transitory instrument" is taken from Castro's speech of March 13, 1968, at the University of Havana. See *Granma*, Weekly Review, Mar. 24, 1968, p. 7. A key compilation of revolutionary ideas about the role of money in past, present, and future societies is "El dinero a través de su historia," *El Militante Comunista* (monograph), Aug. 1968. The 38 citations in this monograph are distributed as follows: Fidel Castro, 18; Engels, 10; Marx, 7; Raúl Castro, 2; Che Guevara, 1.

in this long-term vision. That is, the argument does not say that in the new society basic goods and services must be brought within the reach of everyone. It says that they must be given, unsullied by the necessity of giving even one centavo in return. On the fifteenth anniversary of his attack on the Moncada Army Barracks, Castro articulated this theme in all its starkness:

> In the past, the capitalists slandered revolutionary ideas and reviled Communism. Nevertheless, that society, that way of life—in which no young person had a chance, in which even the sick were forsaken, in which each man was an isolated, desperate human being left to shift for himself in the midst of a society of wolves—can in no way be compared with what a Communist society really means in the realms of human relations and morality. We hope to achieve that Communist society in absolutely all ways some day. Just as books are distributed now to those who need them, just as medicine and medical services are distributed to those who need them, and education to those who need it, so we are approaching the day when food will be distributed in the necessary amounts to those who need it, and clothing and shoes will be distributed in the necessary amounts to those who need them. We certainly aspire to a way of life—apparently utopian for many—in which man will not need money to satisfy his essential needs for food, clothing, and recreation, just as today no one needs money for medical attention or for his education. Nobody takes money to a hospital; nobody takes money to a high school; nobody takes money to a scholarship school; nobody takes money to a sports event.*

If the attack on money as a bitter and transitory instrument is a hearkening back to one of the earliest tenets of Marxism, it is also an outcropping of a basic reaction against the pre-revolutionary social order in Cuba. As we have seen, from the very outset the revolutionaries rejected the old (especially urban) culture as inequitable, materialistic, corrupt, and hopelessly oriented toward consumption. Pre-revolutionary Havana, viewed as a city in which sufficient money could get you anything—a high political office, membership in the country club, a blessing from the bishop, a beautiful woman, first-rate medical care, or protection from the law

* *Granma*, Weekly Review, July 28, 1968, p. 4. At the time of this speech, local phone calls and burials, as well as sports events, education, medical care, and some housing, were free in Cuba. The personal experiences of myself and others who have visited the island would seem to indicate that removing such transactions from the marketplace has been extremely well received, even among those who are less than enthusiastic about the revolution.

—became the very antithesis of the social order that the revolutionaries wished to construct. It is not just that great inequalities existed in pre-revolutionary Cuba, that senators drove Cadillacs and ate steaks while shoeshine boys went barefoot and hungry; it is that money and the concomitant capacity to buy and consume were the key bases of human differentiation and the final arbiters of human relations. Cuba, in the revolutionary view, did not even have the dubious virtue of being a highly stratified traditional society. Certainly it was not a meritocracy or a technocracy either. It was—at least in the cities—a dollarocracy, the most vulgar, demeaning, exploitative, and uncreative social order imaginable.[6] Dollars and pesos were the measure of both men and things, the universal standard of value. It is thus not at all surprising that the revolutionaries selected money and commercial relations as one of the prime targets of attack in their war on the old order.

The promise and importance of youth. As was suggested in Chapter 1 and emphasized repeatedly in the discussion of the literacy campaign, from the days of the Sierra Maestra young people have occupied a special place on the revolutionary stage. Not only did young men and women figure prominently in the struggle against Batista, but since that time they have continually been given important positions and opportunities in the revolutionary scheme of governance. As many observers have pointed out, the Cuban Revolution has been made largely by and for the young people of the island.

The Cuban emphasis on youth, however, should not be confused with the acceptance of youth culture of the kind that has developed in other societies. Neither in theory nor in practice is there any tendency for Cuban revolutionaries to elevate youth culture—with its various contemporary connotations of seeking after individual experience, freedom from conventional constraints, and challenges to established authority—into a life-style to be emulated. Quite the contrary, the values and behaviors considered appropriate for young Cubans are, if anything, almost directly opposed to those usually associated with contemporary youth culture elsewhere. According to official Cuban publications, young people are expected to exhibit personal abnegation, self-discipline, a sense of duty, service to society, and love of country. Not only do these virtues and behaviors emphasize the importance of patriotism, they also signify "the moralization of work," a Cuban revolutionary variant of the Protestant ethic, stripped of its overtones of salvation by means of private accumulation.[7] Like other Marxist and also capitalist prescriptions for youthful behavior, the Cuban doctrine fuses work and societal service into an idealized vision of a clean, hard, and useful life.* Clearly such values and behaviors are not now typical of the life-styles either professed or practiced by the trend-setting young in the more developed nations, either Eastern or Western.

What, then, is the meaning of the Cuban emphasis on youth? In part it is a response to the manpower needs of the developmental effort, made even more acute by the exodus of tens of thousands of Cubans. Just when thousands of persons were needed to staff the bureaucracies, schools, factories, and farms created or reorganized by the Revolutionary Government, thousands of professional, white-collar, and skilled blue-collar workers were going into exile. In staffing the developmental effort, the Revolutionary Government often had nowhere to turn except to young people, who had very limited experience but a great deal of energy and enthusiasm.

* An interesting perspective on youth culture and revolutionary virtues was given in a Havana radio broadcast of March 7, 1968: "The young boys [of Havana] think that the new man is one who wears tight pants. One sees how these ill-mannered brats talk back to their parents and how they act in their homes, on the streets, and in the schools. They are disrespectful and use improper language.... Perhaps not so many of them have taken up their little guitars after Fidel spoke about them, but there are many left. They wear tighter pants every day and they let their bangs grow longer until they look like girls. We could say that these are the new men of a bankrupt universe. They are the ones who like to sing and dance to modern music.... What do they call modern music? A Yankee rhythm which is imported so that they can dance their epileptic dances? They themselves say that they are sick, and they are. They need to be cured. They need a radical cure. The coffee plantations are waiting. The miniskirt, a type of urban bikini, is another of the styles we import with the greatest shamelessness. It is temptation in the middle of the street.... Is that the new world? Is that the human being of the coming third world so heralded by the intellectuals? No! ... Lack of respect and lack of clothes are not qualities which will characterize the new man." Foreign Broadcast Information Service, *Daily Report: Latin America*, Mar. 7, 1968, pp. HHHH 3–4.

Thus throughout Cuba one finds engineering students supervising highway construction, twenty-one-year-olds running schools, and young workers in charge of factories.

The emphasis on youth, however, is more than a response to manpower needs. It derives from a fundamental belief that, in general, only the young come to the revolutionary experience uncorrupted and pure enough to be formed into true Communists. The "integral man" so celebrated during the Cultural Congress of 1968 can grow only in an environment that has, in the revolutionary view, just begun to be created in Cuba. Although members of pre-revolutionary generations are or can become the best of citizens and militants, only members of post-revolutionary generations can achieve the proper fusion of beliefs and patterns of action that determine the character and the life-style of the new man. Thus young people are valued not only because of their actual and potential contributions to the developmental effort, but also because they are seen as bearing the seeds of the new culture. They have both the opportunity and the responsibility for being better men than their fathers.

The burden of the past. "It is well known that to build Communism we must confront, in the economic sphere, the underdevelopment imposed on us by imperialism and, in the ideological sphere, the extraordinary weight of the ideas, habits, and concepts that society has accumulated for centuries. The past has its claws into the present."[8] One of the developmental lessons the Cubans have been longest in learning is that the inertia of a cultural system is very great indeed. That is, the revolutionary leaders have had to do their best to learn to live with some of the ideas, habits and concepts that were well integrated into the pre-revolutionary way of life. This inertia can be seen in the traditional reluctance of peasant families to send their children to the new schools, in the absenteeism of workers long accustomed to days off after hard nights on the town, and in a slipping back into social isolation on the part of ordinary citizens who feel abused by constant pressures toward participation and public service. The developmental effort is constantly and inevitably slowed down by the persistence of old values and patterns of behavior, even in the bosom of the newest and most disciplined of revolutionary institutions.

There is, of course, nothing surprising about this state of affairs, for no theme in the literature of social change is as frequently underlined as the dialectic between the old and the new. What should be noted, however, is that the revolutionary leaders have recently emphasized the burden of the past more frequently as an integral part of their doctrine. For example, on January 1, 1969, in his speech commemorating the tenth anniversary of the triumph of the rebel forces, Castro underscored the legacies of both economy and political culture against which the revolution still had to do battle.* He also repeatedly reminded his audience of how long and tortuous the road out of underdevelopment would really be. In an elaboration of the counterpoint of struggle and utopia mentioned in Chapter 1, the developmental doctrine has thus come to incorporate very explicitly the notion that, while steadfastly moving toward the Communist society, one must never underestimate the tenacity of the old ways or the perverse vitality of the old culture, with its materialism, self-centeredness, and indiscipline. Just as ten years of revolution have taught that only the young can be formed into the citizens of the new order, so the same decade has taught the related though bittersweet lesson that the claws of the past are not easily or painlessly torn from the flesh of the present.

The five themes sketched above organize the doctrine but not necessarily the practice of mobilization and cultural change in Cuba. Without going into the details of various new programs, is it possible to generalize about the institutional manifestations of this doctrine after more than a decade of revolution? Particularly, is it possible to discern the directions mobilization and cultural change are taking?

At the risk of oversimplifying a complex situation, we can say that the main thrust of current practice seems to be toward engag-

* *Granma*, Weekly Review, Jan. 5, 1969, pp. 2–6. Castro used the expression *cultura política* to refer to "the organization, discipline, consciousness, and sense of duty" of the masses.

ing as many citizens as possible for as long as possible in productive work in rural (and openly anti-urban) environments. This is, of course, the experience of the brigadistas generalized to other sectors of the population. Thus for schoolchildren there is the Schools to the Countryside plan, which each year takes tens of thousands of students with their books and teachers to rural areas for 45 days of study and work. For other young people there is semipermanent residence on the Isle of Pines—renamed the Isle of Youth—with its special emphasis on forming the first generation of true Communists in a setting of equality and sacrifice. For the adults of the capital there is the *Cordón*, or greenbelt around the city, a program to make the urban complex self-sufficient in foodstuffs by bringing adjacent lands under cultivation. Sometimes called the Isle of Youth for the middle-aged, the Cordón represents the implementation of the strain in revolutionary doctrine that views agricultural work as essential for liberating the urban masses from their city ways and bourgeois values.[9]

Programs like these all attempt to fuse as intimately as possible the participatory and the learning components of cultural change. That is, they represent an effort to make available to more and more Cubans the integrated, formative experiences seen by the revolutionary elite as central to the radical transformation of men and institutions. These programs are thus a direct continuation and expansion not only of the brigadista movement, but also of such movements as the attack against manualismo and the concurrent attempt to introduce practical education and "learning by doing" into the Schools of Revolutionary Instruction. Furthermore, such programs underline the elite's continuing emphasis on the inseparability of attitudinal, value, and behavioral changes. In this view, significant cultural shifts do not depend in linear fashion on changes in attitudes that in turn produce changes in behavior.* Rather, the starting point of change is when more and more citizens take part in the right kinds of activities, activities

* Social scientists concerned with development are beginning to appreciate, albeit somewhat grudgingly and incompletely, the importance of this view. For instance, Albert O. Hirschman, in "Obstacles to Development: A Classification and a Quasi-Vanishing Act," *Economic Development and Cultural Change*,

that direct attention away from the self and toward the collectivity, activities that wordlessly but dramatically teach the lessons of development and underdevelopment. The Schools to the Countryside plan, the Isle of Youth, and the Cordón are all examples of what the revolutionary leadership considers the right kinds of activities.

Although only a decade of the Cuban Revolution has passed, we must ask what kinds of changes in political culture have taken place in the first ten years and how lasting or rooted these changes seem to be. Such an evaluation is tentative not only because the revolution is still in progress, but also because it is difficult to obtain data on the outcomes and consequences of revolutionary programs. Available information serves relatively well for assessing the ideology, organization, and practices employed on behalf of developmental efforts, but we lack the necessary behavioral data on those who are participating in the revolutionary process.

XIII, 4, Part I (July 1965), pp. 385–93, devotes considerable attention to the possible uses of cognitive dissonance theory for an understanding of the attitude-behavior matrix in development. In brief, Hirschman argues that "Dissonance theory deals with the possibility of replacing the 'orderly' sequence, where attitude change is conceived as the prerequisite to behavioral change, by a 'disorderly' one, where modern attitudes are acquired *ex-post*, as a consequence of the dissonance aroused by 'modern' type of behavior which happens to be engaged in by people with non-modern attitudes." The quoted passage is from p. 392. What the author fails to consider is the role of developmental elites in creating institutional settings and mobilizational practices in which this "disorderly" change can get started. Thus, although disorderly change may enable one to bypass at some stage in the developmental process certain attitudinal and value patterns, elites must still be viewed as first-order obstacles to change insofar as they fail to create institutions that encourage "disorder" in this sense. The failure of many social scientists in the United States to face squarely the logic of such situations would seem to derive in part from their belief that this way of shaping behavior entails unacceptable authoritarian control or infringements on individual liberties. It should also be pointed out that an interaction between behavioral change and attitudinal change might possibly be established right from the outset, thus rendering the "disorder" model (with its reverse linearity) quite inappropriate for understanding the way change takes place—or could take place. Dialectical or cybernetic models that begin with behavioral change certainly seem the most appropriate for representing the attitudinal-behavioral interaction in revolutionary Cuba, as well as in many other situations. See the position taken by Milton Rokeach, "Attitude Change and Behavioral Change," *Public Opinion Quarterly*, XXX, 4 (Winter 1966–67), pp. 529–50.

What is clear is that the revolutionary elite has demonstrated an impressive capacity for mobilizing the Cuban citizenry. As defined in Chapter 1, mobilization means getting out the troops to do whatever the leadership feels needs to be done. But however impressive this performance, one cannot infer from it the extent to which individual people are being transformed. That hundreds of thousands of Cubans belong to the Committees for Defense of the Revolution, that tens of thousands of workers and bureaucrats occasionally cut sugarcane, and that thousands of Cubans passed through the Schools of Revolutionary Instruction should not be taken as evidence that their basic values and attitudes have been transformed, that the "new man" has arrived. Mobilization of the type and scale achieved in Cuba certainly attests to the organizational capacity of the leadership and to the place given to such activity in the system of ideology and action that guides them. It also demonstrates the extent to which the new politics have proven workable in Cuba. But the fact remains that mobilization is primarily an instrument, rather than the consequence, of cultural transformation.

As a starting point for our evaluation of the transformation of political culture, it should be emphasized that neither the revolutionaries nor outside observers claim that the utopian vision outlined at the beginning of this chapter has been achieved. By no stretch of the imagination is Cuba a society in which egoismo has disappeared, in which every man sets societal service above personal gain, in which Communist *conciencia* and the patterns of behavior commensurate with it characterize the average citizen. To deny the fulfillment of the utopian vision, however, is not to deny that profound changes have taken place. Though it is difficult in the absence of better data to be specific about the content and scope of these changes, the broad outlines and thrust of the transformation seem relatively clear. The following four propositions help to organize speculation about these matters.

There is a great deal of revolutionary behavior that does not stem from the internalization of new values or even from political attitudes and orientations consistent with the behavior observed.

Revolutionary behavior in this context refers to any behavior that is deemed proper, useful, or appropriate from the point of view of the Cuban leadership. Most social psychological perspectives on the relationship between values, attitudes, and political behavior carry the implicit—if not explicit—assumption that values and attitudes are rather good predictors of action.[10] For instance, if we know how a citizen views the political parties in a two-party system, it is thought that we can predict fairly accurately how he will vote at election time. Or if we know what kinds of expectations a person has about being able to get access to politicians and bureaucrats, we can hypothesize, it is thought, with some confidence how frequently and in what way he will attempt such contacts. As has been emphasized in this book, however, such models of the nexus between values, attitudes, and behavior are suspect when applied to Cuba.

In a system like the Cuban, in which political institutions and work environments are oriented toward shaping participation, and in which alternative opportunities are limited, a great deal of revolutionary behavior is evoked from persons who if left to their own devices would probably behave differently. We shall return to this theme in more detail later, but it is well to point out here that in this situation, although group and institutional norms have changed under the impetus of revolutionary leadership, many who participate do so not because their values necessarily fit with those of the leadership, but because they have few if any alternatives and are subjected to substantial peer-group pressure. Thus individual values and attitudes may differ from institutional norms without being reflected in differences of individual behavior. This is not to say that revolutionary behavior—and therefore revolutionary institutions—can persist indefinitely in conflict with individual values and attitudes. The point is that the revolutionary environment makes considerable disjunction both possible and probable.*

* For those who have difficulty accepting this point of view, the analogy of the wartime Army in the United States is instructive. Although military institutions and their norms often seemed in conflict with the values and attitudes of individual soldiers, acceptable military behavior was evoked from most enlisted men during both the Second World War and the Korean War. Further-

The modification of some aspects of the traditional value system is perhaps the most important long-term consequence of attempts to transform the political culture. Whereas the first proposition emphasized that in a system like the Cuban it is possible to evoke revolutionary behavior from individual persons without prior large-scale changes in their values, here it is suggested that, in fact, some changes *are* taking place. An example will help to make this clear. One of the value dimensions most discussed by theorists of development is what Seymour Lipset calls equalitarianism-elitism. Among other things, this means that "nations defined as equalitarian tend to place more emphasis than elitist nations on universalistic criteria in interpersonal judgments, and . . . tend to de-emphasize behavior patterns which stress hierarchical differences."[11] Furthermore, the argument continues, the equalitarian orientation supports developmental efforts by fostering social mobility and the rise of new talents, by facilitating the formation of associations and working coalitions, and by liberating individual energies in a host of other ways while at the same time encouraging collective efforts.

This theme in the developmental literature frequently carries with it an ethnocentric bias. There is a tendency to generalize out of the American experience certain constellations of values that are assumed to be causally related to the impressive economic growth of the United States and, to a lesser extent, of Western Europe. Thus, the argument continues, less well-developed nations, nations that are also characterized by value patterns quite different from those of the United States, will begin to progress economically only as they become more "Western," more oriented toward achievement, more universalistic in evaluating persons and performance, more equalitarian in social relations, and so forth.[12] The most interesting and important aspect of this argument, however,

---

more, the soldiers were not generally coerced into this acceptable military behavior except in the sense that members of all closed and authoritarian social organizations are coerced. In both military and revolutionary organizations, the small primary living or working group (itself closely guided by the organizational leadership) would seem to be the most important single factor influencing individual behavior.

is that it is probably strengthened if stripped of its ethnocentrism. That is, a nation can become more oriented toward achievement and more equalitarian socially without at the same time becoming more like the advanced Western nations institutionally, organizationally, or in terms of other values. In short, it would seem that although shifts in value patterns as outlined by Lipset and others are in fact related to development, and particularly to economic development, there is no reason to assume that the North American way of life is a necessary concomitant or outcome of cultural systems that stress equalitarianism and achievement.

To return again to the Cuban case, there is evidence that the lessons learned on the farm, in the factory, in school, and in the mass organizations have already shifted the cultural center of gravity significantly away from elitism and hierarchy and toward equalitarianism. Furthermore, the environment of material scarcity, coupled with the relative evenness of remuneration, reinforce the dominant anti-elitism of social relations and opportunities. This does not necessarily mean that the lessons of equalitarianism being learned by the Cuban masses will in the long run direct popular energies into exactly those kinds of behaviors desired by the revolutionary leadership. The basic cultural realignments instigated by the Cuban Revolution are open-ended enough to support a variety of political and economic arrangements. But no matter how value changes as basic as the shift toward equalitarianism manifest themselves in the Cuba of the future, a major cultural shift is clearly taking place behind the immediate effort to inculcate specific attitudes and encourage certain kinds of behavior. While the regime devotes most of its attention to the mobilizational and educational objectives deriving from the exigencies of the present, the value constellations of Cuban society are being moved in exactly those directions advocated by many Western theorists concerned with the relationship between culture and national development.*

* It would seem that the entire general syndrome of Hispanic-American upper-class and middle-class values is breaking up in Cuba under the impact of the revolutionary experience. John P. Gillin, in "Some Signposts for Policy,"

Youth is, in general, the group most exposed to the revolutionary experience. Earlier in this chapter it was mentioned that Cuban doctrine on cultural transformation gives special attention to the promise and importance of youth. Not only are young people seen as the hope of the future, they are also given special opportunities to participate, to immerse themselves in revolutionary activities in ways not open to most adults. In fact, such opportunities are characteristically thrust upon them (e.g. in the Schools to the Countryside plan) more directly than any that are thrust upon adults.

It would seem, moreover, that young people are especially available psychologically for being recruited into and affected by the revolutionary experience. They are encouraged by the regime to participate precisely at that stage of life when—as Erik Erikson has emphasized—they are searching for a sense of the self that is relatively unambiguous, action-oriented, and ideological (providing a convincing world image). As the examples and case materials suggest, the formative environments for young people in Cuba seem to be very conducive to ameliorating many of the most profound difficulties and uncertainties that are usually associated with the search for adult identity. In the more extreme instances, environmental exposure and psychological readiness come together in what Erikson calls the indoctrination experience. Although not all youth environments in Cuba can rightfully be thought of as leading to indoctrination, Erikson's formulation of the extreme case remains very relevant to the fusion of personal identity needs and system requirements in revolutionary Cuba:

---

in Richard N. Adams et al., *Social Change in Latin America Today* (New York, 1960), characterized this syndrome as follows: personalism, the strength of family ties, the importance of hierarchy, a variant of materialism (the importance of land), the weight of transcendental values (the *pensador* tradition), emotion as fulfillment of the self, and a sense of fatalism. If these were, in fact, among the dominant values of the national (middle and upper) sectors of pre-revolutionary Cuba, there is little doubt that they are less so now. Contrast the characterization of Cuban values given by Wyatt MacGaffey and Clifford R. Barnett, *Twentieth Century Cuba* (Garden City, N.Y., 1965), chaps. 2 and 4, with the descriptions contained in Appendix A below and in Elizabeth Sutherland, *The Youngest Revolution* (New York, 1969).

> It stands to reason that late adolescence is the most favorable period, and late adolescent personalities of any age group the best subjects, for indoctrination; because in adolescence an ideological realignment is by necessity in process and a number of ideological possibilities are waiting to be hierarchically ordered by opportunity, leadership, and friendship. Any leadership, however, must have the power to encase the individual in a spatial arrangement and in a temporal routine which at the same time narrow down the sensory supply from the world and block his sexual and aggressive drives, so that a new needfulness will eagerly attach itself to a new world-image. At no other time as much as in adolescence does the individual feel so exposed to anarchic manifestations of his drives; at no other time does he so need oversystematized thoughts and overvalued words to give a semblance of order to his inner world. He therefore is willing to accept ascetic restrictions which go counter to what he would do if he were alone—faced with himself, his body, his musings—or in the company of old friends; he will accept the *sine qua non* of indoctrination, lack of privacy.... Needless to say, good and evil must be clearly defined as forces existing from all beginning and persevering into all future; therefore all memory of the past must be starved or minutely guided, and all intention focused on the common utopia. No idle talk can be permitted. Talk must always count, count for or against one's readiness to embrace the new ideology totally—to the point of meaning it. In fact, the right talk, the vigorous song, and the radical confession in public must be cultivated.[13]

Erikson's formulation implies that the ideological reordering and thus the sense of identity that is communicated to young people must make sense in terms of their own needs, confusions, and tribulations. Adult leadership must provide both personal models and developmental programs consistent with youthful concerns.[14] In this respect the Cuban revolutionary leadership has been exemplary, not only because it is itself relatively young and much admired, but also because its action programs meet quite closely the implied conditions of Erikson's analysis. Not only are the young able to tolerate (and even enjoy) the scarcity, the physical discomfort and dislocations, and the interruptions of routine that accompany mobilization efforts in Cuba, but their sense of self-importance is profoundly reinforced by participating in activities that are clearly of national importance, that result quite rapidly in a palpable transformation of some aspect of the physical environment, and for which they are often given serious responsibilities. Whatever shortcomings the formative experiences of most young

Cubans may have, they are seldom irrelevant to the problems at hand, nor do they entail endless postponement of involvement and responsibility. Owing to the closure of debate and self-examination, the channeling of energies into societal service, and the conformism encouraged by the attacks on egoismo, Cuban youth may not be growing up with highly developed critical skills—with regard to either themselves or the new social order. But neither are they—in Paul Goodman's phrase—growing up absurd. The possibility of rebelliousness in the face of continuing regimentation exists, and certainly it is too early to predict what the increased leavening of Cuban society with young adults formed under the revolution will bring. But it is already clear that the growing-up experiences of these future adults differ profoundly from those of their parents. They may not turn out to be the "true Communists" prophesied in the developmental doctrine, but many will be "new Cubans" to about as great an extent as sons can ever differ from their fathers.

There is presently substantial fragility in new Cuban patterns of belief and behavior. This proposition is meant to emphasize the importance of environmental supports for new constellations of thought and action. Put briefly, after ten years of revolution the emerging Cuban political culture should be viewed as still very dependent on the revolutionary environment itself, rather than on internalized and deeply ingrained values and patterns of behavior. This follows quite naturally from the previous three propositions on the disjunction of behavior and beliefs, the probability of long-term changes in values, and the special exposure and susceptibility of young people. The radical attempt to transform the political culture of Cuba is, after all, only a decade old, and no full generation has yet been raised to adulthood in the hothouse of the revolutionary society. A decade is a short time compared with the time spans ordinarily observed in evaluating the internalization of new values and behaviors.

Note that this proposition does not predict the failure of the radical experiment or even its attrition. It simply says that observed and hypothesized changes to date have not become so much a part of the general culture that they can be considered independent of the mobilization environments now sustaining and encouraging them. At one level, this simply says that were the revolutionary leadership to abandon its radical efforts to transform the political culture (if one can imagine that!), much of the behavior now evoked from the citizenry would also cease. Thus any meaningful amount of volunteer labor in Cuba would stop if all the intragroup pressures and organizational encouragements now sustaining it were discontinued. But the proposition also implies something more. Volunteer labor as a continuing pattern of behavior, particularly when the labor involves agriculture, is difficult to imagine in any modern society without intragroup pressures and organizational devices of the kind now arranged by the Cuban Revolutionary Government. Such cultural values as equalitarianism and such political orientations as strong identification with the nation—and the patterns of action related to them—may, however, eventually become independent of the specific contexts in which they were originally practiced and learned. To pick a common example, people who must exercise patience while waiting in line for rationed goods and practice equality while cutting sugarcane will carry consonant attitudes and behaviors over into other situations if, in fact, the original lessons have been well learned. One would expect, and certainly the revolutionary leadership expects, that when the days of cutting cane and waiting in line are over, Cubans will not simply revert to their earlier ways. But it is wise to emphasize that ten years of revolution is a relatively short period in which to accomplish the kinds of fundamental, internalized transformations that the radicals seek. The revolutionary environment thus is still the single most important determinant of states of mind and behavior, even in those domains of thought and action that one would expect to become much more fully internalized during the second decade of the Cuban experiment.

The phrase "the second decade of the Cuban experiment" implies a prediction about the viability of revolutionary institutions and their continuing innovativeness during the 1970's. Neither aspect of this prediction should be allowed to pass unexamined.

From 1959 on, there has been no dearth of persons willing to testify to the imminent collapse of the Castro regime. Economy-watchers have been firmly convinced that mismanagement in general and Socialism in particular would combine to destroy the productive base of the island; society-watchers have been equally convinced that the Cuban people would not long endure the inefficiency, the autocracy, and the mobilization tactics of the Castroites. They have predicted that the Revolutionary Government is doomed—if not directly because of its own incompetence and irrationality, then indirectly because of the massive defection of sub-elites and the estrangement of the general population. But such has not been the case, and there are important lessons to be learned from an examination of why the Revolutionary Government is still so fully in command despite admitted economic failures and despite the real costs of autocracy and mobilization.

The easy explanation for foes of the regime is that Castro rules by terror. Couched as it frequently is in general and clearly condemnatory language, this charge is so loaded and so vague that it is not easy to refute. If it means that there are people in Cuba who obey because they fear the Revolutionary Government, it is true but nevertheless irrelevant to any reasonable understanding of rule by terror. If, however, the charge is that Castro rules by bureaucratized and arbitrary exercise of police violence against selected segments of the population (a charge that links the Cuban Revolution with the Stalinist and Hitlerite experiences), then the explanation is demonstrably false.[15] The entire thrust of the three preceding chapters and of most serious scholarship and reportage on Cuba testifies that the regime—while harsh and unrelenting at times—is not even a pale approximation of Stalinism or Hitlerism. The rules of the revolutionary game are quite well understood in Cuba; there is little or no arbitrary violence directed against any sector of the population (as opposed to sporadic harassment); and the quasi-coercive shaping of environments to channel citizen energies toward revolutionary activities is relieved by an easiness of interpersonal relationships and a widespread—though often grudging—feeling among the citizenry that all must contribute to the development of the nation.

But if terror does not explain the staying power of the Castro government, what does? A partial explanation is found in the factors outlined in Chapter 2: the integration of Cuban society, the socioeconomic potential of the island, the political skill and charisma of Castro, and the rich heritage of Cuban nationalism combined with the peculiarities of the Cold War. As this combination of factors suggests, the Revolutionary Government has had much to work with; and many of its developmental undertakings have been successful because they have fit relatively well with the resources and potentialities (human, situational, and material) of the island and the historical period. As exorbitant as it may sound both to critics and to some admirers of the Cuban experiment, the leadership has in fact been quite realistic as well as quite audacious in what it has attempted—particularly since 1963. The first ten years have seen (in addition to hardship, dislocation, and bewildering change) considerable material progress, increased distributive justice, and a veritable explosion of opportunities for education, social mobility, and occupational responsibility; and these positive and palpable achievements go far toward explaining the continuing popularity and viability of the revolution.

There is, however, a still more basic explanation to be made. Over the past decade Cuba has achieved a more rapid rate of political development than that achieved by any other nation in Latin America and perhaps by any nation in Africa or Asia, and this dramatic progress in political development undergirds the above prediction of the continued viability of the revolutionary effort. To understand and delimit the substance of this claim, it is necessary to be clear about the definition of political development being used. Political development, as seen by Huntington, is the "institutionalization of political organizations and procedures" in the direction of adaptability, complexity, autonomy (insulated from the pull and haul of social forces), and coherence (having a distinctive and internally shared spirit and style).[16] The organizations of the Cuban Revolutionary Government have grown rapidly on all of these dimensions over the past ten years. Note that this claim does not deny the continuing importance of Castro or the personalistic aspects of his style of rule. Clearly, revolutionary institutions would be deeply affected by his death and would probably move in the directions of rigidity and disunity, the polar opposites of adaptability and coherence. Nor does the definition depend on a high degree of individual freedom being practiced or allowed within the system. In fact, in real political systems—at least in less developed ones—institutionalization probably takes place in part at the expense of conventional democratic practices. What this formulation does emphasize is that the strength of governmental institutions vis-à-vis the society in which they are embedded is critical for predicting the viability of a regime and its problem-solving capabilities. On this score, the performance of revolutionary organizations in Cuba has been impressive indeed, and there are no signs of decreasing capacity.

The claim that during the first decade the Cuban revolutionary system of rule has shown impressive levels of institutional performance is substantiated by the cases presented here. By the standards that prevail in most poorer countries, and even by the standards of more affluent nations, the campaign against illiteracy and the continuing work of the CDR could only occur in a political system with relatively well-developed organizational capabilities. Even the less impressive history of the Schools of Revolutionary Instruction supports this point of view. During their truncated existence, the schools responded flexibly and successfully to the many responsibilities thrust on them. That they were eventually closed should be taken not as an index of the weakness of the revolutionary system of rule, but rather as an index of the leaders' capacity to control and redirect organizational resources as they perceive goals and circumstances to change. The revolution has not been allowed to become a living museum of outmoded organizations and procedures. This bears witness to the vitality of its organizational life.[17]

The prediction of continued innovativeness within the Cuban Revolution is not, however, based primarily on an assessment of the institutionalization of revolutionary rule. More important factors are the personality and style of Fidel Castro and the characteristics of his ideological system. As was emphasized in Chapter 2, nothing that is known about Castro or that can be inferred from his behavior to date suggests that he will routinize or otherwise cease to experiment with the process of governance and development. The metaphor Castro chose to express his feelings about the revolution in his interview with Lee Lockwood is very instructive in this regard:

> *Castro:* We love the Revolution as a labor. We love it just as a painter, a sculptor, or a writer may love his work. And, like him, we want our work to have a perennial value.
> *Lockwood:* You consider the making of a revolution a work of art?
> *Castro:* Yes, I certainly do. Revolution is an art. And politics is also an art. The most important one, I think.[18]

In Castro's view only hack or pseudorevolutionaries—like hack or pseudoartists—would cease trying to improve their creations or the genre that they have evolved. The first decade of the revolution is replete with examples of experimentation that can be understood only in the light of Castro's profound personal need to advance the art of revolutionary transformation. Thus, although at times he appears as merely capricious or reactive, the overall level of innovativeness he has displayed is best seen as the consequence of this "urge to create" as manifested in his political personality. In short, an appreciation of Castro's view of himself as both revolutionary artist and revolutionary warrior goes far toward explaining the intensity and energy with which he has sought and continues to seek new strategies for waging the political struggle and new tactics for winning the battle against underdevelopment.

This restlessness and relentlessness in the search for tactics and strategies that work under Cuban conditions has its direct counterpart in the realm of words and symbols. Out of Castro's voluminous production of speeches it is difficult to codify anything approaching an elegant or even wholly consistent doctrine of man, society, politics, and change. Elements of the New Testament, Marx, Martí, Fanon, and a great deal of Fidel Castro are mixed together in what is best described as a set of postures toward a range of issues rather than a philosophical system. But this does not mean that the revolution has no ideology. Quite the contrary—as was argued in Chapter 1—if ideology is taken to mean a symbol system linking particular actions and mundane practices with a wider set of meanings, then the revolution has a well-developed, flexible, and seemingly successful ideology.[19] It is successful precisely because it is personalistic, adaptive, and artful.

When viewed this way, the ideology of the revolution clearly depends for its success not on its literal truth, but on its evocative and motivating power under prevailing conditions. As Clifford Geertz has pointed out, one ought to take the key metaphors of such an ideological system very seriously, not because they are true in some scientific way, or even because they are plans for action, but because (if successful) they multiply meanings and enlarge understanding for the audiences to which they are directed.* One of the basic themes of this book has been that Castro is a very effective metaphor-maker for large segments of the Cuban population, and that developmental programs of many types are quite successful in translating the citizen energies thus evoked into prescribed patterns of behavior. Thus part of the revolutionary art is the art of making an ideology that fits with the times and the circumstances. For more than a decade Castro has practiced this

* See Clifford Geertz, "Ideology as a Cultural System," in David E. Apter, ed., *Ideology and Discontent* (New York, 1964), esp. pp. 57–60. For example, if Cuban rhetoric concerning the new man is taken as a design for an action program, then the appropriate measures of success and failure are "before and after" tests of the modalities of individual values and social behavior. However, if the rhetoric is also seen as metaphor, then the appropriate measures of success and failure involve the evaluation of the understandings of self and society that are achieved by, and the political and organizational consequences attributable to, the multiplication of meanings. Obviously, the accounting scheme needed to capture the results of a metaphor that is "working" are extremely complex. As Geertz has indicated, many social scientists tend to evaluate ideological systems as if they were either blueprints or descriptions, rejecting them as foolish or unimportant when they find them to be unworkable or untrue. To do this in the case of the Cuban Revolution and Fidelismo is to run the risk of misunderstanding the significance of the ideology while at the same time underestimating its capacity to be regenerated by Castro as circumstances change.

art with consummate skill, and there is every reason to believe that he will continue to do so.

Yet even practicing the revolutionary arts with consummate skill will not protect Castro and his lieutenants from having to face certain dilemmas during the coming decade. The history of all radical movements—in China, in the Soviet Union, and in the new governments of Africa and Asia—illustrates that the politics of mobilization, scarcity, sacrifice, and enthusiasm cannot be continued indefinitely. Eventually some substitute must be found. Both successes and failures in the economic sphere carry with them potential for eroding or at least calling into question the politics and developmental style of the first decade. Rising productivity and increasing distributive payoff, if sustained for a number of years, will undermine the *ambiente* of emergency, threat, and sacrifice. On the other hand, because a great many promises have been made, failure to increase productivity and ameliorate living conditions must eventually cost the regime dearly in the coin of support and credibility.

The Cuban leaders are well aware that either success or failure —or even a mixed performance—in the developmental effort will bring critical new problems of governance to the fore. This is one reason why they attach such great importance to linking increased productivity and more equitable distribution to the creation and internalization of new values. A transformed citizenry, they hope, will not turn soft and turn inward when exposed to increased abundance. The vision is of a revolutionary citizenry living under post-revolutionary economic conditions. This is, as has been emphasized earlier, a profoundly radical and even utopian posture. If the economic effort fails, the vision is clearly doomed. But what if the Cubans can manage their economy well enough to make good on a number of their promises of increased goods and services? When the psychology of siege is lifted and goods return to the stores, the true and enduring test of the radical experiment will be precipitated. Will the process of cultural transformation have been profound and widespread enough to withstand the tendencies toward increased egoismo and diminished conciencia? Can participation, national service, and sense of community be normalized and incorporated into a nonheroic way of life in Cuba; or are such feelings and behaviors inevitably dependent on an environment of plena revolución?[20] No definitive answer to such questions can be given. At the least, however, the Cuban leaders have given us reason to believe that they are very serious in their attachment to radical goals. Passionate commitment is not, of course, tantamount to achievement. But in speculating about the future of the Cuban Revolution, one should not lightly brush aside the utopias of the men who have already made the most profound social transformation ever seen in the Americas. Their visions may not be an accurate prediction of the shape of the future, but they are a promise that it will be very different from both past and present.

Appendixes

APPENDIX A

The Cuban Countryside, Spring 1968

TO UNDERSTAND what is happening in Cuba today, it is absolutely necessary to get out of Havana and into the countryside. In the city, one is at first struck by shortages, by the *colas,* or lines, that result from these shortages, and by the run-down condition of buildings and facilities. The recent rationing of gasoline, the closing of the bars and nightclubs, and the nationalization of the remaining private businesses have made the atmosphere even more one of siege and shortage. Although *Habaneros* still maintain much of their gaiety in spite of their troubles, it is apparent that spirits have been rubbed a bit raw. One does not sense in the capital the movement, the optimism, and the change that one sees in the countryside.

The Cuban countryside offers a wide variety of landscapes. There are the mountains of the extreme southeastern corner, the Sierra Maestra, from which Castro launched his attack against Batista in the first months of 1957; the Escambray Mountains of the central province of Las Villas, which were a center of counterrevolutionary activity in 1960 and 1961; and the coastal swamps to the southeast of Havana, which were the site of the invasion of April 1961. There are the rich, flat sugar lands of the western part of Oriente Province and the adjoining province of Camagüey, and the red tobacco lands of the easternmost province, Pinar del Río.

Sandino City

Sandino City is southwest of the city of Pinar del Río, only about 25 miles from the eastern coast of the island. It was established in

This appendix is elaborated from field notes taken in Cuba during March and April 1968.

1960 in an area that before the revolution had contained a number of large vegetable farms, the homes of a few peasants, and little else. Sandino now has approximately 3,500 residents housed in neat concrete buildings. About 70 percent of the inhabitants are rehabilitated political prisoners of peasant origin who have been reincorporated into the work force. Most of these ex-prisoners were rounded up at the time of the counterrevolutionary activity in the Escambray Mountains. Few are from the Province of Pinar del Río, and it is probable that few ever fully understood what was happening during the early 1960's. Sandino City has more than 600 houses, a day nursery for children from one to five years old, a regular primary school extending to the fifth grade, a special primary school where boys learn construction trades while at the same time studying standard school subjects, and a 70-bed hospital that is scheduled to open soon. Future plans include a secondary school, various boarding schools designed to free the women for work in agriculture, and a center for the artificial insemination of cattle.

Sandino City is the political, administrative, and service center for two large granjas, or peoples' farms. One, Granja Simón Bolívar, is devoted primarily to the cultivation of citrus, other fruits, and coffee. The second, Granja Sandino, is concentrating on the cultivation of blond or light tobacco. This kind of tobacco, used in cigarettes rather than in cigars, is a post-revolution crop in Cuba. It lends itself to far more mechanization than the darker cigar tobaccos for which the area is famous, and at Sandino the Cubans are developing this newer industry with the help of Canadian technology and machinery.

For a foreigner, a trip through Granja Sandino starts with an introduction to a member of the local branch of the Communist Party of Cuba, who will serve as both host and guide. In this case it was Luis, a tall and articulate man of about forty. Like most of the revolution's leaders, Luis is entirely self-taught in the areas of agriculture and administration. Before the revolution he had been a singer of some repute. During 1960 and 1961 he fought against the counterrevolutionaries in the Escambray, and he then returned to Havana to be director of entertainment at the Havana Libre Hotel—once the Havana Hilton and still the city's most luxurious hotel. He came to Sandino City as a full-time Party functionary early in 1967, and he will remain there as long as he is asked to do so by the Party. His wife, also a Party member, remains in Havana, and Luis makes the four-hour trip back to the capital about once a month to see her.

The dirt road into the heart of Granja Sandino leads past a seemingly endless nursery containing, according to Luis, 20 million young coffee plants. Many of the plants are approaching the age at which they can be transplanted, and already the nursery has been stripped of some of the maturing young trees. The nursery is almost entirely under the care of women, who water, fertilize, and tend the young trees, relinquishing their care only to the few men who operate the machines spraying insecticide. This particular plant begins to bear after only two years; and, given the present shortage of coffee in Cuba and its popularity as a national drink, there will be an island-wide sigh of relief when the fruits of the ambitious coffee program—of which this nursery is only a part—begin to find their way into the cup.

From the nursery, the road continues on past corrugated iron tobacco drying sheds and into a machinery yard. The men who work in the fields and in the sheds earn on the average slightly more than four pesos a day (the Cuban peso is officially valued at one dollar, but its purchasing power on the island varies greatly, depending on the goods and services bought). During the tobacco harvesting season, the fastest workers can earn more than their base pay if they gather the ripening leaves at a rate exceeding the norms established in the industry. The Cubans insist that this modified form of piecework does not offer a "material incentive," which would violate their stated policy of offering "moral incentives" only, but the distinction is not easily apparent.

At one edge of the machinery yard are two long lunch halls for the workmen. The food is cooked indoors over wood-burning grates and served over a low counter on metal trays. The lady in charge of the kitchen is a good-natured peasant woman known to the workers as "grandma." On that day Grandma was offering her flock a meal of stewed beef, sweet potatoes, black beans, and bread.

Just off to the other side of the machinery yard are a number of long dormitories housing dozens of boys and girls from a preparatory school in Havana. As part of their training—or "formation," as the Cubans say—schoolchildren from the cities are taken to encampments in the countryside, where they work for periods of up to three months each year. The program is known as the "schools to the countryside" movement, and it is designed to instill in all students respect for the dignity of physical work as well as to teach some basic knowledge of the technology and problems of agriculture. Of course there are also direct, short-term benefits to the state from the contributions made to the agricultural labor force, but these are seen as less important than the changes wrought in the young people themselves. The students working at Granja Sandino were from a rather selective technical boarding school, ranging in age from about fifteen to nineteen years old. The boys were working in the sugarcane fields and were temporarily out of the area; the girls were working in the nearby tobacco fields and drying sheds.

Shortly after lunch, the girls gathered near a raised platform to hear some announcements and to discuss plans for the "Jornada de Girón," which in 1968 lasted the entire month of April.* The Jornada de Girón is an annual period of national mobilization commemorating the defeat in 1961 of the invading exile forces at the Bay of Pigs, or Playa Girón. During this 30-day period, tens of thousands of city dwellers are mobilized to go to the countryside to work on agricultural projects. Those already working in agriculture are expected to dedicate themselves to making some extra effort in support of the national mobilization.

Since the girls of the encampment at Granja Sandino were already working eight hours a day in the fields, there was little else for them to do except dedicate their evenings and part of their weekends to more work. Caught up in a wave of schoolgirlish enthusiasm, they jumped onto the platform singing and clapping and called on the regular workers of the granja to join them. Of the several dozen workers standing about, three or four joined the girls immediately, some wavered for a few minutes before joining, and others tried to make themselves as inconspicuous as possible. It was clear that the girls favored certain workers over others, and the favorites paid for their popularity by being actively sought out, teased, danced around, and almost lifted bodily onto the platform to join the rapidly expanding evening and weekend work force. There they were surrounded, sung to, congratulated, and teased

* There is no good translation for this usage of the Spanish word *jornada*. About the best translation of the phrase would be "the effort of Girón." Before 1968, the Jornada lasted only two weeks.

some more by the exuberant girls. At the end of the meeting, it was difficult to say whether most of the workers on the platform had really volunteered or not. But there they were, and the girls were delighted with their success in recruiting so many.

Heroic Vietnam

The mobilization of bureaucrats and workers in Havana for the Jornada de Girón is done through the various state ministries, departments, service centers, institutes, and organizations that make up the administrative and political infrastructure of Cuba. On Sunday, March 31, and Monday, April 1, 1968, hundreds of trucks, buses, automobiles, and motorcycles left the capital—some bound for the rural area immediately surrounding the city, others for the outlying areas of the Province of Havana, and a few for the neighboring provinces of Matanzas and Pinar del Río. Each governmental organization has a certain rural area to which its officials and workers go. Usually the organization has a permanent encampment on a granja in this area. During most of the year, the granja operates with its regular agricultural work force, aided from time to time by volunteers from the city. But during the first week of April, there is a massive migration of city dwellers to these encampments, leaving only skeleton crews in Havana to man the bureaucratic apparatus of the state.

Like the "schools to the countryside" movement, the mobilization of urban workers to spend a number of weeks in the rural areas has at least two purposes. First and perhaps most important, it is a learning and formative experience for those who participate. In the dust, the sun, the rain, and the backwardness of the countryside, city people are forced to confront the realities, the problems, and at least some of the hardships of rural life in what is still predominantly an agricultural economy. Second, there is the contribution made to the general agricultural effort by this arrival of urban workers. It is costly to transport, house, feed, and equip the urbanites for rural work, and their productivity is undoubtedly lower than that of their rural counterparts; but the work they do in the countryside is work that otherwise would not get done. It is safe to assume that the administrative life of the island does not suffer greatly from their absence, and some wags insist that it is improved.

The encampment of the Cuban Ministry of Foreign Relations is in the southwest corner of the Province of Havana, slightly more than an hour's drive from the center of the city. It is situated among low rolling hills devoted mainly to sugarcane, cattle, and various vegetable crops. The Ministry's encampment, known as "Heroic Vietnam," consists of a cluster of low concrete buildings: two men's dormitories; one women's dormitory; a kitchen with a wood fire; a dining hall adorned with pictures of Ho Chi-Minh, José Martí, and Che Guevara; cold-water showers; outdoor toilets; and a small stall selling beer, soft drinks, crackers, and cigarettes. The roads are all of dirt and are well rutted from the oxcarts that haul the cut sugarcane of the granja to the narrow-gage railroad siding on the property.

The day at Heroic Vietnam starts at 5:30 in the morning, when more than a hundred diplomats, office workers, and service personnel tumble out of their closely packed double-decked bunks and make their way to the outdoor washstands and toilets. After a quick breakfast of coffee and milk and a few hard rolls, the city folk of the Ministry of Foreign Relations are off to work in the cane fields. By far the hardest job they are called on to do is to cut cane, a nasty business that involves swinging the machete, bending, tugging the snarled cane into the clear, trimming the leaves, cutting the cleaned stalk, and tossing the usable pieces into piles to be stacked and collected later. While some cut cane, other members of the Ministry, including the women, do the easier work of cleaning, weeding, and fertilizing the cut fields by hand.

The lunch break comes at eleven, after more than four hours of work. This time there is a full hot meal of meat and vegetables. Almost all the workers collapse into their bunks after lunch; many sleep, although a few play chess, talk, or read. The afternoon work shift runs from two until six, followed by a meal very similar to lunch. After dinner some watch television in the dining hall; others sing, talk, or play chess or dominoes. The lights go out at ten. On special occasions the encampment is visited by groups of singers and entertainers from Havana, who travel from camp to camp during the Jornada giving shows.

Life in the dormitories, dining hall, and cane fields of Heroic Vietnam is extremely egalitarian. No one is above doing any particular job or above being made the brunt of a joke. Everyone addresses everyone else informally by first or often simply by last name, as is the custom in Cuba. Neither dress, nor physical appearance, nor rhythms of work enable one to guess what job a person might have in the city during the rest of the year. Here all wear boots, rough olive drab or blue pants, long-sleeved denim shirts, and usually a peasant's broad-brimmed hat. Some of the best and hardest workers are members of the diplomatic corps, whereas some of those who spend the most time talking and smoking are from the service section of the Ministry, drivers, mechanics, and maintenance men.

After months in the city, the first days in the cane fields are hard on almost everyone. In such an encampment, however, no one wishes to be branded a complainer or a quitter, no matter how much he might dislike the work and the style of life. Those not genuinely moved by the revolutionary ethic of struggle and sacrifice are brought into line by subtle but pervasive peer-group pressures. There is one office worker, for example, who is totally blind, yet who is led every day by a friend to the cane fields. There he takes his machete and, by touch, he cuts, cleans, and stacks cane. Although slight of stature, he seems to bear the heat and discomfort of the cane field better than many. His is an example that makes it difficult for others to slack off on the job.

The Isle of Youth

The Isle of Pines lies to the south of the eastern edge of the Province of Pinar del Río and is separated from the main island at its nearest point by about thirty miles. It can be reached either by a one-hour flight from Havana or by a six-hour ferry ride. The island has an area of slightly over one thousand square miles, and although it receives more than the average amount of rainfall for Cuba, its sandy, porous soil soaks up the water and gives the landscape a semiarid and somewhat desolate look. A large swamp cuts the southern third of the island almost completely off from the northern two thirds, and except for a few scattered fishermen and farmers the southern portion is uninhabited.

At various times during the seventeenth, eighteenth, and nineteenth centuries, the Isle of Pines was a haven for pirates, smugglers, escaped prisoners, and fishermen and the home of a few English settlers. Later, though it continued to be known as a place slightly outside the law, it also became the site of the so-called "model prison," a group of austere, many-tiered, circular concrete buildings used in the 1940's, 1950's, and early 1960's for both common and political prisoners. It was here that Castro and his companions were held after their abortive attack on the Moncada Army Barracks in 1953.

During the first years of the Revolutionary Government, little changed on the Isle of Pines. It remained a place of detention, this time for political opponents of the Castro government. To supplement and replace the model prison, a number of new detention and rehabilitation camps were built. Some of these were quite modern and well constructed, suggesting their purpose only by the mushroom like concrete guard towers between the barracks. It is possible that as many as fifteen thousand men were held on the island during the mid-1960's, the peak years of political imprisonment. Some were hard-core political opponents, kept under full security. Others were held as trustees, their degree of freedom determined by how much they had demonstrated their willingness and readiness to be reincorporated into the new social order. Today all these camps and the prerevolutionary model prison have been either closed or converted into schools. Perhaps half of their former occupants have been rehabilitated and set free, and the rest have been taken to camps on the main island, there either to continue in the process of rehabilitation or to be held for their full sentences.

The phasing out of the detention and rehabilitation camps on the Isle of Pines set the stage for one of the most audacious of all the social experiments of the Castro government. Beginning in the autumn of 1966, the first contingents of young Cubans started arriving on the island. Some came to live and work only for short periods; others pledged to remain on the island for two years. Soon the place became known as the Isle of Youth, and as more and more young people came, a philosophy of social and political formation was articulated to explain and to promote the venture. In brief, it is felt that on this sparsely populated, scarcely developed, and poorly endowed island a new breed of young Cuban, a true Communist youth, will be forged. Away from the influences of city life and the older generation, and under the direction of the Party, these Cubans will become the first generation of truly "new men." The Spartan atmosphere of the Isle of Youth will teach them the meaning of sacrifice, cooperation, selflessness, discipline, and hard work. It is the philosophy of the "schools to the countryside" movement carried to its logical extreme. Thus the island's prerevolutionary population of about ten thousand has now swollen to more than forty thousand. No one knows exactly how many people there are, because much of the population is made up of transient youth and because the new arrivals are scattered throughout the encampments that dot the areas being brought into production.

The agricultural plans for the northern two thirds of the island are extremely ambitious. By 1970 it is hoped that more than a hundred thousand acres of citrus will be cultivated with an even larger amount of land made into pasture to support some four hundred thousand head of cattle. By the same date it is hoped that there will be four large earth-fill dams and about sixty smaller ones to catch the runoff from the seasonal rains and supply water to the cultivated land. Officials say that after the northern part of the island is made productive, attention will be turned to the less accessible and less promising south.

Except for those in the central area of Nueva Gerona, the capital of the Isle of Youth, the few roads on the island are badly potholed or unpaved and are fit only for trucks and jeeps. In the areas where land is being cleared, and particularly where the dams are being built, dust hangs thick in the air, so that by the middle of the day the people working there have taken on the yellow, red, and brown hues of the earth around them. Even in the center of Nueva Gerona there is no escape: every passing jeep leaves a trail of fine sand and dirt in its wake. The frontier atmosphere is seen in the appearance and customs of the people: almost everyone is dressed in rough work clothes and boots, and the informality of greetings and talk is even more pronounced here than it is on the main island.

For the most part, the young people on the Isle of Youth live in encampments close to where they work. These encampments are of various sorts. Some are true work camps of dormitories and mess halls where men or women in their late teens and early twenties live and eat when they are not working in the fields. Most of the young people who live in such camps have pledged to stay on the island for two years, although the force of this pledge is moral rather than contractual. A few never return from their first trip back to visit on the main island, but others return bringing with them friends and relatives. Even from a distance it is easy to tell which of these encampments are inhabited by men and which are inhabited by women. The women's camps, although just as modest as the men's, are usually painted and decorated with flowers and curtains, and they stand out in the raw landscape as little spots of color and order. The men's camps are serviceable but drab, and they could easily be mistaken for warehouses or army barracks.

At other encampments, particularly those for younger people, schooling is combined with agricultural work. A typical schedule includes four hours of digging, watering, cultivating, and planting in the morning followed by class instruction, sports, and drill in the afternoon. The school encampments are usually of a vocational sort; the one housed in part of the old model prison, for instance, trains technicians for the construction industry. Both on the Isle of Youth and on the main island these technological schools have a decidedly military cast, and in fact they are run by a special section of the Ministry of the Armed Forces. The internal discipline of the schools resembles that of basic training, and the male students can fulfill their military obligation while they work and study.

One of the most interesting encampments on the Isle of Youth is a set of wooden barracks not far from Nueva Gerona. This is a special school for what the Cubans call predelinquent boys. Government organizations from all over Cuba send boys to this school to be rehabilitated and made into useful citizens. Some have actually run afoul of the law; others are simply street urchins, drifters, abandoned or uncared-for illegitimate children, or boys from broken homes. They share a common background of poverty and neglect, and it is hoped that here they will be able to begin life anew. Although they are not confined or physically mistreated, they are subjected to strict discipline and rigorous training in school and in the field. As the training officer of the encampment said, "When they come here they are like animals. Some know how to eat only with their fingers, and others know no form of human relations except to take what they want. The kind of discipline we give them here is the only kind they understand." In truth, the collected urchins do not look like the most promising sons of the new Cuba. But the directors of the encampment express unqualified optimism that here on the Isle of Youth even these youngsters can be transformed. This optimism echoes that of Castro's speech on March 13, 1968, from the steps of the University of Havana:

> We cannot encourage or even permit selfish attitudes among men if we don't want man to be guided by the instinct of selfishness, . . . by the wolf instinct, by the beast instinct. . . . The concept of Socialism and Communism, the concept of a higher society, implies a man devoid of those feelings, a man who has overcome such instincts at any cost, placing above everything his sense of solidarity and brotherhood among men. . . . We don't feel that the Communist man can be developed by encouraging man's ambition, man's individual desires. *If we fail because we believe in man's ability, in his ability to improve, then we shall fail, but we shall never renounce our faith in mankind!*

Such is the vision that energizes the Isle of Youth, Heroic Vietnam, Sandino City, and many other encampments, schools, granjas, and experimental settlements throughout the Cuban countryside. It is a vision full of optimism, with strong overtones of utopianism, couched in a language that is more Castro's than Marx's, that looks to Vietnam rather than to Eastern Europe for examples of revolutionary behavior.

By rubbing his peoples' noses in the countryside, Fidel Castro is smashing the traditional class distinctions and social relations of what was once a very Latin society. In all of Latin America, only in Cuba are boots, rough hands, dirty clothes, first names, and agricultural talk among the marks of honor and status. What difference will this sociocultural transformation make? Will it put coffee in the cup, fruit in the market, gasoline in the tank, and foreign exchange in the national bank? By itself it clearly will not; but combined with modern technology, hard work, some degree of economic realism, and a little luck, it will. The sociocultural transformation may well be a necessary prelude to the economic transformation of the island. The Cuban leadership thinks that it is, and there is much, both in contemporary social science and in contemporary history, to support this view.

APPENDIX B

Fidel Castro's Speech at Varadero to Departing Conrado Benítez Brigadistas and Their Families, Mother's Day, May 14, 1961

LADIES, Mothers of the brigadistas; compañeros and compañeras of the brigades: *

I am going to say just a few words, really, because we must also attend another event like this one—an homage to the mothers of young peasant girls studying in Havana.

But as I watched this event on television, I could not resist the temptation to join you for a few minutes. When we first organized this literacy army, our plan was to always be on hand when the young people were being sent off to the countryside to do literacy work. That has not been possible, as you know. I wish I could have talked with all those who have already left, in order to try to explain to them the importance of this campaign and the extraordinary worth of the task you are about to accomplish.

An Army to Combat Ignorance

At the time of the mercenary attack against our nation, what worried us, the threat that bothered us most of all, was that the attack might interrupt the literacy campaign. We knew that each

This speech is translated and slightly abridged from *El Mundo*, May 16, 1961, pp. 6, 8. Most subheads are from the original.

* *Compañero*, sometimes translated as "comrade," is left in the Spanish throughout this translation. Its closest ordinary English rendering is "companion," but in revolutionary Cuba it has become the official, egalitarian form of address, even among those who are not compañeros (or buddies) in the more usual Latin sense. Campesino, or peasant, has also been left in the Spanish in much of the translation. By "campesino," Castro means what we would ordinarily think of as "rural resident." Thus he also includes some who are not really peasants by more standard definitions.

and every invader would be defeated; we were confident that our soldiers would wipe them out within a few hours. What did worry us, though, was that the events might hinder or slow down the movement of this other army—this army that is fighting a much longer and far more difficult battle. For there are two armies in our nation: one armed with rifles and cannons to defend the work of the revolution, and one armed with books to advance the revolution; one army to combat foreign enemies, traitors, and those who would destroy what we have accomplished, and another army to combat lack of culture and illiteracy.

The revolution needs both of these armies; one can do nothing without the other. The militiamen and soldiers can do nothing without you; and you, without the support of the soldiers and militiamen, cannot carry on in this campaign.

Yours will be the longer struggle; you will need more patience. Your struggle will not be a matter of hours or of days. If illiteracy could be liquidated as easily as a band of mercenary invaders, by the end of the month there would be no more illiterates in our country. But, since illiteracy is an illness that has existed in our country for centuries, an endemic sickness of all the peoples of Latin America, the struggle against it is long and hard. You'll need constancy and force. Just as much heroism is needed to defeat illiteracy as is needed to conquer the mercenaries of imperialism.

And the battle that defeats ignorance will give our country more glory than any military battle we have waged so far, or any military battle we shall wage in the future. There have been many military battles throughout history, but a battle like the one being waged by this force armed with pencils and primers has never before been fought in any part of the world—this battle of one year. Other peoples have struggled and won against illiteracy, but no people has ever before proposed to eradicate illiteracy in the space of one year. Our country is the first in the world to confront so serious a problem in so short a time; it is the first in the world to commit itself to eradicating illiteracy in one year.

We have not even had the whole year at our disposal; during this same year we have had to spend much of our energy guarding against foreign threats. It would have been much easier if struggling against ignorance had been our only task. But we have found ourselves confronting two great tasks: defending the revolution and the Fatherland from threats of aggression, and, at the same time, doing battle against ignorance.

We must realize that our task is difficult and that all of us must exert our maximum effort; we should be aware that in our country there are more than a million illiterates. Each one of you must teach at least six to ten people how to read and write, and we must mobilize, from among the young people and the adults, from among teachers and workers, no less than 250,000 literacy workers. Furthermore, we must search for and find the illiterates, wherever they may be; often illiterates live right next door without our knowing it.

This battle involves the total eradication of illiteracy in our country. That is, we must find, persuade, and teach every last illiterate in the most remote corner of our nation. And when that job

is done, we shall have to make an accounting, so that we can know whether or not we have won the battle—whether our youth has won or lost, whether or not our army of literacy workers has been able to win as crushing and brilliant a victory against ignorance as that won by our soldiers and militiamen against the mercenaries at the Peninsula of Zapata.*

Sixty thousand young people have already registered. It is now necessary to augment this figure; we must make sure that not one young person capable of literacy work remains at home. There were sixty thousand registered long before enthusiasm became as strong as it is today, long before our young people witnessed this formidable mobilization.

We are certain that we shall reach our goal of one hundred thousand literacy workers, and that this force of one hundred thousand will make our campaign against ignorance a total success.

We know that these one hundred thousand young people, working arduously and traveling to the most remote corners of our country, will manage to wipe out illiteracy from one end of the island to the other. Rarely has the youth of any nation been faced with such a task; rarely has any country's youth been called on to do a job as important as this one; rarely has any people placed so much confidence and hope in its youth.

* The Peninsula of Zapata is the name given to the swampy area surrounding the Bay of Pigs.

You Will Teach and You Will Learn

You are going to teach, but as you teach, you will also learn. You are going to learn much more than you can possibly teach, and in the end you will feel as grateful to the campesinos as the campesinos will feel to you for teaching them to read and write. Because while you teach them what you have learned in school, they will be teaching you what they have learned from the hard life that they have led. They will teach you the "why" of the revolution better than any speech, better than any book. They will show you what life has been like in the countryside and how our campesinos have lived deprived of everything. They will teach you how hundreds of thousands of campesinos have had to live without roads, without highways, without parks, without electricity, without theaters, without movies, and without entertainment. They are going to teach you how the peasant boys and girls have had to live without light bulbs, and how it has been never to have gone to a movie, to a museum, to a park, to a botanical garden, or to a zoo. They will show you that there is a harder life than the life we have led; they will show you how human beings have suffered because of exploitation by selfish and mean interests. They are going to teach you what it is like to live with a deficient diet; they will show you what it is like to have lived months and months without consuming even one pound of meat or one pound of fish. They will teach you what it is like to live without doctors and without hospitals. And they will teach you what it is to have lived, working constantly, forgotten by every government.

But at the same time, they will also teach you the real meaning of sacrifice, and how honest and healthy the hard life is. They will show you the clean life of the campesinos and the rural workers. They will teach you what moral rectitude is, what duty is, and what it means to share with others, to take a crust of bread from your own mouth and give it to a guest, to one who has come to help.

And when you return, satisfied with what you have done and proud for the rest of your lives, you will also carry in your hearts a profound feeling of appreciation. Each of you is going to feel that you have become more of a man or woman than you were when you left for the countryside.

Each of you is going to feel like a better citizen and a better revolutionary, because you will better understand the necessity and the duty of studying and preparing yourselves for the Fatherland of tomorrow. And each of you will also understand the need for all of our people to study and improve. You will realize that much effort will be needed, that much learning will be needed, and also that much science and much technology will be needed in our nation if we are to bring to your friends in the mountains and fields, and to their sons, the opportunities that you yourselves have had. All this will be required if we plan to bring thousands of doctors to our countryside; to bring thousands and thousands, tens and tens of thousands of technicians to our countryside; to bring thousands and thousands of machines to our countryside; to accomplish there the work that has yet to be done to give those long-suffering campesinos a standard of living as high as that in the city.

The Same Development in the Countryside as in the City

Then you will have a better understanding of the relationship between the country and the city, and you will see that it is impossible to achieve greater progress in the city if the rural economy does not develop at the same time. You will have the opportunity to see how the campesinos work to supply the cities, and how each cup of coffee that you drink owes its existence to a thousand sacrifices by those campesinos. Year after year those campesinos, who have never received credit, who have always lived under the threat of eviction, have been creating that wealth, a wealth that represents tens and tens of millions of pesos in the mountains. You will realize that each grain of coffee has its story of sacrifice and human effort; it tells of families struggling all by themselves to grow those few crops.

Thus we can be sure that when you return again to school you will be much better students. The success of the literacy campaign will mean not only that we have taught more than a million illiterate Cubans to read and write, but also that we have made a hundred thousand young people from the cities better, more revolutionary citizens.

The Efforts and Sacrifices of Your Parents

And when you return to your homes, you will also be less demanding and more understanding of your parents. After you have learned to live without electricity, without movies, without television, without theaters, without parks, and without paved streets, and after you have learned to live the life that you will live while you are in the countryside, eating only what is produced out there, the chances are that you will never again find the soup at home tasteless or the meat tough. When you sit down again at the tables in your homes, even though they be modest tables (and however modest they may be, the tables of the campesinos are more modest), you will feel grateful for the efforts and sacrifices your parents make so that you can enjoy such benefits. Then you will better understand life. Be careful to see that you never forget what you have learned in the countryside, where there is pain and sacrifice, but where there is also much happiness and beauty—physical beauty and spiritual beauty. You are going to do unforgettable work in our countryside: you are going to sow the seeds of culture. And afterwards all of us will have to struggle so that he who wishes to can continue studying. For it is not enough that the campesinos simply learn to read and write. You must sow in them the desire to continue studying, to continue reading, and to continue learning. They should be encouraged to stay in contact with the National Literacy Commission and the Ministry of Education, so that they may continue to request books and facilities in order to continue studying.

Everything Comes as a Result of the Work of Our Workers

It will not be enough to teach them their first letters. It will be necessary for the Republic to continue creating conditions that permit all peasant boys and girls to have the same opportunities to study as any of you. And you should know that today each and every one of you has an opportunity that formerly only a handful of young people had. All of you today—pupils who have reached the sixth grade and pupils who are already beginning secondary school or pre-university—are given this opportunity by the revolution. It is the gift of the people, the gift of wealth produced by the hands of our campesinos and our workers. Students receive books and scholarships, and where do these books and scholarships come from? Where does their food come from? Where do the clothes they wear come from? That food, those books, and that clothing come from the people, our workers and our campesinos.

The nation does not have these resources at its disposal because they fell from the sky. The nation has these resources because they are the product of the work of the people. And think of all the teachers, university instructors, and professors who have to spend hours and hours with you, and who also have to live, who have to eat and satisfy all their needs. If the country has at its disposal tens of thousands of teachers and professors, it is thanks to the work of our workers and peasants.

That is to say, wealth is created by the manual worker as well as by the intellectual, and part of that wealth is dedicated to you. Those same campesinos that you are going to teach are also working so that you can have your teachers and your good schools, so that any humble student can have a scholarship to study in an institute or a university, and so that any humble student can tomorrow become a doctor, an architect, or an engineer.

Go from here conscious of the fact that you are going to work for those who have worked for you, that you are going to help those who have helped you. Go from here conscious that these people will return one hundred fold what you are giving them. Go conscious of the fact that to every man and woman in our country we shall guarantee opportunity and security. We guarantee that every person will be able to learn and to train himself to the extent he wishes, and that today the Fatherland will give all of its children the same opportunity that yesterday was held selfishly by a few.

The Work of Youth

This is the work that the revolution carries forward, and for this work the revolution enlists the support of everyone. It is for this work that the revolution has rallied its young people. After all, what were the young people going to do during these months? Were they going to remain idle, waiting for the problems to resolve themselves? Was our youth going to pass up this opportunity to write a page in the history of their Fatherland?

Youth had to participate. Though you are young, you are already conscious of your obligations to your people. Because you are young, you know that the future belongs to you. You are young, and you know that the revolution works primarily for you and for the generations to come. Because you are young, you are the ones who will one day harvest the fruits of the gigantic efforts being made by the people of today. You are young; you know that it is for you that the revolution is creating the Fatherland of tomorrow.

And tomorrow you will have the satisfaction of saying that this work was also yours, that you helped to build this edifice. Tomorrow you will be able to feel infinitely satisfied that you were part of this revolution. People will come from all over the world to see the results of this campaign. From all over the world they will come to ask how it was possible to eradicate a whole country's illiteracy in one year.

What We Do Will Be an Example to the World

It is essential that you realize how much everyone is expecting from this task, that this task is one of those most admired by visitors, and that what we do will serve as an example to the world. Our success will give courage to other peoples.

Whereas the imperialists, to defend their immoral interests, wish to destroy the revolution by armed force, we plan to destroy imperialism by example, by our success in this venture. Therefore we must achieve that success. The armed victories we obtain on the fields of battle are not our only victories. No, other victories are every bit as important; our literacy victories are just as damaging to imperialism as the victory won by our people at Playa Girón.

They try to destroy our country physically with airplanes, armies, and battleships. But what can they use to destroy the example of the Cuban Revolution? What do they have that can possibly destroy the example the Cuban Revolution is giving to the world in this battle against ignorance? When you have achieved this victory you will have accomplished something that cannot be destroyed. No cannons, no airplanes, no atomic bombs, no hydrogen bombs can destroy the example our country will be giving to the world. Against this example there are no nuclear arms; against this example there are no military weapons; against this example there is absolutely nothing in the world. These are our guided missiles! These are our nuclear arms! The effects of this literacy campaign will be felt all over the world. They will yield results and create havoc everywhere, in every country exploited by imperialism, in every colony exploited by colonialism, in every corner of the world where there is ignorance, imperialism, or exploitation. The effects of our arms, of our "guided missiles," will reach all of these countries. Such is this campaign against ignorance. Such is this example, unique in the history of the world. And such is the task for which our country has called together its youth.

Teach the Peasant About the Revolution

You—and I'm about to finish; I must go—are going to get along well in the countryside. As I've said, you won't have all the comforts there; but the countryside is healthy, it is good, and it is quiet. I, for one, very much miss the countryside. You will live a tranquil life, noticeably different from that of the city. When the time comes for taking in the harvest—and this harvest will be large, because according to estimates this coffee crop will be twice the size of last year's—those of you who are in the mountains will help the campesinos gather coffee. And those who are not in the mountains, those on the plains, will help the campesinos manage the cattle, help them sow, and help them with their other work. Not only must you teach the campesinos, you must win them over. You must win their sympathies in order to teach them what the revolution is all about. We shall send along material to help you explain the problems of the revolution, but it is more important that you teach the campesino by your example. None of you may rest on your laurels as teachers while the campesinos and their wives and children do all the work. No, you are not going there as mere intellectuals; you will have to sweat through your shirts alongside the campesinos. While you are there you must help them with their work whenever you have a free moment. You must help organize them, and you must teach them everything you are capable of teaching. Do not make a burden of yourself. No campesino should ever have cause to say that his teacher has come there to eat and nothing more.

Discipline, Obedience, and Correctness

With your work, with your efforts, with your generosity, and above all by your example, you will teach the campesinos. Moreover, you must have discipline. It is very important that you obey your teachers and the leaders of the brigades. Remember that we are responsible for you: the Revolutionary Government, as a pledge to your parents, has assumed responsibility for your safety as well as for your conduct and behavior. The revolution has a responsibility to your parents, and nobody can collaborate with us better than you in making us worthy of their confidence.

Remember that any fault, any misconduct, or any incorrectness can affect the revolution. No error is too small to harm the reputation of the revolution, both within the country and abroad. Because tomorrow people will come to ask us how we arranged things, how the young people behaved and how they solved problems, how their parents accepted the arrangements, what guarantees the revolution could give the parents to help them overcome their prejudices and fears—in short how the whole operation was handled. And the better the outcome, the better for the revolution. Success will contribute to raising the prestige of our people and the reputation of our Revolutionary Government.

The Idea of What a Revolution Is and Should Be

Because of all this, you must take with you the idea that you are no longer children and that you must behave correctly. Because each campesino is going to be looking at you to see what a revolutionary is like; and if he gets the idea that a revolutionary is a person who is correct, respectful, and disciplined, that will also form his opinion of the revolution itself. But if any one of you gives the wrong impression because of your behavior, you will be deceiving that campesino about the revolution, just when you could be giving him a clear and precise idea of what the revolution is and what it should be.

Above all, maintain discipline and obedience to your chiefs; for when difficulties arise you won't be able to pretend that you are in the heart of Havana. How often are there no communications? How often are letters late? How often does the material we need fail to come? You are going to understand why these things happen after you have spent a day walking through the rough terrain of the mountains to the places where you will be teaching.

We sometimes hear protests when we send boys to the most isolated places and girls to places closer to towns. By no means does this mean that we have any discriminatory ideas about women. The fact is that we are responsible to your parents, and we must take every precaution to put them at ease. We must make sure that this effort does not conflict with the concerns and feelings of your parents, because for them it is a sacrifice to be separated from you.

Every mother thinks that she should have her son and daughter at her side, where she can watch over them; parents are making a sacrifice by permitting you to travel to the countryside. We are very grateful for this sacrifice, but it also places us under an obligation to take every precaution to put them at ease.

To Those Who Participate in the Educational Campaign

You are young, and tomorrow people are going to ask you what you did. Tomorrow your sweethearts will ask how you behaved yourselves. I'm sure that none of you will want to say you had to leave. None of you will want to confess to your friends and sweethearts that you didn't have enough willpower to spend the necessary time in the mountains. You won't want to admit that, while tens of thousands of other boys and girls remained in the battle, you gave up and withdrew. Because afterwards, if you should want to become milicianos, you would be told that they have no use for the kind of miliciano who leaves his companions and withdraws from combat. When they organize athletic teams, they will ask you whether or not you were in the campaign, and then whether or not you stayed to the end. It will always be humiliating to have lacked the willpower to stay to the end; just as it will always be a source of pride for all of you—until the time of your grandchildren—to have belonged to this literacy army. And it will always be a source of pride for your parents.

Think of your parents: are they making the sacrifice of being separated from you only to have the pain later of seeing you return home simply because you were tired and could not stick to it? Remember your parents, so that next year on Mother's Day you can tell your mothers that you have fulfilled your duty and that they can be proud of their children.

Veterans of the Literacy Army

During the remainder of this month and throughout the next month the mobilization will continue to grow. Young people are very enthusiastic. After they have seen the television programs and the movies about what you have been doing, no young person will want to stay at home. Tomorrow, when all of you are veterans of this campaign, no stay-at-home will want to be asked if he participated. But listen well: when I say "veterans" I mean that you'll be there until the end; you won't be veterans if you get homesick and return. How humiliating it will be at the beginning of the school year if there is someone who, for lack of will, for lack of character and patience, did not remain as long as he was needed and thus was a deserter from the literacy army.

You are the future generation of this country. You are the ones who tomorrow will have to do all the things that we are doing today. Tomorrow you will be the ones who will run the factories, direct the institutes, teach in the centers of higher education, and work in the large industries. Tomorrow you will have to govern the country, and you will have to concern yourselves with housing, education, universities, industry, and all the other problems of the country. You are the ones who, tomorrow, will have to do all that. We see in you the generation that is going to continue the work of the revolution. It is you that will carry all of this forward. Everything that we are doing today will be the base on which you will build your tomorrow.

Thus you will have a series of advantages tomorrow: you will be able to count on tens of thousands of trained men to do all the things that we have had to do as best we could. We are not the ones who will be able to take advantage of all that is being done today. It is you who will profit from all this. You will have a thousand engineers if you need them, a thousand architects, hundreds and thousands of professors and researchers, and thousands of artists. In other words, whereas we are doing what we do with the few resources that we have, you will be able to advance the work of the revolution with the many advantages made possible by everything that is being done today.

You Will Be More Revolutionary Than We Are

You are the ones who, tomorrow, will have to continue this work. That is why we are preoccupied with youth and why we don't think selfishly of ourselves. We think instead of the future, of you, and we look forward to the time when all that will remain for us will be the satisfaction of having started this revolutionary work. We believe that you will be better revolutionaries than we have been, and that you will be better governors and better builders than we. You'll be more disciplined, better trained, freer of prejudice, and more competent in all ways to continue this work of the revolution.

I wish you success! I wish you triumph! I hope that you will return wearing the laurels of victory! I hope that you will bring prestige to our country! I hope that you will win the hearts of the campesinos! I hope that you will always feel pride in what you are today going out to do!

Fatherland or Death! We Shall Triumph!

APPENDIX C

Fidel Castro's Speech on the First Anniversary of the Committees for Defense of the Revolution, September 28, 1961

COMPAÑEROS and compañeras of the Committees for Defense of the Revolution from the Province of Havana:

Exactly one year ago today, we embarked upon a program of organizing the people to defend the revolution. Only one year, and already there are in the Province of Havana—in the Province of Havana alone—thirty thousand Committees for Defense of the Revolution! And in all the island, one hundred seven thousand Committees for Defense of the Revolution! What's more, each committee has no fewer than ten members, and there are some committees with as many as a hundred.

The Origin of the Committees

Why did the Committees for Defense of the Revolution arise? Could the Committees for Defense of the Revolution have arisen if there had not been a revolution? Where did the idea come from?

The counterrevolutionaries began organizing themselves within a few months after the triumph of the revolution. Imperialism began to act: the former privileged classes, affected by revolutionary laws, began to stir. The larvae began to appear; the CIA set to work.*

We had arrived in power by means of revolutionary battle; the masses, with weapons in their hands, had won power. Furthermore,

This speech is translated and abridged from *Revolución*, Sept. 30, 1961, pp. 12–14. This translation contains approximately one half of the material in the original speech. All subheads are by the translator.

* "Larvae" refers to the *gusanos* (worms), the term used by Castroites to refer to counterrevolutionaries.

the people had fought against a regime of oppression, against a regime of injustice run by a privileged minority.

And how had the minority been able to stay in power? The minority kept itself in power by force. Supported by thugs and repressive organizations, the minority made use of economic resources, propaganda media, and instruments of force. When privilege was in power, when the exploiting minority was in power, they needed a small, well-trained professional army to control the masses. They acted on the false assumption that their professional army, well armed and well trained by imperialist technicians, could never be defeated by the people.

Upon coming into power, the masses, because of the interests they defended and because of the nature of the revolutionary regime, had at their disposal other arms and other resources for battling the exploiting minority. The masses had other ways to fight a minority that desired a return to power, and to fight, above all, the masters of that minority, the powerful empire that begins ninety miles from our coast.

How were the masses to defend themselves? The revolution in power was not a privileged minority; the revolution in power represented the great masses of the people. It did not intend to defend itself against its enemies with an army of professional soldiers. The revolution did have an army, an army made up of the masses, principally from the peasant and worker strata. But the masses could also depend on that incomparably superior force: the force of a liberated people. The people couldn't rely on several thousand soldiers to defend them. They had to rely instead upon themselves. The people depended on the hundreds and hundreds of thousands of workers, peasants, and young people ready to defend their cause.

Only exploiting regimes, regimes that haven't the support of the people, must resort to setting an armed minority against the masses. When the masses are in power, they themselves become a powerful, invincible army. They organize and arm themselves. This is how the National Revolutionary Militia and the new Revolutionary Armed Forces arose: simply by arming the masses, by arming the people. Cuba was the first nation on this continent in which the organized masses armed themselves. Cuba was the first nation on the continent that, with a revolutionary program, armed its workers and peasants—yesterday's exploited masses—so that they might defend their rights against an exploiting imperialist minority seeking to return to power.

If in any exploited country, in any country under the rule of a privileged minority, the workers and the peasants receive arms, that privileged regime will last no more than twenty-four hours.

The Revolutionary Armed Forces were the organization destined to defend our national territory and to battle the enemy on any front where it appeared armed and organized.

Organization on the Home Front

The Revolutionary Armed Forces needed a complement. An organization was needed to fight counterrevolutionary terrorists, saboteurs, and those agents of imperialism who sought to hinder production, sabotage our industries, and sow terror among the people. The Revolutionary Armed Forces needed another organization for this job, and thus arose the Committees for Defense of the Revolution. It is the organization in the rear guard, a rear guard that sometimes also becomes the front line of battle against fifth columnists, saboteurs, terrorists, and agents of imperialism.

Thus the masses that had organized themselves into revolutionary militia, that had trained themselves in camps and had organized their battalions to confront the enemy, had also organized themselves in the rear guard. Whereas the brothers, husbands, and sons might be in the front line trenches with their militia battalions, their relatives—the wives, sisters, parents, and sons too young to go—remained in the rear guard at home. In the rear guard also stayed those workers who were indispensable to production, as well as everyone who for one reason or another could serve neither in the trenches nor in the battalions, but who nevertheless desired to be useful to the revolution. They did not want to feel impotent; they wanted to do what they could for the revolution. The masses were everywhere, and they were especially well represented in the most populous areas of the city.

All of us knew how the population was distributed throughout the city. Except in the most aristocratic neighborhoods, where the richest class lived, men and women of the people were everywhere. People of the revolution were in every neighborhood, on every block, in every apartment house.

In order to act, in order to carry out their terrorism and sabotage, the counterrevolutionaries had to meet, had to hide, had to move from place to place. Although they could count on the United States for all the dynamite, live phosphorus, and money they needed, they nevertheless had to act in the city. They had to arrive at diverse hours at predetermined places, and they had to find places to store their equipment. In other words, their plans against the people involved them in a series of secret activities.

The people did not need spies; the people did not need a small group to defend them from the activities of those criminals. Before, when it had been the people fighting against an exploiting tyranny, that tyranny had needed an army of spies. But when it was the minority fighting the masses, the masses were there conscientiously to defend their rights! The people could take care of themselves; they did not have to seek out and hire someone to watch over them. The people were everywhere, and they were able to organize their own defensive apparatus. The wives, sisters, sons, and parents of factory workers and of militiamen in the trenches could organize themselves and carry out this duty.

It was impossible for the worms and parasites to stir as long as the people—who knew only too well who the worms and parasites were—kept an eye on them. And that was what the imperialists—the Yankee Central Intelligence Agency—had not counted on. The CIA had not counted on finding its criminal, counterrevolutionary objectives opposed by a vigilant people. And that is another lesson the people of Cuba have taught imperialism.

Each revolutionary man or woman, in his house, on his block, in his apartment building, or in his neighborhood, became an active defender of the revolution. The counterrevolutionaries were faced with a new and unforeseen apparatus, an apparatus that is the historical product of the Cuban Revolution. It is because the Committees for Defense of the Revolution are an apparatus of the masses that they arose for the first time in our country. This organization of the masses came to fill a need that the other mass organizations could not fill.

The Militia had its function, the Federation of Cuban Women had its function, the young people's and children's organizations had their functions, the workers' unions had their functions, and the ORI [Integrated Revolutionary Organizations] had its function as a leadership organization. But there were still countless persons in the homes who did not belong to unions or to units of the Militia. There were housewives with numerous obligations who could not participate in the Federation of Cuban Women. And these were persons who wanted to help, who wanted to act and do something for the revolution. They did not have in their buildings, blocks, or neighborhoods a revolutionary organization to belong to.

The Importance of Organization

All the people should be organized, because for people in the midst of a revolution the most important task is organizing their forces. No matter how great its enthusiasm, no matter how great its morale and fighting spirit, an unorganized populace is ineffective because it disperses its forces. The people are like a battalion or a regiment in camp, with each person occupied by a different activity. When this military unit is suddenly faced with an enemy, the first thing it must do is organize itself. As long as the soldiers are dispersed around the camp, it has no strength. Its strength begins to exist when each soldier goes to his unit, squad, platoon, or company; its strength really exists when all the soldiers have joined in formation, when that dispersed mass has acquired the shape of a combat unit, perfectly commanded and perfectly organized.

So it is for the people: the most important part of the revolution is becoming organized. Every man and woman, every young person, every old person, and even every child must be organized. The isolated citizen, no matter how great his patriotism and his revolutionary fervor, lacks strength and efficiency. The revolution cannot count on isolated persons. The revolution must and will always depend solely on organized persons.

Thus every man and woman of the people must seek his organization. Whoever works in a factory will have his union there; if he also belongs to a militia battalion, that battalion will be another organization in which he will fight if he is needed. If the battle is one of production, he will be there in the factory; if the union calls a meeting, he will attend it; if the workers proclaim a motto or a goal, he will participate with his fellow workers in that program; if he is called to a training camp, he will report to his unit, receive his instruction, and report afterwards to his work center;

if there is a parade, he will parade with his unit; if the Fatherland is in danger and calls up his battalion, he will report immediately to his battalion, and his battalion will report immediately to the place assigned it; if the Fatherland is attacked, he will join his unit immediately and leave to fight in the front ranks.

That gives an idea of what organization means, and of how strong an organized people can be. For example, there might be a man who belongs to the union, but who cannot also belong to a battalion because he is an indispensable worker at the factory. That man, returning to his home, might find a Committee for Defense of the Revolution organized on the block where he lives. And there he can help out by participating in the various activities of that committee.

The Committees Integrate the Masses

The Committee for Defense is also the organization for a worker who has retired and who no longer belongs to a union or to a work center, and who, because of his age, has been convinced that he should not belong to a battalion (often it is difficult to convince him of this). Such a worker has, in the Committee for Defense, an organization for which he can work.

But above all, the Committee for Defense of the Revolution is the organization that complements all other revolutionary organizations. It is the organization that permits those citizens who cannot belong to any other organization to work for the revolution.

There are even cases of persons who cannot do physical work; there are cases of compañeros who are invalids but who nevertheless work actively in a Committee for Defense of the Revolution. We've been told of one such invalid compañero who could move only in a wheelchair, but who nevertheless is one of the most outstanding members of the Committee for Defense of the Revolution in the town of Madruga. In other words, the committee has given that compatriot, who must feel shame at not being in a militia battalion and who must frequently worry about not being in a factory producing, an opportunity to defend his country and the revolution. It is said that especially in the evening he patrols the town in his wheelchair and takes note of the state of vigilance.

All the true people are organizing themselves. Who are those that do not organize? Who are the ones who have no interest in organizing themselves? The worms, the parasites, the bums—those who do not work. By this I do not mean to say that everyone who does not presently belong to some organization is necessarily a parasite or a bum. There may be a few persons who have not yet entered the body of the revolution, although they are really a small minority. But those who neither have nor ever will have any interest in organizing or in joining any organization of the masses are enemies of the people, enemies of the masses, parasites, exploiters, slackers, those who don't work, those who live off the work of others.

And that is precisely what the revolution is all about. It is the grand union of all honorable persons, of all useful persons, of all studious persons, of all worthy persons, of all persons who produce for the populace. The revolution is for all those who do useful work for the public: the worker who raises a building for a factory, a school, or a hospital; the musician who entertains and excites the public; the teacher or professor; the doctor (one of the revolution's many honest doctors who are doing the work of those who left); the engineer; the architect; and the artist.

The Old Society

We have not spoken of gamblers, of corrupt politicians, of thugs, of landowners, of loan sharks, or of any other type of parasite. In the old society there were those who worked, and there were those who did not work but who nevertheless dressed, ate, wore shoes, slept, and lived. They did not produce one single useful thing. They did not play in a band, work in a theatre, build a building, teach a child, cure a patient, grow a plant, or fish. They did absolutely nothing useful, and nevertheless they ate, drank, slept, wore shoes, dressed, drove—drove cars—and lived in elegant houses.

Of course there were various kinds of parasites. There was the large parasite and there was the small parasite. That policeman who walked with a nightstick, wearing a hat with the brim turned up, he was a small parasite. The general, any one of those generals, was a large parasite. There were national parasites, and there were foreign parasites, like the great imperialist "mister" who owned shares in the electricity company, the telephone company, the sugar refinery, or the huge plantation. What kind of people were they? How can we describe that plague of parasites who did not teach children, raise buildings, cure patients, or sow the earth? What kind of people were those double-dealers who bought from the peasant at half price and sold to the people at triple price? What were those gentlemen who paid the farmer a third part of his own produce? What was that gentleman who charged a poor family sixty, seventy, and eighty pesos for a two-room apartment? What were those speculators? What were those smugglers, those exploiters of vice, those loan sharks, those thieving and corrupt politicians, those crooks—what were they? How did they live? Who worked for them? At whose cost did they eat, dress, wear shoes, and live? At whose cost? At the cost of the workers, at the cost of the peasants, at the cost of the humble, at the cost of the men and women of the masses, and, at times, even at the cost of the children.

And together with the exploitation of a people by a caste of parasites, there were all the other vices as well: chronic unemployment, men standing idle while the land went uncultivated, factories not producing at maximum capacity, tens of hundreds of thousands of families living in ignorance in slum neighborhoods, more than a million adults not knowing how to read or write. There was gambling, prostitution, discrimination, informing, lies, exploitation, interminable abuse against the people, and widespread injustice. The Fatherland was underdeveloped, the economy was in foreign hands, and criminals sowed terror among the people. Ours was a nation without a future, without honor, without liberty, without equality, without rights, and without hope.

What is the revolution but the great rebellion of the workers and the peasants, of the good and the honest, and of the useful against the parasites, exploiters, bums, and hangers-on?

The Remnants of the Old Society Linger On

Has parasitism been completely eradicated in Cuba? No, and it would be an error to think so. No people can rid itself of all its parasites with only one purgative. It would have to be such a terrible vermifuge that it would endanger the health of the social body. Just as some parasites require a long treatment because they are especially hard to kill, social parasitism, one of the most difficult types of parasitism to eradicate, requires an especially careful treatment. So although we have rid ourselves of many of the parasites, we have not yet come near to wiping them all out. We can still see, every day, even in the street, various forms of parasitism.

Occasionally there will arrive at a restaurant an impeccably dressed gentleman who bears not the slightest sign of ever having worked a day in his life. His companions are also elegantly dressed. They sit, they eat the best filet, they drink the best wine, and they leave in an automobile, wasting gasoline. When one asks "Who is that gentleman? What does he produce? What does he live on?" one finds out that there are still many people who produce nothing, who do no work, yet who waste gasoline, gasoline for the payment of which a worker has to cut and carry cane and other workers have to produce and ship sugar. And that gentleman—who neither cuts cane, nor refines petroleum, nor runs trains, nor attends to anyone—uses gallons and gallons of gasoline, arrives at the restaurant, and eats the best filet, the filet produced by workers from the farms, cooperatives, or fields. The chances are he lives in a fine house with three or four rooms or has two or three apartments. When one asks "What does he produce?" one finds out that he consumes everything and produces absolutely nothing. Furthermore, he speaks ill of the revolution and thus speaks ill of a people at whose expense he is still eating and living as a parasite.

And what right has anyone to live as an idler? What right has anyone to be a parasite? Why do they speak ill of the revolution? Why are they enemies of the revolution, spreading counterrevolutionary rumors? Why do they buy their little passage to Miami? Ah! Because each day our country becomes more a country of workers, a country of honest men and women, a country of producers and of useful, worthy people. Thus the atmosphere in the Fatherland is becoming more and more asphyxiating for the parasite, for the idler and exploiter.

There were many people here who were accustomed to a very comfortable and abundant life. For example, after the war, during which money accumulated in the banks because the country was necessarily prevented from acquiring many articles, there was an inflow of large sums that were then spent on automobiles, houses, dresses and the best laces, French perfumes, and vacation trips to the United States and Europe. For these people there was no housing shortage, because for people with enough income there were always more than enough houses. Whoever could afford to pay 100 or 150 pesos for a house never had problems, because the pages of the newspapers were full of such houses.

The difficult thing, the impossible thing, was to find a house for

15, 20, or 25 pesos where a man of humble income could live. That man could search the newspaper for an entire year. With three or four children and a salary of 100 or 120 pesos, he could never pay 60 or 70 pesos. For him there was no overabundance of houses.

For the others, the ones with high incomes, there were more than enough houses. For them there were luxurious automobiles in the agency windows. For them there were imported articles, laces, perfumes, and dollars. That stratum lived well; they had plenty of articles. And they lived a thousand leagues away from social reality, far removed from the slum neighborhoods where hundreds of thousands of families lived without schools and often without work during most of the year. Those poorer families had no luxurious automobiles; moreover they never once thought of flying to Miami to go shopping at the stores on Flager Street. Those families never dreamed of going to aristocratic clubs, having big parties, or spending vacations in Varadero or in other large recreational centers. They never even dreamed of having their children's bread assured to them!

The Revolution Is Changing All That

Then the revolution came. The revolution did not come about in order to maintain that elegant stratum's standard of luxury. The revolution had to use all its resources and all its efforts to benefit the immense majority of the nation: those without houses, recreation centers, or schools; those who had no trips to Europe, no trips to the United States, and no luxurious automobiles.

Would it be logical for the revolution to invest its resources—the few resources it can count on during the blockade—in building palaces and importing luxurious automobiles to maintain a bourgeois facade that can still be observed in our country and especially in our capital? The revolution was not going to buy Parisian perfumes with the money needed to buy material for dentures for the farmers of our Fatherland! No, the facade of the country had to change. The facade of luxury, which reflected the elegant life of a minority that was always giving parties, driving luxurious cars, and traveling in and out of the country, had to change. Only then could we acquire the physiognomy of a country of workers and producers, a country without parasites, a country with neither exploiters nor exploited.

The bourgeois facade of Cuban society had to change, and it will have to keep on changing! Each day the streets of our cities will see fewer luxurious cars. By contrast, the fields of our Fatherland will see more tractors and agricultural machinery every day! Our country will see no more new palaces of 100,000 or 200,000 pesos; it *will* see each day thousands and thousands of houses where the worker will pay only 10 percent of his salary!

That facade, which belonged to a society of parasitism and exploitation, will change a little more each day toward becoming the physiognomy of a working country, of an austere country where there are no luxurious cars for the minority. Instead we will have what matters. Bread will be assured to each child of each man and each woman! Schooling will be assured: there will be schools, institutes, technical centers, and universities! There will be education for the young and for the adults! There will be work for all! And the cement we use, the steel we use, and the labor we hire will not go toward building palaces for millionaires. They will build schools for young people and children, factories, streets, aqueducts, roads, and hospitals! Then everyone will have clothes and shoes; everyone will have bread; and everyone will have a right to life, to culture, and to happiness.

They Danced While We Died

Is it possible that the people still do not understand how completely their lives were surrounded by a society of shameless exploitation, and to what extent they were the victims of lies and ridicule?

When I learned that I would be speaking to you today, to the members of the Committees for Defense—which we all know are made up of the most fervent defenders of the revolution in each neighborhood—I went to the National Library to look over some newspapers from the past. I brought some of those newspapers along with me to remind you of that era.

I have brought [he holds up a newspaper] a *Diario de la Marina.**

"Photographs from the *Crónica Habanera.*" A photograph: "In the Country Club. The Havana Country Club canasta parties are

* *Diario de la Marina* was the largest and most successful of the well-established, conservative, pre-revolutionary newspapers.

becoming more and more popular and animated.* This photo, taken last Thursday, shows a group of those attending."

"A lively cocktail party. Last Thursday evening, Miss So-and-so gave a cocktail party at the home of her parents, Doctor and Mrs. So-and-so."

"A ladies' luncheon at Tarará. A lovely society ladies' luncheon was given last Thursday noon at the Tarará Yacht Club by the Association of Owners of that beach and by the distinguished ladies who offer their help for the traditional holiday parties celebrating Santa Elena, which, as we know, will take place August 16–23." A whole week. "The luncheon was presided over by Mrs. So-and-so, etc." When we turn the page we see:

"An exciting reception at the inauguration of the new American International building. A modern building, American International was inaugurated at the corner of F and 23rd Streets in Vedado. In it are found the offices of Insular Underwriters de Cuba, S.A. A brilliant reception was given, attended by well-known figures from Havana society, banking, commerce, industry, and business. It was a magnificent party in every sense, and it began with the blessing of the modern construction by His Eminence Manuel Cardinal Arteaga, Archbishop of Havana. Present at the ceremony were Mr. Cornelius V. Star, president of the board of directors of C. V. Star and Company, Inc., and Enrique Fernández Silva, president of the Insular Underwriters de Cuba, S.A." Everything was perfectly blessed by "His Most Illustriousness," the Cardinal. Date: July 26, 1953.†

And on the front page: "Some seventy dead is the tragic toll from the coup attempted against the military barracks of Santiago and Bayamo. The armed forces still pursue groups implicated in the attempt, who are presumed hidden on farms in the eastern province. It is reported that normalcy has returned after Sunday's bloody events."

[He shows another *Diario de la Marina.*] Date: December 2, 1956,

* Many phrases like "canasta party" and "cocktail party" appeared in English in *Diario de la Marina* and in other newspapers, as well as in the conversation of middle-class and upper-class Cubans. In his speech, Castro of course read these phrases in English whenever they so appeared in the original.

† July 26, 1953, was the date on which Castro and his followers attacked the Moncada Army Barracks in Santiago, Cuba. The 26th of July Movement took its name from this event.

the day of the landing from the *Granma*.* "The national sugar industry toasts its success. At a magnificent gathering Friday night, plantation owners and planters gave public homage to the President of the Republic, General Fulgencio Batista, in a gesture of appreciation for the astute economic policies that the government has been following, especially with respect to our primary industry.

"Friday's banquet was one of the most beautiful social events of the week, not only because of the sense of justice prevailing, but also because of the instructive illustration of cohesion and brotherhood among the various sectors of the sugar industry, which depends on a harmonious relationship for its best development and for its reputation."

[He shows another newspaper.] Date: December 25, 1956, the night of the "Bloody Christmas." "Nineteen persons dead—seventeen shot, two hanged—in the eastern zone. The circumstances under which they lost their lives are as yet unknown." Those were the seventeen workers and the labor union leaders, the nineteen assassinated during the Bloody Christmas season in the east.

Well. "One of the best Christmas parties has been the Christmas dinner held at the Havana Yacht Club last Tuesday night in honor of its members and the members of the Havana Country Club.

"Countless small parties met on that exquisitely decorated terrace, contributing to the brilliance of the affair, which began at eight o'clock and lasted until past two in the morning." It is possible that while they danced and drank champagne, Cowley's thugs were assassinating the labor leaders.†

[He shows another newspaper.] From the *Crónica Habanera*: "Cocktail parties, fashion shows, the Lastre-Rebordeo wedding, receptions, dinners." And on the front page: "Sixteen rebels and eleven soldiers died in two skirmishes in the east."

"The nuptial walkway began next to the home's swimming pool. It was built of wood and its entire length was covered by a lovely pearl gray rug. At the head of the path stood two small, leaf-bedecked columns whose tops were covered with masses of white

* The *Granma* was the converted yacht that brought Castro and his armed force from Mexico to Cuba to begin the guerrilla struggle that eventually led to the overthrow of Batista.

† Colonel Fermin Cowley was in charge of the military garrison at Holguín, the second largest city of Oriente Province. He was one of the most brutal and

gladiolas. From both sides of the columns extended arms of stone, which were also decorated with gladiolas. The altar, which had two levels, was set above a large platform. In the background was a huge wall of green foliage interrupted by square columns also covered with leafy greenery and topped by spheres covered with white gladiolas. There stood a statue of Our Lady of Carmen, etc. . . .

"The central table was covered with a cloth of Brussels lace and adorned with large silver candelabras, each bearing three long, thick, white candles. In front of this table were placed the chairs for the bride and bridegroom, the wedding party, and the President, Major General Fulgencio Batista Zaldívar, etc. . . .

"Within that marvelous and distinguished setting was celebrated the resplendent ceremony, which brought together representatives from the official world, the diplomatic corps, and Havana society.

"The bride, radiant with beauty in her finery, etc. . . .

"And after listening to the classic sermon, etc."

Such Was the Contrast

This small sample gives us an idea of what our country was, what it stood for and what our people had to work for: so much frivolity, so much luxury, so much waste, so much ridiculousness. And the dates of the newspaper accounts I brought were dates of heroism, mourning, and pain, of suffering to which those "ladies" and "gentlemen" of the aristocratic clubs were unconscious. Those millionaires, birds of prey, and looters of the people who went [to the Christmas wedding] to celebrate the birth of the Baby Jesus (who was born in a stable, according to the Bible) and who lived in palaces, surrounded by laces, by gold and by silver, by opulence and by millions—those were the Christians! His Eminence the Cardinal blessed imperialist business ventures; there were laces and luxuries, English names and French firms; there was the Yacht Club, the Miramar Club, and the Country Club, where not one single name could even be pronounced in Spanish. And only they could go there: those who produced not one single grain of food,

corrupt of Batista's military commanders. Less than a year after the "Bloody Christmas" of 1956, Cowley was assassinated by members of the 26th of July Movement while he was shopping in Holguín.

the well-dressed, well-perfumed, well-fed, well-transported, and well-served parasites.

And who took care of their children? Who looked after their homes? Who washed their clothes? Who scrubbed their floors? Who prepared a hot meal when the "lady" arrived tired? And don't you believe that they were tired from work. No, they were tired from playing canasta, from chatting and talking with their big and little girlfriends of the same ancestry, from eating, from drinking, from dancing, and from gossiping.

How did they get their luxuries? How were they able to live such a life? How if not by forcing the laborers to work at the sugar refineries? How if not with the help of loansharks at the banks and of exploiting landowners? They had the people at their service. As long as there were enough poor men and women and enough workers with large families and no schools, they could have maids for their wives. Their wives could play canasta and never miss a meal, a tea, a cocktail party, a social event, or any other folly.

How Long Could It Last?

How long were we to live like that? How long would the workers' and farmers' daughters have to continue becoming domestic servants, barmaids, and prostitutes so that all those wives could treat themselves to fashion shows, cocktail parties, canasta parties, and trips to Paris and Miami? How long? How long were our people supposed to stand for all that? And why should our people have stood for such atrocity even if it was sanctified by all the reactionary, falangist priests in the country?

That was the "Christian" sentiment of those gentlemen; that was their "religious" sentiment: to live as parasites and idlers, as if they were superior beings whom the people were obliged to fatten like suckling pigs, as if they had a right to be waited on forever. How long? It had to end. All those privileges had to end. All the exploitation, the discrimination, the high society, and the world of business and banking had to end. That fatuous world of privileges, with its exclusive clubs, English names, French perfumes, and laces, had to end. All that ridiculous, frivolous garbage had to end. Those aristocratic clubs had to be opened up, and the people's children had to stop swimming at the rocks of the Malecón and start swimming at the Yacht Club, Miramar Country Club, and all the other places that are no longer called clubs, no longer called "country," and no longer called by English names.* They are now called "workers' circles" and "popular circles"!

Of course! And who used to say the world would end the day that high society ended, the day that the world of business and banking, exclusive clubs, and cocktail and canasta parties ended? Who used to say the Republic would end the day that all parasitism ended? They believed that society was a natural order, one in which they were destined to remain on top, raised upon the heads and shoulders of the people who were by nature destined to suffer enslavement and exploitation. And now it turns out that they are far from here; and the people—a people that no natural order obliged to be the slaves and servants of parasites—are the ones who have power in the Fatherland.

Of course as far as the ladies and gentlemen of the Country Club, the Biltmore, and other such places were concerned, the people were rabble. How could they let the rabble bathe there? That was all they needed! At the same place, the same beach, in the same water? Never! How could their children study in the same schools with children of the working class? No, never; get a passport to Miami! Quick, even if you already have a passport, get another, and then leave!

Of course, all that had had its antecedents. The problem was not just the issue of their children. The revolution had attacked the most fundamental part of an evil society: the exploitation and parasitism at its base. The revolution had instituted agrarian and urban reform, and it had nationalized all the large industries. In short, the revolution had affected the economic interests of that exploiting stratum and its satellites.

And of course that is what they can neither forgive nor get used to. And so the parasites have been leaving. And what do they want? Well, they want to destroy the rule of law and justice that the revolution has brought. They want the country to return to all

* The Malecón is the seaside drive bordering the newer section of Havana. There is no beach there, only surf and tumbled rocks. Almost all the beaches in the greater Havana area were in private hands before the revolution, and therefore the children of poorer Havana families swam from the rocks at the Malecón.

that is past. That is what, with the help of imperialism, they want to reestablish here. That is what the counterrevolutionaries and turncoats defend. Today when you open a newspaper you won't find all that frivolity; nor will you find grand ladies. Today you will find laborers and farmers working; and the newspaper's praise is not for the greatest parasite, but for the greatest worker, the laborer who has made the greatest effort. Today the newspaper speaks not of the most distinguished club, but of the most distinguished work center, the best cooperative, the people's farm that is in first place, the literacy teacher, the work brigade leaving for the mountains, the militiaman in his training camp, and all the activities of the people. Because the world of exploiters has been entirely replaced.

And all the parasites are joining together in an effort to destroy the revolution of the Cuban workers and farmers. How far they were from suspecting that a revolution was developing. How far they were from imagining that the world they believed had divine benediction (after all, they went to mass every day at eleven, after sleeping all morning of course) was threatened. Since they gave a little charity every once in a while, they believed that their social regime was blessed and sanctified and, furthermore, that it was eternal and indestructible.

The Committees Are Stronger Than Ever

The Committees for Defense of the Revolution are organs of revolutionary power. Organizing the masses is only one of the various revolutionary tasks that you are called on to carry out. These tasks are essential to the revolution, and you must perform them responsibly and with a high sense of sacrifice. Because one thing you must always remember is that being part of a Committee for Defense involves having the spirit of sacrifice. You must be an example for the rest of the citizens. You must work and observe the counterrevolutionaries. Moreover, part of being a committee member is doing a job of proselytism and conversion. As you know, many of those arrested back at the time of Girón have changed.* Many of them have joined the revolution. So keep in mind that one task of the committee is to proselytize and convert,

* "Girón" refers to the invasion at the Bay of Pigs in April 1961. The main beach used by the invading force is known as Playa Girón.

just as another task is to maintain severe and implacable vigilance against the enemies of the revolution.

You now have much more experience and the apparatus is much more developed. In any emergency you will be able to perform your tasks more efficiently, more fairly, and with more care so that all the citizens in the neighborhood will look upon your Committee for Defense as a friendly organization as well as a revolutionary organization—an organization that is ready to help, just as it is also ready to act with the necessary energy when ordered to do so by the revolution.

We must continue to be more and more organized, in the committees as well as in the Militia. The more organized the people are, the stronger they will be. We are organizing all the decent, useful working people so that they will never be conquered by the parasites; so that those loyal to the Fatherland, to the humble, and to the poor will never be defeated by the exploiters, parasites, and privileged worms; so that reason and justice will never be defeated by crime.

Onward, compañeros of the Committees for Defense of the Revolution! Forward to fight, to begin as many battles as are necessary! When the enemy launches its attack again, not only will it find a much stronger Army and Militia, but also it will have to confront a much stronger revolutionary organization, the Committees for Defense of the Revolution!

Long live the Committees for Defense of the Revolution!

Long live the workers!

Long live the Socialist revolution!

Fatherland or Death! We Shall Triumph!

APPENDIX D

Fidel Castro's Speech to the Seventh National Meeting of the Schools of Revolutionary Instruction, June 27, 1962

COMPAÑEROS, directors of the Schools of Revolutionary Instruction:

To begin, I want to tell you our impression of this meeting. Really, this meeting gives us a very good impression; although in general we can never feel completely satisfied with what we have achieved, because all revolutionary work—especially in the first stage of the revolution—has many shortcomings and defects. It could not be otherwise.

One truly gets the impression, in a meeting like this, that a great movement of revolutionary education is on the march—stumbling, falling, rising up again, struggling, and little by little conquering all natural obstacles.

The compañeros that have spoken, members of the National Directorate of the Schools of Revolutionary Instruction representing each province, have talked here in a serious and responsible manner. They have demonstrated that there is a group of compañeros deeply involved in the work of revolutionary instruction who have assumed their task with a deep feeling of responsibility.

Moreover, we know that this instructional movement, this movement of revolutionary education, has been organized from practically nothing. We know that a great number of you were yourselves students in the first courses organized. It is logical that we find ourselves today with many more human resources—which are the most important kind—than we found ourselves with when we began organizing the schools. And it is also evident that all of you are young compañeros who have every possibility and every

This speech is translated and abridged from *El Mundo*, June 30, 1962, pp. 6–8. This translation contains slightly less than one half of the material in the original speech. All subheads are by the translator.

opportunity to continue developing yourselves, preparing yourselves, and qualifying yourselves for work that is just beginning.

Really, this organization has been created from nothing. And the possibility that from the schools themselves will continue to come revolutionary young values as well as first-class material for forming more cadres of the movement of revolutionary education encourages us to have an optimistic vision of the future.

The Most Complex and Difficult Science

We have been, perhaps, less exacting than the academies, universities, and institutes. This is as it should be. The well-established centers of learning and technology can afford the luxury of being very exacting, for they can count on a number, small though it may be, of trained professors. And they can always hire professors to teach engineering, medicine, and technology.

The Directorate of the Schools of Revolutionary Instruction could not count on such a team of highly experienced professors. Even less was it conceivable that we could hire foreign professors and technicians to give this kind of revolutionary instruction here in Cuba. Nevertheless, what we are teaching is more important than medicine, more important than engineering, and more important than architecture. It is more important than any technical subject; it is more important than any university subject. Moreover, what is being taught is more difficult, for it is also a science, the most complex, difficult, and profound science. It is not a dead science, but a science in full historical development. What could be more difficult and more complex in the first instance than a revolution? What in the life of a people could be more difficult and more complex than politics? And what could be more difficult than what has to be learned in the heat of daily battle, when from the struggle itself and from each battle more and more knowledge has to be extracted? This study has to be elucidated in the midst of passions, in the midst of class warfare, in the midst of tremendous conflicts of interest. Thus politics and the revolution are something far more difficult than anything one might study in the universities.

We Have Made Marxism Ours

We have adopted the very rich experience of more than a century, the extraordinary intellectual abundance that Marxism contains. This means we have an extraordinary advantage in the struggle. Marxism is not only the sole true science of politics and of the revolution; it is also the only true way of interpreting the development of human history. With what little we have, we have entered this immense terrain of experience and knowledge in order to develop something as extensive as our movement of revolutionary education.

But we are not studying Marxism out of simple philosophical or historical curiosity. No, for us it is vital, fundamental, and decisive to study and to teach Marxism. For ordinary politics, and for make-believe revolutions like those we have seen here many times, those that have been called revolutions by demagogues and tricksters in order to confuse the people about true revolutions, one does not have to study Marxism—or anything else for that matter. To study to be a political schemer is quite sufficient. In the age of political chicanery no one had to study anything. But in the midst of a true revolution like this one, in the midst of a change so profound and so audacious, in the midst of a conflict of such historical dimensions, you have to study. You have to really study; you have to reach down deep; you have to sharpen all your weapons and all the forces of science and truth. To orient ourselves in the first instance, and to know how to orient our people correctly, we must learn and we must teach. No one may be irresponsible or superficial. One cannot brush aside study; one must stick to it, because it is by studying that we find our best weapons. When historical forces confront each other and ideologies clash, the enemy avails himself of *his* best weapons. The enemy uses all the resources at his disposal: ignorance, the most subtle lies, and all the weight of tradition. As revolutionaries, we too must avail ourselves of our best weapons: of truth, and of the clearest possible arguments for the masses. With the weapons of truth, reason, and revolutionary passion we must teach the masses and carry them victoriously forward.

Some Mistaken Ideas

I think that by now no one doubts the importance of the Schools of Revolutionary Instruction. Lamentably people sometimes misunderstood the objectives of the schools. There were irresponsible people who thought of the schools as an amusement park for elders, a kindergarten for problem children, or a body shop for the politically damaged.

Unfortunately, our Schools of Revolutionary Instruction suffered because of mistaken ideas. The schools also suffered because of misconceptions about the role of the masses in the revolution—as did the mass organizations and the political apparatus of the revolution. Cadres were taken from the schools, from the mass organizations, and from the political committees in a policy that tended to produce permanent anemia, depriving all the organizations of their best leaders.* For example, it didn't seem at all strange when the director of a school was taken away to be appointed administrator of a warehouse, or when the secretary of a union section was appointed foreman of a machine shop. And that is nothing more than the result of a mistaken idea.

Either one has faith in the masses or one doesn't have faith in the masses. And from one's attitude toward the masses comes the method: a method that is either with the masses or against them. The anti-masses method is characterized by subjective selection, by "tapping," by self-importance on the part of officials who want to drag people along by their hair instead of leading and cultivating them.

Mistaken methods were leading us to form a party filled more and more with opportunists and mediocre people; in other words, there wasn't any party at all. Mistaken methods led us to spend millions and millions of pesos—pesos that came from the sweat of the workers—to "patch people up" and to educate not the working class but in many cases the petite bourgeoisie.

The Party and Revolutionary Education

Surely the task of revolutionary education has to be intimately linked with that of organizing the revolutionary vanguard by forming a party of the working class. The two activities are inseparable. Without a revolutionary party, without a revolutionary method, there can be no revolutionary education. And if there is no revolutionary education, there will be no revolutionary party.

A party of bureaucrats can be organized easily. Mechanical methods can be applied, to which revolutionary instruction will then respond. Education has to respond to that conception, because it cannot escape the consequences of those errors.

* Here Castro is referring to the selection policy practiced by certain discredited leaders of the ORI.

But as I said to the compañeros of the School of Revolutionary Instruction in the Province of Havana, the spirit of an office clerk who works in a ministry is not the same as that of a miner who works a thousand meters under the earth. We see this constantly. The spirit of the office worker is not the same as that of the peasant who climbs hills every day. This peasant, who is not a member of the proletariat but who has to face a hard and unyielding natural landscape, develops a firmer spirit, a greater capacity for self-denial, and a more pronounced capacity for sacrifice.

The selections for the schools were made by tapping: So-and-so is going to the provincial school; this other one is going to the national school. In absolutely no way were the characteristics, qualities, or merits of the individual person taken into account. Of course from time to time many good people were tapped, because among those tapped some were bound to be worthy. In the Party cells there were many good people who had gotten there by being tapped; but clearly their positions as members of cells had nothing to do with their behavior or their merits. It was simply that they were known; the one who had organized the cell knew that such a person existed. It had nothing to do with the masses or with the opinion of the masses. And so it happened with the schools. Clearly, all the efforts that the compañeros were putting forth in the schools were limited in their results by these methods.

Henceforth, the functions of the schools will be very different. From this moment on, the schools will cease to exist for patching people up. The schools must be converted into schools primarily for the working class.

The social composition in the schools is already changing, and in the future—as Compañero Lionel explained—80 percent of the students who go to the provincial schools will be selected from the basic schools on the basis of merit. To the basic schools will go the members of the Party cells and the best workers selected from each work center. That is, workers who are not members of the Party cells will be able to go to the basic schools. Even a worker who is not a member of a Party cell could conceivably be such a good student—so exact, so punctual, so clearly revolutionary in his behavior—that he would go to a provincial school.

The schools won't be only for the members of the Party cells. They will also exist to educate the masses, the working class. And they will serve to discover revolutionary minds and revolutionary characters. They will help fortify the revolutionary cells not only ideologically but also numerically.

The Schools Will Give No Privileges

Well now, what is one of the first things you have to explain to the students in each course? That the course is not going to give them any privileges or any special rights; that they are not going to emerge from the course as leaders simply because they have taken it; that the school is an opportunity for fortifying their political knowledge, but that when it is over they will return to the work centers from which they came. What happened in the case of one agricultural worker who went to the Sierra Maestra School must not happen again. After finishing the course, and upon finding himself with some compañeros back at the farm, he said to them, "Look, they've forgotten me here. I'm still digging with my hoe on this farm." This man passed a three-month course, and when he returned to the countryside he thought he was no longer required to work as he had before.

Even those who attend the provincial schools should remind themselves frequently that from there they will return to their work centers. After all, how could we possibly convert all nine hundred provincial school students into cadres? We did have to recruit many cadres and professors from the first courses, but this is not the function of the schools. Students will return from the provincial schools to their work centers. When the Party needs to convert a militant into a cadre, the best-prepared militant will of course be chosen. But this does not mean that as soon as one graduates from a school he automatically becomes a cadre. Rather, he returns to his Party cell or to his work center.

What the revolution wants is well-prepared workers in each work center—workers with a high level of political education, workers who can orient their compañeros and explain Socialism, who can argue with the defeatists and the ignorant, argue against the enemy, explain the intricacies of every problem, and explain the past, present, and future.

It is an elementary principle that neither the revolution nor the Party is an instrument of personal benefit. Clarify this for every student as the first principle: to be a revolutionary means abnegation, sacrifice, and humility; it means being first in the most difficult work, first in effort, and first in danger. Erase from the mind of each and every one any idea that the school and the Party are vehicles for personal benefit. They are *not* for exchanging hoes for tractors. No, hoes are exchanged for tractors in a school for tractor operators. One type of work is exchanged for another by improving one's technical skills, not by attending the Schools of Revolutionary Instruction or by belonging to the Party. The Party doesn't provide a sinecure. The Party requires sacrifice. One does not go to the Party in search of anything.

We ought to defend every revolutionary from those administrators who, when a student comes from the schools, want to take him away from his work and convert him into a boss or an administrator of something. Administrators who act this way are enemies of our effort to build a great revolutionary Party, because they encourage people to go to the schools just to better themselves at work when they return.

There are schools specifically for administrators: it is necessary to turn to the masses to find administrative cadres, because the masses are a great reservoir. But we must set up conditions to prevent a person from being promoted simply because he has been to a school for cadres or because he is from a Party cell. Moreover, each cell should strive to create conditions in the work center that permit any worker from the masses to be promoted to a more important administrative post because of his merits, his capacity, his qualities. It is important that any worker from the masses be allowed to rise, and that no worker see the Party cell as composed of privileged persons or as a springboard to personal advantage.

Cadres and Administrators

If at any given moment it becomes necessary to promote the most capable and knowledgeable worker in a department, and if that worker happens to be a militant from the Party cell, that's fine. But he should not be promoted just *because* he is a militant. Within this same department there might be someone who is not a militant, yet who has more knowledge and experience. In this case what should the militant do? He should advance the cause of the other. If they plan to promote him, the militant should say, "No, don't choose me. That compañero has more knowledge, he has more experience, and he can do the job better than I. He can't fill my shoes here as a militant and a soldier of the revolution, but he can fill the job of chief of this department or some other job in the productive process better than I."

These are the conditions we have to create in all the work centers. We must make sure that from the masses rise up the most worthy and those best suited for each task. It is inconceivable that if a theater lacked a violin player they would want to convert their janitor into a violinist just because he was the best militant of the revolutionary cell. They would have to look for a real violinist. The janitor would not do. If he had no ear for music, he should be made anything but a musician.

It will be our policy to preserve the cadres of the Party, of the mass organizations, and of the schools. When we lack an administrator for a factory, it is important that we do not take away a director of a school in order to put him in the factory. By doing this we would possibly be taking a compañero away from what he knows how to do and placing him in work that he does not know how to do. We have to defend the cadres of the schools. We have to defend the cadres of the mass organizations. And above all, we have to defend the political cadres, because they cannot be wasted or lost to the organization. It takes a great deal of effort and years of experience to make a good cadre. It would be an outrage and a mistake to take away the cadres.

The position of administrator is not the "ne plus ultra." It is clear that a bad administrator causes more damage than an elephant in a china shop; he fouls up the work of the mass organizations. He fouls up the work of the political cadres and the mass organizations frightfully. And what can an administrator accomplish alone—no matter what a marvelous administrator he may be—without a spirit of work among the workers? What can he accomplish if there is not a vanguard in his particular work center, if there is not someone to set the example and someone to set the pace? The position of a political cadre, of a cadre in a mass organization, has to be the highest honor the revolution can bestow on any revolutionary. And how much greater the honor is when that cadre is poorly paid. To a true revolutionary, income should not be important. To be a revolutionary means to march in the vanguard in everything.

The Schools and Class Warfare

Compañeros, directors, along with the first lessons—those to which we referred concerning the role of the school and the spirit of sacrifice with which one goes to the school and belongs to the Party—we should explain to the students that our revolution is going through a period of enflamed national and international class warfare. It is necessary to explain why there still exists a large rural bourgeoisie of middle-sized property owners; why there still exists a large urban bourgeoisie with cars, money, telephones, resources, gadgets, and a cultural style of their own. These are the people who harbor a profound class hatred of the proletariat. Their eyes are turned toward the foreigners, the enemies of the Fatherland. Their eyes are fixed on the might of imperialism; and they dream of tearing down the proletarian revolution and of reestablishing in our land their hated regime of exploitation, parasitism, hunger, and death. They would reestablish their heartless regime, in which the masses were obliged to live without a future and without hope.

Teach the students that a revolution is not completed on the first day, or in the first year, or in the second, third, fourth, or fifth. Teach them that the revolution is a long struggle, as was the battle to gain power, and that now that we are in power, we have to continue struggling harder and harder against that class, against its influence, and against its reactionary spirit. They are the ones who create difficulties. When we freed the peasants from restrictions and when we adopted measures that would help the peasants in the sale of their products, the bourgeoisie were the ones that paid ten pesos for a hen and fifty pesos for three turkeys. They are the ones who in these troubled times augment our difficulties by promoting speculation, by bribing, and by behaving like the parasites they are, feeding themselves at the expense of those who don't have cars, who don't have resources, and who can't pay fifty pesos for three turkeys.

And since our country is only ninety miles from Yankee imperialism and from the greatest reactionary power in the world, it is only natural that the bourgeoisie should feel hopeful and bold. For this reason, we must turn to the theory of the class struggle. We must give a clear explanation to the students, so that they won't have any of the illusions that have fooled many into thinking the revolution was just a stroll or that it was already completed. We must not be like those who fell into that unrealistic position, oblivious to the reality of history and to the essence of what a true revolution is. We have to struggle arduously and conquer formidable obstacles so that each student who leaves the schools will understand the stage in which we are living. Each student must understand this struggle and be able to explain the "why" of the revolution. It is necessary to create in every student who passes through the schools the consciousness of a true revolutionary, of a combative revolutionary, of a revolutionary ready at any moment to do battle.

It is the attitude of the convinced believer and the true defender of a cause not to look at how many enemies there are. Rather, he thinks about the cause he is defending, about his convictions, and about the interests he is protecting from the unhealthy interests of the enemies, from the turncoats, cowards, exploiters, and traitors.

The revolution today faces the class enemies of the proletariat, the lumpen bourgeoisie, the parasites of all types, the instruments of imperialism who are disposed to play the game of the imperialists that blockade us. Those are our enemies, and they will be so forever. And for the enemy, no consideration; for the compañero, every consideration. For the compañero peasant and for the compañero worker, for the one who works for society with his intelligence or with his muscle, our heart and our life. For the enemy wherever we meet him, our fist; for the enemy wherever we find him, destruction by our hardened hand.

You will understand from meditating on the problems of the revolutionary process that we must necessarily strengthen our mass organizations, our revolutionary apparatus, our cadres, and the ideological and political level of the masses.

The Revolution Advances

Compañeros and compañeras, the thrust of our revolution in these times is impressive. The advance of the people on all fronts is impressive, as is the effort being put forth at this moment in every sector. This very movement of revolutionary education is impressive. The number of schools for teaching Marxism and the tens of thousands of men and women passing through these schools exceed anything that we had dreamed of. Seldom has there been anywhere such a dizzy assent of the masses toward education and truth. All of it is impressive; and it is even more impressive when one thinks of the difficulties we face, of the booby traps imperialism has set.

It is clear that we have had—in the midst of our difficulties—more luck than other revolutions. We have had three and a half years in which to do this, whereas the Russian revolution, for example, had to spend its first three years on the battlefields combating foreign intervention. They were not able to do what we have been doing and are doing at this moment—giving a push to the revolutionary education of the masses. That allows us to strengthen ourselves; that permits us to give solidarity to the revolution; that enables the revolution to put down deep roots and to build a solid and indestructible base; that permits us to think of our revolution as an irreversible event, a shining episode in the history of our continent. It permits us to have more security and more faith in the final victory of our people.

We should explain, we should teach, and we should study. That way we shall be able to see more and teach more. We shall be able to understand reality, and there won't be any mystery for any of us about the revolutionary struggle. We shall know how to recognize our friends and our enemies, and how to recognize the allies of the working class in the smallholding peasantry, those admirable mountain peasants who have given to the armed forces of the revolution tens of thousands of valiant, stoic sons. We should know how to recognize this ally, and how to reinforce ourselves on every front of production in order to bring him clothes and shoes, doctors and medicine, teachers, and economic aid.

Clearly, we know that we don't have all the teachers we need or all the doctors we need. We know that there are teachers who offer classes barely two days a week and unworthy doctors who do not tend to the sick. We know it, but it doesn't matter. Not only are we making an effort to elevate the revolutionary consciousness of the teachers, but we are also making new generations of teachers, doctors, and technicians, just as we are making new generations of fishermen and administrative cadres. We are stimulating the future of our country with faith and conviction. We do not fool ourselves about today's difficulties, because we know that they will pass. Furthermore, we know that they give us honor and strength: the people are strengthened not by abundance but by sacrifice, by struggle, and by adversity.

Everything depends on what we ourselves understand and what we can make others understand. We know that a revolution is not a stroll or a bed of roses. It is a sacrifice, a hard and selfless struggle. We know that we do not live in normal times and that the revolution is a tremendous struggle, a war that changes its form, appearing sometimes as an armed struggle and at other times as a class struggle.

We also know that the people are unbreakable; that they are capable of the most unimaginable sacrifices; and that when the chickenhearted and the faithless begin to get weak in the knees, the people react with energy and efficiency against their enemies. Their enemies fortify them. The reaction of the people is not long in coming; already it is seen in all parts, and it will be seen more and more.

Compañeros, with this spirit of struggle, of combat, and of offense, you must begin this new step in the schools. With this spirit you must go to teach your students.

Fatherland or Death! We Shall Triumph!

APPENDIX E

Chronology of Organizational Events and Data on the Number of Students in the EIR

December 2, 1960:

First national meeting of the EIR. Castro, directors of the PSP and the 26th of July Movement, and the newly named directors and cadres of the first twelve provincial schools and the Ñico López School meet to launch the program.

January 1961:

First classes are held in the provincial and national schools. At this time there are twelve provincial schools with approximately seven hundred students in a three-month course and the one national school with sixty students in a six-month course. The provincial schools offer three courses a year, and the national school offers two.

April 26, 1961:

Third national meeting of the EIR. The program for the development of schools at the basic level (EBIR) is announced.

May 15, 1961:

The first EBIR open in Havana and Oriente, the boarding EBIR offering 45-day courses and the part-time boarding schools offering 60-day courses.

August 1961:

The special national school for teachers opens, the first of a series of specialized national EIR.

January 1962:

The Ñico López School begins offering an eight-month course; other special national schools begin operating as shown in Table

7; the provincial schools begin offering two five-month courses each year; the EBIR lengthen their courses, some to two months, others to three months.

June 12, 1962:

An official circular, signed by Castro and Soto, centralizes the direction of the EIR, outlines new procedures for selecting students, and defines the criteria for inclusion in the EIR system. These and other changes are announced after Castro's speech of June 27.

June 27, 1962:

Castro speaks to the seventh national meeting of the EIR and attacks the errors of selection, management, and policy that have existed in the schools.

August 1962:

The special national schools of the Federation of Cuban Women, the Committees for Defense of the Revolution, and the Association of Small Farmers open with three-month courses.

January 1963:

The Ñico López School lengthens its course of study from eight to ten and a half months. The provincial schools of the UJC are brought formally into the EIR system, offering two five-month courses a year. The rural EBIR are retained as boarding schools, and all urban EBIR are made night schools. The normal EBIR course of study is set at three months.

October 1963:

The first issue of the monthly bulletin *Theory and Practice* is published.

November 28–December 1, 1963:

Tenth national meeting of the EIR. Plans for beginning the political-technical cycle in the schools are announced. Plans for developing the capacity to conduct social science research in the EIR are also announced.

January 1964:

Because the new curriculum (which includes technical education) is more demanding, the courses in the basic schools have been extended to five months for 1964. Also, those national schools that have had courses of three or three and a half months will now also have five-month courses. The provincial schools begin a nine-month course. The Ñico López School begins a year-and-a-half course. The Marx-Engels-Lenin School is established. Its purpose is to educate the cadres of the EIR.

January 1965:

The 30 EBIR boarding schools begin a ten-and-a-half-month course. The other EBIR continue with two five-month courses a year. The provincial Party schools, the provincial UJC schools, and the special national schools begin ten-and-a-half-month courses. The Ñico López School will begin a two-year course after the current class graduates in June 1965.

The Plan for Technical Education in Soils, Fertilizers, and Cattle goes into operation under the National Directorate of the EIR. The special national school for agricultural workers becomes a technological institute under the Plan, as do other training centers not previously associated with the EIR.

The National Commission of Social Research and Studies begins to function under the National Directorate of the EIR.

Autumn 1965:

The first two monographs from the commission of social research of the EIR are published. One concerns costs in the sugar industry, and the other concerns the founding of the Communist Party in 1925.

November 1965:

The Marx-Engels-Lenin School is incorporated into the Ñico López School. The National CTC-R School for high labor officials is incorporated into the other CTC-R national school as a special, advanced course. The provincial schools of the UJC cease to function as such. The special national school for the Federation of Cuban Women is closed.

November 1966:

The national schools of the CDR and the teachers are closed. Henceforth, CDR and teacher cadres will go to the regular Party EIR.

November 1967–February 1968:

The entire EIR system is phased out.

Graduates of Schools of Revolutionary Instruction and Academic Years of Instruction Represented by Those Graduates, 1961–66

Year	Basic schools	Provincial Party schools	Provincial UJC schools	National schools	Total graduates for each year
1961					
No. of graduates	16,661	2,061	did not	219	18,941
Academic years	2,777	687	operate	83	3,547
1962					
No. of graduates	31,070	1,661	did not	3,756	36,487
Academic years	7,767	830	operate	1,332	9,929
1963					
No. of graduates	25,524	1,532	880	3,759	31,695
Academic years	8,508	766	440	1,334	11,048
1964					
No. of graduates	19,100	879	610	2,125	22,714
Academic years	9,550	879	610	1,092	12,131
1965					
No. of graduates	15,101	797	358	708	16,964
Academic years	8,739	797	358	708	10,602
1966					
No. of graduates	16,276	779	special	609	17,664
Academic years	9,458	779	courses only	609	10,846
Total graduates	123,732	7,709	1,848	11,176	144,465
Total academic years	46,799	4,738	1,408	5,158	58,103

Note: The number of academic years of instruction represented by the graduates is an estimate based on the length of the courses offered. For instance, in 1962 the basic schools offered both two-month and three-month courses; if we take two and a half months as the average course length and ten months as the academic year, the 31,070 students thus represent approximately 7,767 academic years. For purposes of this table, the academic year varies from nine to ten and a half months, depending on the school cycle in operation. Consult the chronology of organizational events for more information on these school cycles.

The total number of graduates of the national schools in 1962, 1963, and 1964 was inflated by the existence of the national Sierra Maestra School for agricultural workers from the granjas del pueblo, or people's farms. In 1962, for example, 2,356 students graduated from the three three-and-one-half-month courses in this school. The academic work in the Sierra Maestra School was roughly at the level of the work in a basic school, owing to the generally low educational level of the workers who attended.

The total number of graduates for each type of school except the basic schools is affected by the fact that many if not most of those who attended provincial and national schools had also attended other schools lower in the hierarchy. Thus, although by 1966 there had been more than 144,000 graduations from *all* schools, the actual number of Cubans who had attended a school for revolutionary instruction was somewhat lower (although clearly higher than the 123,732 who had attended the basic schools).

Sources: Data for 1961 and 1963 are from Lionel Soto, "Las Escuelas de Instrucción Revolucionaria en una nueva fase," *Cuba Socialista,* No. 30 (Feb. 1964), p. 75. Data for 1962 are from Lionel Soto, "Dos años de instrucción revolucionaria," *Cuba Socialista,* No. 18 (Feb. 1963), p. 33. Data for 1964 are from Lionel Soto, "Las Escuelas de Instrucción Revolucionaria en el ciclo político-técnico," *Cuba Socialista,* No. 41 (Jan. 1965), p. 72. Data for 1965 are from Lionel Soto, "El quinto aniversario de las Escuelas de Instrucción Revolucionaria," *Cuba Socialista,* No. 53 (Jan. 1966), p. 84. Data for 1966 are from Lionel Soto, "Lo importante es que desarrollemos nuestro camino," *Cuba Socialista,* No. 65 (Jan. 1967), p. 40.

Notes

Notes

EVEN AS the Cuban Revolution moves into its second decade, primary source materials and official publications of the Revolutionary Government are not always easy to find in the United States. When possible, therefore, I have limited references to Cuban periodicals to those few that are most readily available: *Revolución* and *Granma* (available on microfilm from the Library of Congress), *El Mundo* (available from the Foreign Newspaper Microfilm Project of the University of Chicago), and *Cuba Socialista* (available on microfilm from the Hoover Library at Stanford University). Except for *Con la Guardia en Alto* (of which the cited issues are available on microfilm from the University of Florida Library, Gainesville), the Cuban publications mentioned in the notes are held either in the Hoover Library at Stanford or in the author's own collection.

In general, the best guide to the official publications of the Revolutionary Government is Carmelo Mesa-Lago, "Availability and Reliability of Statistics in Socialist Cuba," *Latin American Research Review*, IV, 1 (Spring 1969), 53–91, continued in *Latin American Research Review*, IV, 2 (Fall 1969).

Book epigraph: *Granma*, Weekly Review, Dec. 15, 1968, p. 3.

Chapter 1

Epigraph: Eric Hoffer, *The True Believer* (New York, 1958), p. 71.

1. Universidad Popular, 6th Series, *Educación y Revolución* (Havana: Imprenta Nacional de Cuba, Apr. 1961), p. 271.

2. This definition is modified from Fred I. Greenstein, "Political So-

cialization," in *International Encyclopedia of the Social Sciences,* XIV (New York, 1968), 534. The full statement by Greenstein is as follows: "Narrowly conceived, political socialization is the deliberate inculcation of political information, values, and practices by instructional agents who have been formally charged with this responsibility. A broader conception would encompass all political learning, formal and informal, deliberate and unplanned, at every stage of the life cycle, including not only explicitly political learning but also nominally nonpolitical learning that affects political behavior, such as the learning of politically relevant social attitudes and the acquisition of politically relevant personality characteristics." Notice that we have favored the narrower conception of political socialization while still insisting that inculcation can be either formal or informal, planned or unplanned. See also Richard E. Dawson and Kenneth Prewitt, *Political Socialization* (Boston, 1969); Jack Dennis, "Major Problems of Political Socialization Research," *Midwest Journal of Political Science,* XII, (Feb. 1968), 85–114; and Herbert H. Hyman, *Political Socialization* (Glencoe, Ill., 1959).

3. The phrase is taken from Charles Edward Merriam's early classic, *The Making of Citizens* (Chicago, 1931).

4. Sidney Verba, "Comparative Political Culture," in Lucian W. Pye and Sidney Verba, eds., *Political Culture and Political Development* (Princeton, N.J., 1965), p. 513. Gabriel A. Almond and Sidney Verba, in *The Civic Culture: Political Attitudes and Democracy in Five Nations* (Princeton, N.J., 1963), p. 14, stress that they "employ the concept of culture in only one of its many meanings: that of *psychological orientation toward social objects.*" (Italics in the original.) Similarly, J. P. Nettl, in *Political Mobilization* (New York, 1967), pp. 26–27, argues that the concept of political culture is most useful when limited to orientations that predispose one to action.

5. See, for instance, the view of culture developed in George M. Foster, *Traditional Cultures and the Impact of Technological Change* (New York, 1962), chap. 1. The quotation is from p. 11.

6. How contrary this is to the main current of anthropological thinking can be seen in the following definition of culture by Anthony F. C. Wallace, as quoted from his own earlier work in *Culture and Personality* (New York, 1961), p. 6: "*those ways of behavior or techniques of solving problems* which, being more frequently and more closely approximated than other ways, can be said to have a high probability of use by individual members of society." (Italics mine.)

7. It should be noted that once research is begun it is difficult to maintain a neat analytical distinction between psychological orientations and the patterns of behavior related to them. Thus in *The Civic Culture,* pp. 231–32, Almond and Verba measure subjective political competence

(a psychological variable) with a Guttman scale constructed out of two opinion questions, two projective questions, and one behavioral question ("Have you ever done anything to try to influence a local regulation?"). The fact that this fifth item scales with the other four tells us something about the Guttman technique and the empirical relationship between attitudes and political behavior (in this arena of action), and also reminds us how easily even the purists slip into a view of political culture that includes action components as well as psychological components.

8. In viewing this aspect of the Cuban Revolution I have been more heavily influenced by Anthony F. C. Wallace than by any other single author. In his classic paper on "Revitalization Movements," *American Anthropologist*, LVIII (1956), Wallace formulates the concept as follows (p. 265): "A revitalization movement is defined as a *deliberate, organized conscious effort by members of a society to construct a more satisfying culture.* Revitalization is thus, from a cultural standpoint, a special kind of culture change phenomenon: the persons involved in the process of revitalization must perceive their culture, or some major areas of it, as a system (whether accurately or not); they must feel that this cultural system is unsatisfactory; and they must innovate not merely discrete items, but a new cultural system, specifying new relationships as well as, in some cases, new traits." (Italics mine.) Later we shall be more specific about how the transformation of political culture relates to and forms a part of the transformation of the larger cultural system.

9. Viewing political culture exclusively in psychological terms leads very naturally to viewing political socialization in exactly the same terms. See, for example, Gabriel A. Almond and G. Bingham Powell, Jr., *Comparative Politics, A Developmental Approach* (Boston, 1966), chap. 3, esp. pp. 64–66. It is our argument that such psychological formulations of political socialization, unlike Greenstein's (quoted in n. 2 above), lead one to an excessively narrow examination of processes of political learning, particularly in the Cuban situation, where directed socialization for the purpose of culture change is at the heart of the operation of the political system.

10. See Neil J. Smelser's typology of social movements, and particularly his concept of the value-oriented movement, as developed in chap. 10 of his *Theory of Collective Behavior* (New York, 1963). Smelser is heavily influenced by Wallace's formulation of the revitalization movement. In Smelser's typology the value-oriented movement is the most profound of all social movements because it seeks to reorder the fundamental patterns of belief in a society.

11. In thinking about the interrelationships of participation, new institutions, and political socialization under conditions of rapid and planned change, I have been helped by consulting the rich literature

on contemporary China, particularly Franz Schurmann, *Ideology and Organization in Communist China* (Berkeley, Calif., 1966); James R. Townsend, *Political Participation in Communist China* (Berkeley, Calif., 1967); Frederick T. C. Yu, *Mass Persuasion in Communist China* (New York, 1964); and Frederick T. C. Yu, "Campaigns, Communications, and Development in Communist China," and Robert M. Worth, "Strategy of Change in the People's Republic of China," both in Daniel Lerner and Wilbur Schramm, eds., *Communication and Change in the Developing Countries* (Honolulu, 1967). Significant differences in culture, the scale of national politics, and the ideological thoroughness and clarity of the two ruling elites make direct comparisons of the Chinese and Cuban cases difficult. However, both China scholars and Chinese rulers have thought and written much more about these matters than their Cuban counterparts. For this reason, if for no other, the Chinese case is useful to students of the Cuban Revolution. For more bibliography and information on the Chinese case, see the review article by John W. Lewis, "The Study of Chinese Political Culture," *World Politics*, XXVIII (1966), 503–24.

12. Seymour Martin Lipset, Martin Trow, and James Coleman, *Union Democracy* (New York, 1962), p. 88.

13. For elaboration of these points, see Richard R. Fagen, Richard A. Brody, and Thomas O'Leary, *Cubans in Exile: Disaffection and the Revolution* (Stanford, Calif., 1968), chap. 7. It might be argued that in the Cuban case, as the system settled down to "revolutionary politics as usual" (after most of the major changes had already been introduced), controlled participation became more important in the management of discontent—if only because discontent was by then more widespread.

14. See Nettl, *Political Mobilization*, chap. 9. Nettl's usage of the concept of mobilization refers to a much wider range of phenomena than is referred to here. Similarly, David E. Apter's concept of the "mobilization system" involves a usage that includes but is much broader than ours. As Apter develops the concept it bears striking similarities to a political revitalization movement and thus relates to our understanding of the Cuban Revolution. Paradoxically, Apter's concept of the mobilization system was developed out of his African experience, but Cuba fits the model much more closely than any of the African states. For the most precise formulation, see his "Political Religion in the New Nations," in Clifford Geertz, ed., *Old Societies and New States* (New York, 1963), esp. p. 78. I have used Apter's formulation in an earlier attempt to analyze the Cuban Revolution. See my "Mass Mobilization in Cuba: The Symbolism of Struggle," *Journal of International Affairs*, XX (1966), 254–71.

15. There is evidence from the social sciences that the strategy of directed cultural change as practiced in Cuba and other Leninist systems

promises to give results precisely because it violates certain democratic values and procedures regarding the context in which participation should take place. For elaboration and bibliography, see Ithiel de Sola Pool, "The Mass Media and Politics in the Modernization Process," in Lucian W. Pye, ed., *Communications and Political Development* (Princeton, N.J., 1963); and Ithiel de Sola Pool, "The Role of Communication in the Process of Modernization and Technological Change," in Bert F. Hoselitz and Wilbert E. Moore, eds., *Industrialization and Society* (Paris: UNESCO, 1963).

16. No one has exploited this rich vein of contradictions as pointedly as Theodore Draper in *Castro's Revolution: Myth's and Realities* (New York, 1962) and *Castroism: Theory and Practice* (New York, 1965). It can be argued, however, that if consistency tests of the sort applied by Draper to the Cuban Revolution were to be used in general as the primary standard of evaluation for revolutionary movements (and many non-revolutionary movements), few would fare much better than the Cuban. Furthermore, it might well be that the most consistent movements have attained their consistency by being relentlessly ruthless and dogmatic in the Stalinist tradition. It would seem that Draper really rejects the Cuban experience because it was anti-democratic (as he defines the term), not because it was inconsistent or particularly dishonest. He would not have liked it any better had it shown its "true colors" from the beginning.

17. By ideology is meant a symbol system that "links particular actions and mundane practices with a wider set of meanings." The formulation is Apter's from David E. Apter, ed., *Ideology and Discontent* (New York, 1964), p. 16. See also the penetrating essay by Clifford Geertz, "Ideology as a Cultural System," in the same volume. Franz Schurmann, in *Ideology and Organization*, p. 18, defines an organizational ideology as "a systematic set of ideas with action consequences serving the purpose of creating and using organization." His definition is not at all inconsistent with Apter's, although it ties the symbols or ideas much more closely to the organizational setting that they serve and from which they derive. The Cuban leadership has been less self-conscious and concerned about organizational life than the Chinese leaders. As a consequence, the nexus between organization and ideology was initially and still remains considerably looser in Cuba than in China.

This and the following paragraph have been freely adapted from pp. 225–30 of my "The Cuban Revolution: Enemies and Friends," in David J. Finlay, Ole R. Holsti, and Richard R. Fagen, *Enemies in Politics* (Chicago, 1967). In the same essay I have presented ten revolutionary poems that give some feeling for the public language of struggle and the millennium as it was used in the early 1960's. It should be emphasized that this symbol system can be fully understood only in the context of Cuba and the revolution. The power of these symbols to evoke and condition action in the setting of which they form a part seems much underestimated and misunderstood in the United States.

18. It is in the nature of the culture-transforming movements that we have called revitalization movements (following Wallace) that they include millennial elements—a vision of a "perfect" new order totally different from the old—in their motivating system of symbols. This point has been made by Smelser, among others, in his discussion of value-oriented movements in *Theory of Collective Behavior.* Much interesting and relevant case material is presented in Norman Cohn, *The Pursuit of the Millennium: Revolutionary Messianism in Medieval and Reformation Europe and Its Bearing on Modern Totalitarian Movements* (New York, 1961). The symbolism of struggle is less generic to revitalization movements considered as a class, although it always seems to be manifest in revolutionary politics as a subtype. Wallace, in *Culture and Personality*, p. 148, differentiates the "goal culture" of a revitalization movement from its "transfer culture": "An individual, or a group of individuals, constructs a new, utopian image of socio-cultural organization. This model is a blueprint of an ideal society or 'goal culture.' Contrasted with the goal culture is the existing culture, which is presented as inadequate or evil in certain respects. Connecting the existing culture and the goal culture is a transfer culture: a system of operations which, if faithfully carried out, will transform the existing culture into the goal culture." The millennial vision informs the goal culture and thus is common to all revitalization movements. Struggle is only one of several ways in which the transfer culture can be conceptualized by elites.

19. On the meanings of the concept of modal personality, see Wallace, *Culture and Personality*, Introduction, and the partial criticism of the concept in chap. 3, "The Cultural Distribution of Personality Characteristics." Modal personality, as used here, is very similar to Erich Fromm's concept of "social character," those "relatively permanent passionate strivings" shaped by the social structures in which men live. For a brief explication of Fromm's idea, see Michael Maccoby, "On Mexican National Character," *Annals*, CCCLXX (Mar. 1967), 63–73, particularly the literature cited on pp. 64–65.

20. From Castro's speech on the fourth anniversary of the founding of the Committees for Defense of the Revolution, given on Sept. 28, 1964 (see Chapter 4 below), as reported in *Revolución*, Sept. 29, 1964, p. 3.

21. From Castro's speech on the eleventh anniversary of the student attack on the Presidential Palace, given on Mar. 13, 1968, as reported in *Granma*, Weekly Review (in English), Mar. 24, 1968, p. 7. Since approximately the beginning of 1964, quotations like this abound in the speeches

of the revolutionary leaders. Perhaps the most complete early statement can be found in Ernesto Che Guevara, *El Socialismo y el Hombre en Cuba* (Havana: Ediciones R, 1965). This essay was first written in the form of a continuing letter to the director of *Marcha* (Montevideo) while Guevara was on an extended tour of African countries during the first three months of 1965. The most complete ideological airing of problems in the formation of "new men" came during the international "Cultural Congress" held in Havana in January 1968. For relevant documents, see *Revolución y Cultura,* Year 1, no. 5 (Feb. 29, 1968), and *Revolución y Cultura,* Year 1, no. 6 (Mar. 15, 1968). On Nov. 2, 1967, Dr. Osvaldo Dorticós addressed the planning session of the Cultural Congress in a speech that contained many relevant passages; see "Discurso pronunciado por el doctor Osvaldo Dorticós Torrado en la clausura del seminario previo al Congreso Cultural de la Habana," as edited and distributed by the National Council of Culture, Havana.

22. Edward Boorstein, in his discussion of the "moral versus material incentives" controversy in *The Economic Transformation of Cuba* (New York, 1968), p. 286, quotes the following passage from Lenin: "It [volunteer labor] is the beginning of a revolution that is much more difficult, more material, more radical and more decisive than the overthrow of the bourgeoisie, for it is a victory over personal conservativeness, indiscipline, petty-bourgeois egoism, a victory over the habits that accursed capitalism left as a heritage to the worker and peasant. Only when *this* victory is consolidated will the new social discipline, Socialist discipline, be created." The Cubans did not begin to echo Lenin's language directly before the end of 1963, but from the end of 1959 they were occasionally saying much the same thing in a different vocabulary and acting accordingly.

23. This is the political variant of what Smelser calls the inclusiveness of value-oriented movements. See Smelser, *Theory of Collective Behavior,* p. 313; Apter, "Political Religion in the New Nations"; and Wallace "Revitalization Movements," pp. 264–67.

24. Resocialization ideas and practices in Cuba tend to make "good sense" in terms of what is generally known about changing adult behavior. See, for instance, the brief discussion in Robert Levine, "Political Socialization and Culture Change," in Geertz, *Old Societies and New States,* esp. pp. 301–3.

25. *Granma,* Sept. 27, 1966, p. 2.

Chapter 2

1. See "The Integrative Revolution," in Clifford Geertz, ed., *Old Societies and New States* (New York, 1963).

2. See, for example, Wyatt MacGaffey and Clifford R. Barnett, *Cuba:*

Its People, Its Society, Its Culture (New Haven, Conn., 1962), esp. pp. 31–33; Lowry Nelson, *Rural Cuba* (Minneapolis, Minn., 1950), esp. pp. 154–59; and Maurice Zeitlin, *Revolutionary Politics and the Cuban Working Class* (Princeton, N.J., 1967), chap. 3, and the references cited therein.

3. Theodore Draper, *Castroism: Theory and Practice* (New York, 1965), pp. 97–103. See also Boris Goldenberg, *The Cuban Revolution and Latin America* (New York, 1965), pp. 120–31; and Hugh Thomas, "Middle-Class Politics and the Cuban Revolution," in Claudio Véliz, ed., *The Politics of Conformity in Latin America* (New York, 1967). In his polemical but perceptive essay, Thomas goes to some length to point out the "specialness" of Cuba when compared with the other nations of Latin America.

4. Although based on research conducted in 1946, the best account of the pre-Castro Cuban countryside is still Lowry Nelson, *Rural Cuba.* Rufo López-Fresquet, in *My Fourteen Months with Castro* (Cleveland, Ohio, 1966), p. 10, cites a study done by a private Catholic organization before Batista fled: "The rural per capita income was $91.25. Of the rural families, only 11 per cent drank milk and only 4 per cent ate meat. Thirty-six per cent of the country people suffered from intestinal parasites and 14 per cent from tuberculosis. Forty-three per cent were illiterate, and 88 per cent of those who had gone to school had not passed the third grade. Sixty-six per cent of the rural houses had dirt floors; only 2.3 per cent had running water, and only 9.1 per cent electricity." The design of this study is not discussed further, but López-Fresquet, who was Castro's first Minister of the Treasury and who went into exile in 1960, accepts it as accurately representing conditions in the Cuban countryside in the 1950's.

5. For documentation of this characterization of the Cuban economy, see MacGaffey and Barnett, chaps. 3 and 7; Goldenberg, Part II, chap. 2; Alvarez Díaz et al., *Un Estudio Sobre Cuba* (Miami, 1963), chaps. 32–41; Dudley Seers, ed., *Cuba, The Economic and Social Revolution* (Chapel Hill, N.C., 1946), chaps. 1 and 2; Robert F. Smith, *The United States and Cuba: Business and Diplomacy, 1917–1960* (New York, 1960), *passim*; Robin Blackburn, "The Economics of the Cuban Revolution," in Claudio Véliz, ed., *Latin America and the Caribbean: A Handbook* (New York, 1968); and the literature cited in all of the above.

6. The phrase gained wide currency with the publication of a new children's geography in 1961. See Antonio Núñez Jiménez, *Así es mi país* (La Habana: Imprenta Nacional de Cuba, 1961), esp. lesson 14. Interestingly enough, Núñez Jiménez seems to have taken the expression from Nelson, *Rural Cuba,* whose first chapter was entitled "Rich Land—Poor People."

7. Sidney W. Mintz, "Foreword," in Ramiro Guerra y Sánchez, *Sugar*

and Society in the Caribbean (New Haven, Conn., 1964), p. xxxvi. See also Zeitlin, pp. 144–49, for a discussion of the special characteristics of the Cuban peasantry, their susceptibility to radical politics before the revolution, and their openness to reform measures after Castro came to power. Zeitlin has elaborated this argument in more detail in "Cuba—Revolution Without a Blueprint," *Trans-Action*, VI, 6 (Apr. 1969), 38–42, 61. Those who traveled in the Cuban countryside before 1959 were struck by how intimately linked to the modern sector the Cuban peasant was even though he was unable to partake of its material benefits.

8. Felipe Pazos, before his exile the director of the Banco Nacional de Cuba under Castro, estimated that in the first three months of 1959 there was a "redistribution of income from the propertied classes to the working classes of probably fifteen percent or more of National Income." As quoted in Zeitlin, p. 274. For an insider's view of how the Cuban economy "made progress" during the first years of the revolution by living off its reserves, see Edward Boorstein, *The Economic Transformation of Cuba* (New York, 1968), esp. chaps. 3 and 4.

9. One of the non-Cubans who knows Castro best, Herbert L. Matthews, in *The Cuban Story* (New York, 1961), pp. 162, 149, described Castro as follows: "He is impetuous and, as I said, highly emotional, the reverse of a cold and calculating thinker.... He relies on intuition, instinct, flare, guided—if at all—by a very considerable intelligence.... His is a character of such complexity, such contradiction, such emotionalism, such irrationality, such unpredictability, that no one can really know him." See also Herbert L. Matthews, *Fidel Castro* (New York, 1969), chap. 2. There are no scholarly book-length biographies of Castro, and although he has been promising an autobiography for several years, it has not yet appeared. An extremely useful and insightful portrait is drawn in Lee Lockwood, *Castro's Cuba, Cuba's Fidel* (New York, 1967). In addition see Leslie Dewart, *Christianity and Revolution* (New York, 1963), chap. 2. Even among those who despise the revolution, the more thoughtful generally consider Castro a man of extraordinary character. For instance, Philip W. Bonsal, United States Ambassador in Havana during 1959 and 1960, calls Castro "phenomenally gifted, [although] erratic and unscrupulous." See his "Cuba, Castro and the United States," *Foreign Affairs*, XL (1967), 260–76.

10. I have enlarged on this theme and presented supportive data in "Charismatic Authority and the Leadership of Fidel Castro," *Western Political Quarterly*, XVIII (1965), 275–84.

11. See Richard R. Fagen, Richard A. Brody, and Thomas O'Leary, *Cubans in Exile: Disaffection and the Revolution* (Stanford, Calif., 1968), esp. chap. 2, for data on the sociological characteristics of the exiles and comparisons with the total Cuban population, and chap. 7, on the "costs" to the revolution of the outflow of exiles.

12. See Sidney Hook, *The Hero in History: A Study in Limitation and Possibility* (Boston, 1955). In chap. 10, Hook imagines "A World Without Lenin" in order to demonstrate the impact of the event-making man on the course of history. Those who question the centrality of Castro to the Cuban Revolution, preferring to see only "larger" forces at work, might attempt a similar exercise entitled "A Cuba Without Castro."

13. The best brief discussion of the relevance of this period to the Cuban Revolution is C. A. M. Hennessy, "The Roots of Cuban Nationalism," *International Affairs* (Toronto, XXXIX, 1963), 345–59. In the first part of this section I have drawn freely on pp. 220–23 of my "The Cuban Revolution: Enemies and Friends," in David Finlay, Ole Holsti, and Richard R. Fagen, *Enemies in Politics* (Chicago, 1967). For more detail, see the relevant sections of Charles E. Chapman, *A History of the Cuban Republic* (New York, 1927). For book-length interpretations of nationalism, anti-Americanism, and the revolution, see Ramon Eduardo Ruiz, *Cuba: The Making of a Revolution* (Amherst, Mass., 1968); and Lester D. Langley, *The Cuban Policy of the United States* (New York, 1968).

14. See Smith, *The United States and Cuba*, and Leland L. Johnson, "U.S. Business Interests in Cuba and the Rise of Castro," *World Politics*, XVII (1965), 440–59.

15. Draper, p. 7. See also Jaime Suchlicki, "Stirrings of Cuban Nationalism: The Student Generation of 1930," *Journal of Inter-American Studies*, X (1968), 350–68.

16. Quoted in Smith, p. 103.

Chapter 3

1. United Nations, *Official Records of the General Assembly, Fifteenth Session*, Part I, *Plenary Meetings*, Vol. I, *Verbatim Records* (New York, Sept. 20–Oct. 17, 1960), pp. 117–36. The quoted material appears on p. 126.

2. Fidel Castro, *La Historia Me Absolverá* (Havana: Ediciones Populares, 1961), p. 68.

3. "Manifiesto político-social desde la Sierra Maestra," in Fidel Castro, *La Revolución Cubana* (Buenos Aires: Editorial Palestra, 1960), p. 122. An English version of the Manifesto is available in Jules Dubois, *Fidel Castro* (Indianapolis, Ind., 1959), pp. 166–72.

4. *Revolución*, Sept. 7, 1961, p. 6. See also Gaspar J. García Galló, "La lucha contra el analfabetismo en Cuba," *Cuba Socialista*, No. 2 (Oct. 1961), esp. pp. 71–72.

5. As summarized by Richard Jolly, "Education: The Pre-Revolutionary Background," chap. 4 in Dudley Seers, ed., *Cuba: The Economic and Social Revolution* (Chapel Hill, N.C., 1964), pp. 164–67. This chapter is

the best brief English-language introduction to the pre-revolutionary educational situation in Cuba.

6. *Ibid.*, p. 173.

7. *Ibid.*, estimated from data on pp. 170–75.

8. In International Bank for Reconstruction and Development, *Report on Cuba* (Washington, D.C., 1951), p. 425, a Minister of Education is quoted as saying that the Ministry was "an opprobrium and a shame and, in addition, a dangerous menace to the Cuban nation. It was a cave of entrenched bandits and of gunmen and an asylum of professional highway robbers."

9. The best single English-language source on Cuban (revolutionary) education through the summer of 1962 is Jolly, chaps. 5–8. Much the same period is covered in Comisión Nacional Cubana de la UNESCO, *Cuba y la conferencia de educación y desarrollo económico y social* (Havana: Editorial Nacional de Cuba, 1962). For a brief review of this period from the point of view of Cuban exiles, see José R. Alvarez Díaz, ed., *Un Estudio Sobre Cuba* (Miami, 1963), pp. 1526–34. A number of important articles on revolutionary education have been published in *Cuba Socialista*. In chronological order these are Armando Hart, "La Revolución y los problemas de la educación," No. 4 (Dec. 1961), pp. 33–58; Carlos Rafael Rodríguez, "La reforma universitaria," No. 6 (Feb. 1962), pp. 22–44; José Altshuler, "La enseñanza tecnológica universitaria y nuestro desarrollo económico," No. 8 (Apr. 1962), pp. 13–24; Armando Hart, "El desarrollo de la educación en la período revolucionario," No. 17 (Jan. 1963), pp. 20–39; Armando Hart, "La educación ante la revolución científico-técnica," No. 32 (Apr. 1964), pp. 1–21; Armando Hart, "La enseñanza técnica y profesional de nivel medio y universitario," No. 33 (May 1964), pp. 25–41; María de los Angeles Periú, "Experiencias de la educación obrera y campesina en Cuba," No. 42 (Feb. 1965), pp. 18–38. In the weekly magazine *Bohemia*, Gustavo Torroella has published a number of popular articles that deal with the philosophical underpinnings of revolutionary education as understood by the Cubans. See for instance, "¿A dónde va la neuva educación?," Part I (Nov. 11, 1966), pp. 106 et seq.; Part II (Nov. 18, 1966), pp. 24 et seq.; and Part III (Nov. 25, 1966), pp. 20 et seq. See also, by the same author in the same magazine, "Cuba: avanzada educacional mundial," Part I (Jan. 20, 1967), pp. 106 et seq.; and Part II (Jan. 27, 1967), pp. 22 et seq. A wealth of material on the organization, budgets, plans, ideology, and scale of the educational effort can be found in the various "informes" of the Ministry of Education of Cuba. See, for instance, *Informe a la XXVII conferencia internacional de instrucción pública convocada por la OIE y la UNESCO* (Havana: Ministry of Education, 1964), and publications bearing the same title for the 28th and 29th conferences, published in 1965 and 1966;

also *Informe a la conferencia de ministros de educación y ministros encargados del planeamiento económico en los países de América Latina y del Caribe, Buenos Aires, 20–30 de Junio, 1966* (Havana: Ministry of Education, 1966). For key fragments of some of Castro's early speeches on education, see *Casa de las Américas,* Year II, No. 9 (Nov.–Dec. 1961), pp. 3–37.

10. Comisión Nacional Cubana de la UNESCO, p. 25. The central passages dealing with "the content and orientation of education" in this report are translated in Jolly, pp. 348–51.

11. Certainly the deeply felt belief that one did not have to be a "professional" in order to teach literacy derives from the guerrilla period. In fact, what one needed (according to this view) was to be profoundly revolutionary and highly motivated toward the betterment of the masses, qualities not usually acquired in "normal" professional training. The *ambiente,* or atmosphere, of the Sierra during the guerrilla stage and the way the experience shaped the leadership's perceptions of the role and possibilities of mass organization are best captured by Ernesto Che Guevara in his *Pasajes de la Guerra Revolucionaria* (Havana: Ediciones Unión, 1963). These essays and others are available in translation as Ernesto Che Guevara, *Reminiscences of the Cuban Revolutionary War* (New York, 1968). Out of the work in political education and literacy in the Sierra came the Armed Forces training booklet known as the *Manual de Capacitación Cívica* (Havana: Department of Instruction, Ministry of the Armed Forces, 1960). Many of the themes emphasized in the political materials used in the literacy campaign were first worked out in written form in this manual.

The Cubans are fond of tracing aspects of the literacy campaign to the thought and practice of José Martí. See, for instance, "Maestros Ambulantes," *Trabajo,* Jan. 1961, pp. 40–43, in which one of Martí's essays is reprinted and characterized as a precursor of the educational efforts of 1961. It is from this essay, written in 1884, that the saying "Ser culto es el único modo de ser libre" (To be educated is the only way to be free)—one of the central slogans of the campaign—was taken. The symbolic and philosophical importance of Martí is undeniable, but the organizational style that characterized the literacy campaign grew chiefly out of the experience in the Sierra.

12. See García Galló, pp. 74–75, and Republic of Cuba, Ministry of Education, *Report on the Method and Means Utilized in Cuba to Eliminate Illiteracy* (Havana: Editora Pedagógica, 1965), pp. 17–18. This Cuban English-language publication contains the final report of two UNESCO experts, Mrs. Anna Lorenzetto and Professor Karel Neys, who were invited to Cuba to evaluate the literacy campaign. Hereafter cited as *The Method and Means.*

13. Armando Hart, "Sobre el Año de la Educación," in Universidad Popular Sexto Ciclo *Educación y Revolución* (Havana: Imprenta Nacional, 1961), p. 14. A fictionalized, semiautobiographical account of the impact of the "revolutionary bath" on a city girl can be found in Daura Olema, *Maestra Voluntaria* (Havana: Casa de las Américas, 1962). It is the story of the transformation of a proper middle-class Cuban girl into a revolutionary at a training camp for voluntary teachers in the Sierra Maestra.

14. The official estimate of the number of Cuban adults taught to read and write during 1959 and 1960 under the various programs is 100,000. See "Cuba: Territory Free of Illiteracy," *Cuba* (a monthly in English), Jan. 1962, p. 17.

15. *Revolución*, Oct. 11, 1960, p. 9. In the final declaration of the Congress, the figure of "almost two million illiterate Cubans" was mentioned. Even the census of 1953 had found only slightly more than one million illiterates (ten years or older); hence the figure used by the Congress could have been arrived at only by making some very unfavorable projections of the 1953 data and adding undereducated children and young school-leavers to the total. Eventually, only illiterates of fourteen and older were made the targets of the campaign. See also the discussion in "Honorio Muñoz informa sobre el censo," in *Congreso Nacional de Alfabetización* (Havana: Imprenta Nacional de Cuba, 1961), pp. 97–100.

16. See the organizational charts in *The Method and Means*, following p. 24.

17. Initially, about 500,000 copies of *Alfabeticemos* and 2 million copies of *Venceremos* were printed. *El Mundo*, Jan. 22, 1961 (supplement), p. 3.

18. The 24 themes and a sample from the vocabulary section of *Alfabeticemos* are available in English translation in Richard R. Fagen, *Cuba: The Political Content of Adult Education* (Stanford, Calif., 1964). On page eight of *Alfabeticemos* the themes are cross-referenced to the appropriate lessons in *Venceremos* so that the instructor may introduce political content verbally into the learning process. The overt political content of the primer itself is limited and uneven; most of the practice sentences are of the standard "I will go with the children" variety, but others say such things as "Now the fisherman is not exploited." In order to emphasize the importance attached to the political content of *Alfabeticemos*, one member of the National Commission said, "I think that even Fidel looked over the text and made some corrections, some suggestions." Raúl Ferrer, "El Maestro y el Año de la Educación," in Universidad Popular Sexto Ciclo, p. 52.

19. Comisión Nacional de Alfabetización, Ministerio de Educación, *Alfabeticemos* (Havana: Imprenta Nacional de Cuba, 1961), p. 23.

20. This paragraph is based on data presented in Jolly, pp. 192–93, and *The Method and Means*, pp. 25–27.

21. *Revolución*, Jan. 2, 1961, p. 6.

22. *Revolución*, Jan. 24, 1961, p. 16. Perhaps no young Cuban who did not participate in the struggle against Batista has been as widely eulogized as Conrado Benítez. In addition to the literacy brigades named after him, schools, factories, and recreation centers also carry his name. The most widely circulated poem written in his honor, "Eternamente joven, para siempre, maestro," is available in translation in Fagen, *Cuba: The Political Content of Adult Education*, pp. 19–20.

23. *Revolución*, Jan. 30, 1961, p. 18.

24. See *Bohemia*, Apr. 16, 1961, pp. 66–67. This two-page advertisement invited the parents "to visit the Conrado Benítez Pilot Brigades that have been engaged in literacy work for several months in the Zapata Swamp. There you will receive a definitive answer to your questions about how the brigadistas live and work. Don't deny your child this opportunity to serve the Fatherland." The Zapata Swamp is in the immediate area of the Bay of Pigs. Just before the invasion it was estimated that there were 240 voluntary teachers, members of the pilot brigades, and primary-school teachers working in the swamp. *Revolución*, Apr. 13, 1961, p. 13.

25. See, for instance, Pedro García Suárez and Cuesto Rivero, "El maestro en la mar: cada barco una escuela," *Bohemia*, Apr. 2, 1961, pp. 4–7.

26. *Revolución*, Mar. 15, 1961, p. 3.

27. *Revolución*, May 2, 1961, pp. 10, 14. The private schools were actually nationalized by a law passed on July 6, 1961. For the revolutionary "case" against the private schools, see Raúl Ferrer, "La ley de nacionalización de la enseñanza," in Ministry of Education, *Alfabetización, nacionalización de la enseñanza* (Havana: Imprenta Nacional de Cuba, 1961), pp. 47–71. An English version of this article is available in *Cuba*, Nov. 1961, pp. 19–30.

28. Unless otherwise noted, this discussion of the Varadero training center is based on *Revolución*, May 6, 1961, p. 3; May 16, 1961, p. 6; May 20, 1961, pp. 1, 4; May 26, 1961, p. 3; May 31, 1961, pp. 1, 5; Aug. 18, 1961, p. 10; and *The Method and Means*, p. 43. Many pictures and articles on the center were also published in *Bohemia* for the months of May through August, 1961.

29. *Revolución*, Aug. 18, 1961. pp. 10–11.

30. The Organizaciones Revolucionarias Integradas (ORI) was formed as the preliminary "holding corporation" for the Marxist-Leninist United Party of the Cuban Socialist Revolution (PURSC) that was then being planned. For detail and documents on the difficulties encountered in forming the ORI, the PURSC, and finally the Communist Party of Cuba

(PCC), see "Two Challenges to the Leadership of Fidel Castro," in Richard R. Fagen and Wayne C. Cornelius, eds., *Political Power in Latin America* (Englewood Cliffs, N.J., 1969). Even after the establishment of the ORI, problems of the political control and coordination of the literacy campaign remained. For a rather frank appraisal, see Raúl Ferrer, "Informe de la Comisión Nacional de Alfabetización," in *Congreso Nacional de Alfabetización*, pp. 21–23.

31. For a description of the operation of one Council and its unidades, see Ruben Castillo Ramos, "Así se trabaja en la Revolución," *Bohemia*, July 16, 1961, pp. 10–13. In the rural areas, the unidades were sometimes known as *equipos* (teams) *de brigadistas*. According to the official table of organization, each unidad or equipo was to have both a technical adviser and a political adviser as well as one literacy worker for every two illiterates. See *The Method and Means*, pp. 43–44.

32. See *Congreso Nacional de Alfabetización* for a complete report on the Congress.

33. This paragraph is based on reports published in the following issues of *Revolución*: Sept. 7, 1961, pp. 6, 10; Sept. 11, 1961, p. 5; Sept. 14, 1961, pp. 1, 4; Sept. 21, 1961, pp. 1–2; Oct. 2, 1961, pp. 1, 6.

34. The celebration at Melena del Sur and Castro's speech are reported in *Revolución*, Nov. 9, 1961, pp. 1, 4; and *Revolución*, Nov. 10, 1961, pp. 8–9.

35. *Revolución*, Nov. 29, 1961, p. 4. On the day after Castro's speech, the Council of Ministers of the Revolutionary Government promulgated Law 988, which made it a capital crime "to organize or form part of an armed group for the purpose of committing crimes against the powers of the state" or "to enter the national territory from outside with the purpose of engaging in sabotage or any other counterrevolutionary activity." For the entire text of the law, see *Revolución*, Nov. 30, 1961, p. 1.

36. This and the following paragraph are based on reports published in the following issues of *Revolución* for 1961: Dec. 18, pp. 1, 6; Dec. 19, pp. 1, 4; Dec. 20, pp. 1, 4; Dec. 21, pp. 1, 6; Dec. 22, pp. 1, 10; Dec. 23, pp. 1–4.

37. Castro's speech is published in full in *Revolución*, Dec. 23, 1961, pp. 4–5, 8. Toward the end of the address, Castro described in some detail plans to give scholarships to over 40,000 students, with preference to be given to the brigadistas.

38. A nontechnical definition of a new literate was provided by Raúl Ferrer, Executive Secretary of the National Literacy Congress and a member of the National Literacy Commission: "What is a literate? He can be defined as a compañero who ... has gone through the entire primer, who can read its simple sentences, and who knows how to write well enough to compose a letter to Fidel Castro that ends more or less as

follows: 'Long live our great Socialist Revolution.'" ("Informe de la Comisión Nacional de Alfabetización," p. 19). The final test used by the technical department of the National Literacy Commission to determine if a student had "passed" the literacy course is reprinted in *The Method and Means*, p. 34. For an evaluation of the skill level and the time required to complete the primer and thus be considered literate, see Jolly, pp. 205, 417 (note 9). Jolly and his colleagues estimated that on the average no more than two months of spare-time work would have been required to complete the primer. Thus the large number of new literates officially claimed for the last three and a half months of the campaign is quite within the realm of possibility given the number of literacy workers at that time.

39. During the course of the campaign, the Revolutionary Government became increasingly aware of the necessity of follow-up work and continuing education both to prevent people from slipping back into illiteracy and to raise the skills of new literates to the functional level (officially defined as the sixth grade). For an overview of plans and programs for continuing adult education, see Jolly, pp. 205–19. For more detail, see the literature cited in note 9 above. The political content of the first materials developed for continuing adult education was just as pronounced as it was in the materials developed for the literacy campaign. See, for instance, the introduction and story problems translated from the first arithmetic workbook edited specifically for the new literates, in Fagen, *Cuba: The Political Content of Adult Education*, pp. 59–71.

40. Approximately 13 million pesos (one peso equals one dollar) were officially invested by the Ministry of Education in the campaign. See Comisión Nacional Cubana de la UNESCO, p. 8. The actual costs, however, were much higher. Exactly how high it is hard to say, owing to the immense amount of voluntary labor and goods contributed (for instance, over 100,000 pairs of spectacles were given free of charge to those being taught to read and write). Jolly, p. 195, estimates that the Ministry of Education's costs alone were closer to 52 million pesos.

Cuban pride in the campaign is attested to not only by the leadership's frequent favorable references to it, but also by the invitations issued in 1962 to foreign educators and members of international organizations to visit the island and study the effort. See, for instance, Comisión Nacional Cubana de la UNESCO, p. 93.

41. See "Orientaciones a los alfabetizadores," *Revolución*, Aug. 22, 1961, p. 10. Recalcitrant illiterates were also to be reminded that to learn to read and write is "a moral obligation, a revolutionary duty. . . . Each and every illiterate should contribute to making a reality of Fidel's pledge, spoken before the entire world, that during this year we will eliminate illiteracy in our Fatherland." *Ibid.*

42. *Revolución*, June 12, 1961, pp. 1, 3, 11.
43. *Revolución*, June 19, 1961, pp. 1–2.
44. "El brigadista mas joven de Cuba," *Verde Olivo*, Año II, No. 47 (Nov. 26, 1961), pp. 56–58. The article also reports that Menéndez's father was assassinated during the Batista period.
45. *Verde Olivo*, Año II, No. 51 (Dec. 21, 1961). The Spanish version of the letter, with its original spelling and punctuation, reads as follows:

Finca el Naranjal 12 d Noviembre de 1961
Año de la Educación

DOTOR FIDEL CASTRO RUZ

Estimado Compañero le Ago esta para darle A Conocer que ya yo se leer y Escribir Grasia A nuestra Revolución Sosialista y demacratica por eso es que yo le Ago esta para que Uste la Vea cón Sus propios hojos.
Mas me despido cón un fuerte Saludo Rebalusionario y democratico

Era Analfabeta FELICIA CARPIO BARCELO

Alfabetizador Wilfredo Neyra R.

PATRIA O MUERTE

Alfabetizando Venceremo

As a general rule, when the handwriting was sufficiently legible, such letters were photocopied and published in their original form.
46. From an interview in Geneva, Switzerland, with Dr. Max Figueroa, as reported in *Escuela y Revolución en Cuba*, No. 1 (Feb.–Mar. 1963), p. 44. This was the first issue of the official journal of the Cuban Ministry of Education (MINED) and the National Union of Teachers and Educational Technicians (SNTEC).
47. For the goals and expectations, see Castro's speech to the brigadistas, translated in Appendix B below.
48. I have also drawn on informal discussions with participants and on various accounts of the campaign either previously noted or acknowledged below.
49. García Galló, p. 77.
50. From El Indio Naborí, "Canto del Campesino al Brigadista," as reprinted in *Cartilla y Farol: Poemas Militantes* (Havana: no publisher, 1962), pp. 17–18. This pamphlet (*Primer and Lantern*) is a collection of the most important of Naborí's poems about the Year of Education. For a prose account of the relationship between peasant and brigadista, see José Rodríguez Feo, "Impresiones de un alfabetizador," *Casa de las Américas*, Year II, No. 9 (Nov.–Dec. 1961), pp. 50–57.
51. In Cuba in 1966 and 1968, I spoke with ex-brigadistas, by then fully grown, who still return to "their" families to visit whenever possible.

52. Jesualdo, "Cuba: territorio libre de analfabetismo," *Casa de las Américas*, Year II, No. 9 (Nov.–Dec. 1961), pp. 38–49. Jesualdo (a pen name) was entirely sympathetic toward the revolution, and he wrote very insightfully about the impact of the campaign on its participants—particularly the brigadistas.

53. The adoption of East European practices was most noticeable in the economic sphere. For an insightful analysis of the consequences of this borrowing, see Edward Boorstein, *The Economic Transformation of Cuba* (New York, 1968). The overall learning aspects of the first years of the revolution are discussed in James O'Connor, "Political Change in Cuba, 1959–1965," *Social Research*, XXXV, 2 (Summer 1968), 312–47.

54. The concept of the "operational code" comes originally from Nathan Leites, *A Study of Bolshevism* (Glencoe, Ill., 1953). As used here, however, it derives directly from the critique and reformulation presented in Alexander L. George, *The "Operational Code": A Neglected Approach to the Study of Political Leaders and Decision-Making* (Santa Monica, Calif.: the RAND Corporation, 1967), Memorandum RM-5427-PR. See particularly pp. 27–43 on "The Instrumental Beliefs in an Operational Code."

55. *Congreso Nacional de Alfabetización*, p. 11.

56. See Appendix A below for a description (written from field notes taken in 1968) of several of the rural environments specifically created to contribute to the formation of the new Cuban.

Chapter 4

1. *Revolución*, Sept. 29, 1960, p. 5.

2. *Ibid.*, p. 1.

3. For two accounts maintaining that the genesis of the CDR at the moment of the explosions on September 28 was spontaneous, see Manuel Borjas, "En las zonas montañosas de Oriente," *Con la Guardia en Alto*, Sept. 1963, pp. 24–29; and Blanco Fernández. "Cuando el pueblo se organiza," *Verde Olivo*, Año II, No. 16 (Apr. 23, 1961), pp. 85–87. The magazine *Con la Guardia en Alto* is the official organ of the CDR. It has been published both as a monthly and as a bimonthly. Because the numbering system of *Con la Guardia en Alto* is confused, it will be cited herein by date of publication only.

4. See the coverage of the explosion in *Revolución*, Mar. 5, 1960, pp. 2–7, and Mar. 7, 1960, p. 1. At the funeral oration for those killed, Castro blamed agents of the United States for the disaster. There was no conclusive evidence to support this charge, however. Explanations of the explosion range from sabotage by United States agents to sheer carelessness on the part of Cuban dockworkers.

5. *Revolución*, Aug. 15, 1960, p. 18. This was the third of twelve sec-

tions of the mass oath. This section was used in the early printed propaganda of the CDR.

6. Blanco Fernández, p. 87. Such lists were in circulation well before the Bay of Pigs invasion of mid-April 1961.

7. For a chronology of diplomatic, economic, and political events leading up to and following the April invasion, see A. G. Mezerik, ed., *Cuba and the United States: Complete Chronology of Events Through Mid-1963*, II (New York, 1963), esp. pp. 64–74. On Dec. 31, 1960, Cuba requested an immediate meeting of the United Nations Security Council to consider evidence of a United States plan to invade Cuba. *Ibid.*, p. 65.

8. *Revolución*, Mar. 17, 1961, p. 3; this page carried the complete statement of the National Directorate of the CDR.

9. *Revolución*, Mar. 28, 1961, p. 2; this page carried the complete proclamation of the National Directorate of the CDR.

10. A formal order to this effect was signed by Castro as Commander in Chief and Prime Minister. See *Revolución*, Apr. 18, 1961, p. 4, for the complete text.

11. "La lucha en la retaguardia," *Verde Olivo*, Año II, No. 20 (May 21, 1961), pp. 12–15. The quoted passage is from p. 14.

12. The number of Cubans detained at the time of the invasion is not given in any revolutionary documentation of the events, but it was probably in excess of 100,000. An insightful Italian journalist, Gianni Corbi, estimated the number to be 200,000, although from talks with both supporters and opponents of the regime who lived through the events, I would judge this to be high. See the translations of Corbi's articles for *L'Espresso* in U.S. Department of Commerce, Joint Publications Research Service, *Translations on Cuba*, No. 123 (Apr. 8, 1964), pp. 1–52. The estimate appears on p. 14.

13. *Revolución*, Apr. 24, 1961, p. 11.

14. *Revolución*, Sept. 27, 1965, p. 2. Other semiofficial Cuban estimates on the number of committees at the time of the invasion vary from 7,000 to 9,000, with a high in total estimated membership of 100,000.

15. "La lucha en la retaguardia," *Verde Olivo*, Año II, No. 20 (May 21, 1961), p. 15. For vignettes on individual proselytism, see Eduardo Yasells, "2,100 Comités de Defensa de la Revolución en el Corazón de La Habana," *Verde Olivo*, Año II, No. 23 (June 11, 1961), pp. 14–18.

16. *Revolución*, Aug. 4, 1961, p. 5.

17. *Revolución*, Sept. 28, 1962, p. 4. The beginnings of the system were visible on the first anniversary; see *Revolución*, Sept. 23, 1961, pp. 1, 6. For a third anniversary review of organizational problems and growth, see Radamés Mancebo, "El trabajo de organización en los CDR," *Con la Guardia en Alto*, Sept. 1963, pp. 16–18.

18. *Revolución*, Sept. 28, 1962, p. 4.

19. *Revolución*, Jan. 21, 1963, p. 7. At the section level, and to some extent at the district level, cadres are part-time and unpaid.

20. *Revolución*, Jan. 14, 1963, p. 8.

21. See "Control de las tareas," *Con la Guardia en Alto*, Dec. 1963, pp. 26–29, 81. The elaborate instructions governing the distribution of new cards are included at the end of this article.

22. "Sobre el papel de los CDR en el Año de la Economía," *Con la Guardia en Alto*, Mar.–Apr. 1964, p. 9. See also "Plan de finanzas en los CDR," *Con la Guardia en Alto*, Mar. 1965, pp. 24–25; and "El Nuevo frente de finanzas," *Con la Guardia en Alto*, Sept. 1963, pp. 30–31.

23. *Revolución*, Mar. 22, 1963, p. 8, lists all 35 points. See also *Revolución*, Mar. 7, 1963, p. 6; and "Uno emulación gigantesca," *Con la Guardia en Alto*, May 1963, pp. 2–3. Subsequently, national CDR emulaciones were held on the average twice yearly.

24. *Revolución*, Mar. 28, 1963, p. 8; and *Revolución*, Apr. 4, 1963, p. 8.

25. See the poem published in *Con la Guardia en Alto*, July 1963, p. 59. Emulación in the CDR is primarily organized around performance in the various frentes; this poem pays homage to the fourteen frentes and to emulación as "the motive force of social development."

26. Blanco Fernández, p. 86. For an eyewitness report of a CDR meeting, See José Yglesias, *In the Fist of the Revolution* (New York, 1968), chap. 10.

27. *Revolución*, Sept. 30, 1961, p. 12. See the abridged translation of this speech in Appendix C below. See also "Los CDR, vehículos de unidad," *Revolución*, Sept. 27, 1961, pp. 1, 4. This article speaks of the CDR as "the people, with no political definition other than their support of the Fatherland and the Revolutionary Government" (p. 4).

28. Although the formation of CDR in some of the more exotic settings is largely for publicity purposes, the move into the rural areas had real political and sociological importance. On the CDR in rural areas during the first half of 1961, see "El Comité de Defensa en nuestros campos," *Verde Olivo*, Año II, No. 34 (Aug. 27, 1961), pp. 73–75. For a report on the CDR in the mountains of Oriente, including demographic and organizational data, see Manuel Borjas, "En las zonas montañosas de Oriente." For the seagoing CDR, see Jesús Abascal, "La retaguardia está bien cuidada," *Trabajo*, first fortnight of June 1961, pp. 50–53. The prison story is reported by Manuel Navarro Luna, "Un buen Comité de Defensa de la Revolución," *Verde Olivo*, Año II, No. 26 (July 2, 1961), pp. 60–63.

29. With what was probably unintended humor, José Matar once characterized the CDR as "a heterogeneous organization that conforms fully to the idiosyncracies of the Cuban." *Revolución*, Jan. 21, 1963, p. 7. On

the need to incorporate into the CDR even those who are only marginally favorable toward the revolution, see *Revolución*, Sept. 28, 1964, p. 8.

30. *Revolución*, Sept. 27, 1963, p. 2.

31. *Granma*, Sept. 27, 1966, p. 2.

32. José Matar, "Tres años de lucha en defensa de la Revolución Cubana," *Con la Guardia en Alto*, Sept. 1963, pp. 4–11. The quoted passage is from p. 9; italics mine. See also "La propaganda, factor fundamental," *Con la Guardia en Alto*, Sept. 1964, pp. 58–60.

33. See *Revolución*, Nov. 8, 1960, p. 9. The original civic training manual of the Rebel Army was entitled *Manual de Capacitación Cívica*. For a description of its contents, see below, note 6 to Chapter 5. During 1960–61 the manual was widely used in nonmilitary study groups.

34. The remainder of this discussion is based on the following sources: *Revolución*, Sept. 27, 1962, pp. 1, 4; *Revolución*, Jan. 21, 1963, p. 7; *Revolución*, Sept. 28, 1965, p. 2; "Como de las propias masas se extrajeron 1000 orientadores de los C.I.R. en la Habana," *Con la Guardia en Alto*, May 1963, pp. 21–23; "El frente de Instrucción Revolucionaria, otro triunfo de los CDR," *Con la Guardia en Alto*, Aug. 1963, pp. 29–32; Rigoberto Porras, "Este es año de la organización y de la instrucción revolucionaria en los CDR," *Con la Guardia en Alto*, Sept. 1963, pp. 40–41; and "CIR: fuente de conciencia," *Con la Guardia en Alto*, Sept. 1964, pp. 48–50.

35. See *Revolución*, July 8, 1961, pp. 1, 2; and *Revolución*, July 12, 1961, pp. 1, 5. For areas in which no CDR existed, it was suggested that the citizens would do well to form them if they wanted to receive their allotment of fats and oils.

36. See *Revolución*, Aug. 1, 1963, pp. 1, 4; and Orlando Ravelo, "Los CDR y la batalla de los abastecimientos," *Con la Guardia en Alto*, Sept. 1963, pp. 72–73.

37. See *Revolución*, Jan. 21, 1963, p. 7, for a summary of such activities in 1962.

38. See *Revolución*, Oct. 16, 1963, pp. 1, 2.

39. *Havana Radio and Television*, Aug. 30, 1967. See also the Seventh Anniversary Communiqué of the National Directorate of the CDR, *Granma*, Sept. 28, 1967; and Castro's speech on the seventh anniversary, *Granma*, Sept. 29, 1967, esp. p. 2. For a description of the work undertaken in one town, see Fernando Villar, "El poder local y los CDR construyen en Elia," *Con la Guardia en Alto*, Jan. 1967, pp. 4–7.

40. See *Granma*, Weekly Review, Mar. 24, 1968.

41. For editorials, data, and reports on this phase of the CDR and the Revolutionary Offensive, see *Granma*, Weekly Review, Mar. 31, 1968, p. 2; and *Granma*, Weekly Review, Apr. 7, 1968, pp. 2, 3, 5. The quoted

passage is from "The Revolutionary Offensive," *Granma*, Weekly Review, Mar. 31, 1968, p. 2. For a very detailed explanation of the official rationale for the nationalizations, see "La nacionalización de los establecimientos privados en la ofensiva," *El Militante Comunista* (monograph edited and published by the Secretary of Organization and the Commission of Revolutionary Orientation of the Central Committee of the Communist Party of Cuba, June 1968). For two reports on the CDR during the first month of the Revolutionary Offensive, see *Granma*, Apr. 24, 1968, p. 6; and *Granma*, Apr. 25, 1968, p. 6.

42. For a clear statement of this position, see José Matar, "Tres años de lucha en defensa de la Revolución Cubana," esp. pp. 9–10.

43. As I was told by one knowledgeable and somewhat wry Cuban in Havana in 1966, "The worms [gusanos] were so far underground [after 1962] that even the most assiduous digging failed to uncover any." For a clear statement of the vigilance responsibilities of the CDR during the security phase, see *Revolución*, Sept. 25, 1961, pp. 1, 6.

44. From an interview with José Matar, reported in *Revolución*, Sept. 27, 1962, p. 4.

45. The functional importance of enemies and the symbolism of struggle in the revolution are discussed at much greater length in my "The Cuban Revolution: Enemies and Friends," in David J. Finlay, Ole R. Holsti, and Richard R. Fagen, *Enemies in Politics* (Chicago, 1967). For other examples of watchdog activities in the CDR, see "Frente a los enemigos del pueblo, el pueblo con la guardia en alto," *Con la Guardia en Alto*, May 1963, pp. 15–17 (on the role of the CDR in the control of common delinquency); and "Instrucciones a los CDR sobre el otorgamiento de la Fianza Moral," *El Mundo*, May 13, 1962, p. 5 (on the power of the CDR to guarantee or bond those accused of certain crimes and awaiting trial). In many such activities the committees seemed to act not only as the watchdog of the security and order of the community but also as the guardian of the morals of its citizens.

46. *Revolución*, Mar. 17, 1962, p. 10.

47. José Matar, "Lucha a fondo contra los defectos del frente de abastecimientos," *Con la Guardia en Alto*, May 1963, pp. 32–38, 78. The quoted passage is from p. 34.

48. "Y al cuarto año ... sigue impetuoso desarrollo," *Con la Guardia en Alto*, Sept. 1964, pp. 12–13 (from a speech by Matar given in April 1964).

49. Matar claimed, however, that hatred of the CDR came only from gusanos and counterrevolutionaries. *Revolución*, Sept. 29, 1964, p. 2.

50. Havana Radio, Sept. 26, 1967.

51. See Richard R. Fagen, Richard A. Brody, and Thomas O'Leary,

Cubans in Exile: Disaffection and the Revolution (Stanford, Calif. 1968), chap. 6.

52. The extent to which the general climate of permissiveness, arbitrariness, and self-righteousness led members of the CDR to define their own roles was underlined by an editorial opinion published in *Hoy* on May 7, 1963. In a column entitled "Aclaraciones," devoted to answering questions from its readers, *Hoy* maintained that it was not proper for the CDR to set themselves up as courts of law, to try citizens, to pass judgment, or to levy fines. It is difficult to say how widespread the assumption of formal judicial responsibility was among the committees, but "Aclaraciones" usually treated an issue only if it had already in some sense become a problem. The column is reprinted in Periódico Hoy, *Aclaraciones*, II (Havana: Editora Política, 1965), 213–15.

53. *Granma*, Sept. 29, 1967, p. 2.

Chapter 5

1. The basic data on which this chapter depends come from a series of seven reports by Lionel Soto, published in the party journal *Cuba Socialista*. Some of the material in these reports can be found in other Cuban publications, but the most complete and authoritative versions are those written by Soto, who was national director of the Schools of Revolutionary Instruction from their founding in 1960 until their termination in 1967. Soto was a friend of Castro's at the university; he was at one time a member of the Partido Socialista Popular, and in September 1965 he was named one of the original 100-man Central Committee of the Communist Party of Cuba. In chronological order these seven reports are "Las Escuelas de Instrucción Revolucionaria y la formación de cuadros," *Cuba Socialista*, No. 3 (Nov. 1961), pp. 28–41; "Nuevo desarrollo de la instrucción revolucionaria," *Cuba Socialista*, No. 12 (Aug. 1962), pp. 32–45; "Dos años de instrucción revolucionaria," *Cuba Socialista*, No. 18 (Feb. 1963), pp. 30–44; "Las Escuelas de Instrucción Revolucionaria en una nueva fase," *Cuba Socialista*, No. 30 (Feb. 1964), pp. 62–77; "Las Escuelas de Instrucción Revolucionaria en el ciclo político-técnico," *Cuba Socialista*, No. 41 (Jan. 1965), pp. 67–82; "El quinto aniversario de las Escuelas de Instrucción Revolucionaria," *Cuba Socialista*, No. 53 (Jan. 1966), pp. 72–91; "Lo importante es que desarrollemos nuestro camino," *Cuba Socialista*, No. 65 (Jan. 1967), pp. 37–61. Hereafter, for convenience, the reports will be cited by the author's last name and the number of the relevant issue of *Cuba Socialista* (e.g., Soto, No. 3; Soto, No. 12; etc.).

2. Soto, No. 53, p. 73.

3. *Ibid.*

4. Lionel Soto, *Hoy*, May 31, 1964, p. 2.

5. See Jules Dubois, *Fidel Castro* (Indianapolis, Ind., 1959), pp. 84–85. Castro named this school the Abel Santamaría Academy in honor of his second-in-command, who was captured, tortured, and killed after the attack on the Moncada Barracks in July 1953.

6. Some idea of the content of the training programs carried on in the Armed Forces can be gotten from Departamento de Instrucción, MinFAR, *Manual de Capacitación Cívica* (Havana: Imprenta Nacional, 1960), the study guide–textbook used in these programs. The *Manual* was divided into eight sections: Revolution, Agrarian Reform, Industrialization, Economic Geography, Cuban History, Ideas of Martí, Morality and Discipline, and Documents. Although it is much longer, the *Manual* does not differ greatly thematically from *Alfabeticemos*, the orientation manual used by instructors during the Year of Education. An English translation of *Alfabeticemos* is in Richard R. Fagen, *Cuba: The Political Content of Adult Education* (Stanford, Calif., 1964).

7. In 1961, and usually thereafter, the figure given was twelve provincial schools in the initial group. See Soto, No. 3, p. 30. In 1966, Soto (No. 53, p. 73) wrote of eleven original provincial schools and gave their locations. Since by September 1, 1961, the system had expanded to include sixteen provincial schools, the exact number that existed in January 1961 is not critical. Almost from the outset, the Armed Forces had their own national school, the Osvaldo Sánchez School, which graduated its first class of 750 men in 1961. These graduates then became political instructors at the battalion and company levels. Soto, No. 3, p. 36. The Osvaldo Sánchez School will not be considered in this chapter, for it remained under the control of the Armed Forces Ministry rather than the EIR, and data are difficult to gather. For the most detailed public discussion of the school, see *Verde Olivo*, Jan. 12, 1964, pp. 5–9.

8. Soto, No. 30, pp. 62–63.

9. Soto, No. 18, p. 31. Soto said that during the first course at the provincial level it was not possible to give lessons in dialectical and historical materialism. Rather, "*discussions* about *philosophy*" were offered. Soto, No. 30, p. 64. Italics in the original.

10. Soto, No. 30, p. 76.

11. *Los Fundamentos del Socialismo en Cuba* was originally published in 1943. It was reprinted a number of times, first reaching a truly national audience when it was reproduced in April 1962 in its entirety as a special issue of *Con la guardia en alto*, the official publication of the CDR. Intended as a basic text in the study circles of the CDR, the issue had a press run of 1.2 million copies.

12. Soto, No. 3, pp. 34–35.

13. For a brief official description of the operation of an urban part-time boarding school in the first months of 1962, see "La Escuela Básica

de Instrucción Revolucionaria 'Miguel A. Oramas,'" *Cuba Socialista,* No. 11 (July 1962), pp. 131–34.

14. Soto, No. 53, pp. 78–79.

15. Soto, No. 18, p. 33. After 1962, two more national schools were founded, one for members of the Union of Communist Youth and one school of higher studies for instructors from the other EIR. For a useful introduction to the organization, curriculum, and composition of the student body of the Carlos Rodríguez Careaga School during its first course, see Margot Obaya, "Donde los dirigentes obreros se superan," *Trabajo,* first fortnight of Mar. 1962, pp. 82–85.

16. Soto, No. 3, p. 34.

17. *Ibid.*, p. 33.

18. See Appendix E.

19. Soto, No. 18, p. 32.

20. *Hoy,* Oct. 25, 1963, p. 5.

21. *El Mundo,* June 30, 1962, pp. 1, 6–8; *Revolución,* June 30, 1962, pp. 2, 4–5. This was the first time that a national meeting of the EIR was given more than perfunctory press coverage. Although Castro addressed the sixth national meeting on December 21, 1961, this was not reported in the press, and only small fragments of the speech have been made public since that time (e.g. in Soto, No. 53, p. 74).

22. Soto, No. 53, p. 77.

23. See Boris Goldenberg, *The Cuban Revolution and Latin America* (New York, 1965), pp. 260–68, for a brief description of the political crisis and its antecedents. Goldenberg mistakenly gives March 17 as the date of the second speech.

24. The entire speech was published in *El Mundo,* Mar. 27, 1962, pp. 5–9, and in *Revolución,* Mar. 27, 1962, pp. 2–3, 6, 9–10. It is available in English as *Fidel Castro Denounces Bureaucracy and Sectarianism* (New York, 1962), and in an abridged version in "Two Challenges to the Leadership of Fidel Castro," in Richard R. Fagen and Wayne A. Cornelius, eds., *Political Power in Latin America* (Englewood Cliffs, N.J., 1969).

25. *El Mundo,* Mar. 27, 1962, p. 6.

26. *Ibid.*

27. More than three years later Soto said, "From the best of the students of the national and provincial EIR . . . came the commissions that fundamentally—although in conjunction with other cadres—directed the reorganization of the ORI and the subsequent formation of the United Party of the Socialist Revolution. Furthermore, we can affirm that from March 1962 until the middle of 1963 the schools constituted, for all practical purposes, the only existing national political organism in our country. This was because the old cells of active revolutionaries were almost totally paralyzed as a result of Fidel's criticism, and because the reorgani-

zation commissions were engrossed in the task of purging the ORI and constructing the cells of the PURSC during that entire period." Soto, No. 53, p. 78. Although he is hardly a disinterested party, Soto's evaluation of the key role played by the EIR during this difficult period does not seem to be much exaggerated.

28. Soto said that the provincial schools, under the influence of the provincial ORI organizations, were particularly deformed by improper selection of students. Of all the provincial schools, he singled out the one in Havana as the worst. In that school, Soto said, only slightly more than one fourth of all the students in the first course of 1962 were industrial and agricultural workers. There were no peasants. The clear implication was that many of the other students were bureaucrats on a free ride, friends of Escalante, opportunists, and careerists. See Soto, No. 12, pp. 33, 42–43. For a brief discussion of the provincial school in Havana, see Carlos González, "El Centro Provincial de Instrucción Revolucionaria de la Habana," *Cuba Socialista*, No. 16 (Dec. 1962), pp. 126–29.

29. The list is compiled from Soto, No. 12, pp. 34–44, and *Revolución*, July 3, 1962, p. 8.

30. See Soto, No. 18, pp. 40–41, on the method of choosing the best students (*alumnos ejemplares*).

31. This is not to suggest that no changes were made or that nothing happened from June 1962 to the end of 1963. During this period, among other things, the Ñico López School was lengthened from eight months to ten and a half months; the provincial schools of the Union of Communist Youth (Unión de la Juventud Comunista, UJC) were brought formally into the EIR system; the national schools for women, members of the CDR, and members of the Association of Small Farmers were opened; the first two issues of *Theory and Practice* (*Teoría y Práctica*), the house organ of the National Directorate of the EIR, were published (in October and November of 1963); and there were important additions to the curriculum at all levels. See Soto, No. 12, p. 35. Additionally, of course, during most of this period the EIR were intimately involved in the aftermath of the political crisis discussed above.

32. Soto, No. 30, p. 66.

33. *Ibid.*

34. *Ibid.*, pp. 66–67. Italics in the original.

35. Castro, speaking on the fourth anniversary of the founding of the CDR, Sept. 28, 1964. As quoted in Soto, No. 41, pp. 68–69. Italics in the quoted version. In the official version of Castro's speech (which differs slightly from what is quoted by Soto), Castro added: "What does it matter if a peasant is able to recite from memory the materialist interpretation of history, the dialectical conception of nature, or the problem of the class struggle, if he does not know at what interval to plant cane,

if he does not know what quantity of fertilizer should be added to the soil?" *Revolución*, Sept. 29, 1964, p. 4.

36. Soto, No. 41, p. 71.

37. Soto, No. 53, pp. 80–81; No. 65, pp. 53–56.

38. Soto, No. 65, pp. 55–56.

39. *Ibid.*, p. 56.

40. Soto, No. 18, p. 44.

41. The delay in opening the promised Institute of Higher Studies of Marxism-Leninism came with the realization that the human resources necessary for the founding of such a center simply did not exist in Cuba, and that the Cuban variant of Marxism-Leninism was not yet well enough defined to permit its expression in any institutionalized fashion. In fact, so modest and cautious did the leadership become that in 1966 Soto said that when the Institute finally does open it will be called "The Marxist-Leninist Institute of the Party (later we may be able to call it an Institute of Higher Studies)." Soto, No. 53, p. 88. The Marx-Engels-Lenin School, devoted to economic and philosophical studies and attended by cadres from the EIR and from the universities, was founded in 1964. In 1966 this school, which had been operating more or less as a specialized national school, was absorbed into the Ñico López School. Then, in 1967, the José Martí School for professors of the EIR was established to relieve the Ñico López School of the burden of training middle-level cadres. See Soto, No. 30, p. 70; Soto, No. 53, p. 85; and Soto, No. 65, p. 44. None of these efforts should be confused with the problem of the Institute of Higher Studies, which was planned not as another training center, but rather as an institute of research, ideological innovation, and clarification.

42. Soto, No. 30, pp. 68–69. The first two studies actually published, in 1965, were on costs in the sugar industry and on the founding of the original Communist Party of Cuba in 1925. See Soto, No. 53, p. 87.

43. Soto, No. 53, p. 88.

44. The meeting was held November 24–26, 1966. The motto was taken from Castro's speech of August 29, 1966, to the closing session of the Twelfth Congress of the CTC.

45. Fragments of several speeches of Castro, as quoted by Soto, No. 65, pp. 46–47.

46. Isaac Otero, national Vice-Director of the EIR, was appointed to head this commission. The best description of its work can be found in Isaac Otero, "Las investigaciones sociales en las EIR," *Cuba Socialista*, No. 63 (Nov. 1966), pp. 66–82. The data used in the remainder of this section are taken from Otero's discussion.

47. Lowry Nelson, *Rural Cuba* (Minneapolis, Minn., 1950). The field work for Nelson's study was done in 1945–46.

48. For a description of the multination UNESCO study, see *American Behavioral Scientist,* X, 4 (Dec. 1966).

49. The results of these and other studies were published as monographs, sometimes with very limited circulation. Within the EIR, the main vehicle of publication of research results and discussions of the research and teaching efforts was the journal *Teoría y Práctica.*

50. The exact figures were 21 percent in the provincial schools and 18.7 percent in the basic schools. Soto, No. 30, p. 76.

51. One reason why separate statistics were not given for industrial and agricultural workers attending the EIR in 1966, except in the case of the basic boarding schools, is that the ratio of industrial to agricultural workers at all other levels was probably embarrassingly large. The basic boarding schools—all in rural areas and with a redesigned curriculum by 1966—were the only schools equipped to absorb large numbers of agricultural workers. To a lesser degree, the leadership was also concerned with raising or at least maintaining the percentages of Party members, women, and young people attending the schools. In 1963 and 1965, approximately 27 percent of all students were members of the Party. During the same years, the percentage of students 35 or younger in the several types of schools varied from about 70 to 80 percent. In 1963 about 12 percent of the students in the provincial schools were women, and in the basic schools almost 23 percent were women. In 1965, both percentages were slightly lower. The data for 1963 are from Soto, No. 30, p. 76. The data for 1965 are calculated from Soto, No. 53, pp. 85–86.

52. "The job of choosing and preparing cadres to direct, administer, and give classes in the EIR has been one of the most arduous and . . . trying activities of these three years." Soto, No. 30, p. 65.

53. Soto, No. 65, pp. 41, 42. The quotation is from p. 42; italics in the original.

54. Soto, No. 53, p. 82. For a brief description of the content and the organization of the year-end courses in 1962, see Isaac Otero, "Los cursillos especiales de fin de año para los cuadros de las EIR," *Cuba Socialista,* No. 17 (Jan. 1963), pp. 133–34. For 1964 and 1965, see Soto, No. 41, p. 82, and Soto, No. 53, p. 91, respectively. In certain instances, particularly in the more advanced schools during the earlier years, the regular instructional cadres were joined by professors loaned from the universities and by members of the government and the Party.

55. See Soto, No. 41, pp. 75–76; Soto, No. 65, pp. 49–50; and Isaac Otero, "Las investigaciones sociales en las EIR," *Cuba Socialista,* No. 63 (Nov. 1966), pp. 79–80.

56. *Granma,* Weekly Review, Mar. 24, 1968, p. 2.

57. The technological institutes were placed under the supervision of

the Armed Forces and the Party. The research and investigation that had been located in the schools were passed to the Comisión de Orientación Revolucionaria of the Party, the Cuban Academy of Sciences, and several groups within the University of Havana—all organizations that had already been involved in the research projects under the administration of the EIR. To an extent, the training of revolutionary cadres continued in the buildings that had once housed the EIR. For instance, in November 1968 the first 45-day course for municipal administrators was inaugurated at Ñico López, renamed the National Party School. At the same time, it was announced that courses for municipal administrators would be held throughout the island in 1969. See *Granma*, Nov. 6, 1968, p. 3.

Chapter 6

1. From Castro's speech of July 26, 1968, *Granma*, Weekly Review, July 28, 1968, pp. 3–5. As Joseph A. Kahl has pointed out, there is no easy translation for the word *conciencia* as used by the revolutionaries. It connotes, among other things, "an amalgam of consciousness, conscience, conscientiousness, and commitment." See Joseph A. Kahl, "'The Moral Economy of a Revolutionary Society," *Trans-Action*, VI, 6 (Apr. 1969), 30–37.

2. For a full discussion of the "moral versus material incentives" debate in Cuba, see Carmelo Mesa-Lago, *The Labor Sector and Socialist Distribution in Cuba* (New York, 1968), and the important analysis of Leo Huberman and Paul Sweezy, *Socialism in Cuba* (New York, 1969), esp. chaps. 8–11. A very useful perspective comparing the Soviet Union, China, and Yugoslavia is contained in Richard Lowenthal, "Development vs. Utopia in Communist Policy," to be published in Chalmers Johnson, ed., *Change in Communist Systems* (Stanford, Calif., 1970).

3. For a brief official statement, see "La lucha contra el economismo y por la conciencia comunista," *Granma*, Feb. 21, 1968, p. 4. Despite the title of this article, its main message is that meetings and talk will not build Communism. Only machines and technical knowledge in the hands of men fully aware of their own Communist purposes and destinies can create the material base needed for the new society. For an informed though negative view of the possibilities of rapid growth in the Cuban economy through the methods and investment strategies currently in use, see Carmelo Mesa-Lago, "The Revolutionary Offensive," *Trans-Action*, VI, 6 (Apr. 1969) 22–29, 62.

4. See in particular Castro's speech to graduates of the University of Oriente on December 8, 1968, as published in *Granma*, Weekly Review, Dec. 15, 1968, pp. 2–3, and his speech at the University of Havana on March 13, 1969, as published in *Granma*, Weekly Review, Mar. 16, 1969, pp. 2–5.

5. The most complete development of these ideas is found in the various documents of the Cultural Congress of Havana, held in January 1968. See the literature cited in note 21, Chapter 1 above, and particularly the "Final Resolution of Commission II: The Integral Formation of Man," in *Cultural Congress of Havana* (Havana: Instituto del Libro, 1968). Throughout this aspect of the revolutionary rhetoric one can find echoes of the early Marx, particularly the *Economic and Philosophic Manuscripts of 1844*. See, for instance, Loyd D. Easton and Curt H. Guddat, eds. and translators, *Writings of the Young Marx on Philosophy and Society* (Garden City, N.Y., 1967), esp. pp. 283–337. For a very useful comparative perspective on the variety and uses of Marxist thought, see Robert C. Tucker, *The Marxian Revolutionary Idea* (New York, 1969).

6. Not only revolutionaries hold this view. An American Rabbi visiting Havana in 1968 quotes a deeply religious Cuban Jew as follows: "Rabbi, little girls used to walk the streets of Havana as prostitutes, and teen-agers sold themselves to Americans for food and we merchants made money, not from prostitutes, God forbid, but from the system, from the atmosphere. Today there are no prostitutes, no vice, no Americans, no business. Which is better, Rabbi?" Everett Gendler, "Holy Days in Havana," *Conservative Judaism*, XXIII, 2 (Winter 1969), 15–24. Contemporary Cuban art and literature return again and again to this theme. See, for instance, *Cuban Poetry: 1959–1966* (Havana: Book Institute, 1967), and the cartoons and graphics that abound in Cuban publications.

7. See, for example, Susan Sontag, "Some Thoughts on the Right Way (for Us) to Love the Cuban Revolution," *Ramparts*, VII, 11 (Apr. 1969), 6 et seq. On the clash in Cuba between youth culture as defined by the revolutionaries and the egoismo implied by other youthful life-styles, see José Yglesias, "Cuban Report: Their Hippies, Their Squares," *New York Times Magazine*, Jan. 12, 1969, pp. 25 et seq. See also Arlie Hochschild, "Student Power in Action," *Trans-Action*, VI, 6 (Apr. 1969), 16–21, 67, on generational differences among young Cubans. For a concise statement of the ideal virtues of revolutionary youth, see "Declaración del estudiantado cubano en la Ofensiva Revolucionaria," *Granma*, Weekly Review, July 28, 1968, p. 2. This declaration was read by a student leader immediately before Castro's speech on July 26, 1968. See also "Orientaciones sobre el ingreso al Partido," *El Militante Comunista*, Aug. 1968, pp. 5–30, for an outline of the ideal characteristics of a Party militant. It is not coincidental that most rank-and-file Party-members in Cuba are quite young.

8. "El dinero a través de su historia," *El Militante Comunista* (monograph), Aug. 1968, p. 57. For elaborations of this theme, see Fidel Castro, "Discurso de clausura del Congreso (de la CTC)" *Cuba Socialista*, No. 62

(Oct. 1966), esp. pp. 43–45; and Fidel Castro, "La esencia de esta hora es la técnica y el trabajo" (address on the sixth anniversary of the CDR), *Cuba Socialista*, No. 62 (Oct. 1966), esp. pp. 12–17.

9. The Schools to the Countryside plan was initiated in the 1965–66 school year in Camagüey; 20,000 secondary students participated. In 1967–68, 160,000 students from all provinces took part. For a brief description of the plan, see *Cuba: Report to the United Nations Educational, Scientific, and Cultural Organization, UNESCO, 1967–1968* (Havana: no date or publisher), pp. 25–26. For more detail on the Isle of Youth, see "The Cuban Countryside, Spring 1968," Appendix A below, and the extremely interesting report "Two Weeks on the Isle of Youth," in Elizabeth Sutherland, *The Youngest Revolution* (New York, 1969). The Cordón de la Habana was begun in the spring of 1967. For a map of the area and an outline of the plan, see *Cuba*, Mar. 1968, pp. 3–15. For a brief and enthusiastic eyewitness report, see Timothy F. Harding and Donald W. Bray, "The Green Belts of Cuba," *The Nation*, Aug. 19, 1968, pp. 107–9. Since 1967, all three efforts have been reported in detail in the Cuban mass media.

These aspects of Cuban practice are much closer to Chinese than Soviet patterns of participation and formation. For comparative materials on the Chinese case, see Franz Schurmann, *Ideology and Organization in Communist China* (Berkeley, Calif., 1966), esp. pp. 17–58, and James R. Townsend, *Political Participation in Communist China* (Berkeley, Calif., 1967), esp. chap. 4. As emphasized in Chapter 1 above, the Cubans are not nearly as concerned with theory as the Chinese, nor are Cuban justifications for and explanations of action programs nearly as conscious and doctrinaire. Furthermore, the Cuban leaders do not openly draw upon or cite Chinese political thought, and they have occasionally been sharply critical of Chinese policies. Nevertheless, the Cubans have evolved a style of directed cultural change that has important similarities to the Chinese style.

10. The distinction between attitudes and values that is being used here is that drawn by Milton Rokeach, "The Role of Values in Public Opinion Research," *Public Opinion Quarterly*, XXXII, 4 (Winter 1968–69), 547–59: "I will define an attitude as an enduring organization of several beliefs focused on a specific object (physical or social, concrete or abstract) or situation, predisposing one to respond in some preferential manner.

"Values, on the other hand, transcend specific objects and specific situations: values have to do with *modes of conduct* and *end-states of existence*. More formally, to say that a person 'has a value' is to say that he has an enduring belief that a particular mode of conduct or that a particular end-state of existence is personally and socially preferable to alternative modes of conduct or end-states of existence." The quotation is from p. 550; italics in the original.

11. Seymour Martin Lipset, "Values, Education, and Entrepreneurship," in Seymour Martin Lipset and Aldo Solari, eds., *Elites in Latin America* (New York, 1967), p. 6. See also Seymour Martin Lipset, *The First New Nation* (Garden City, N.Y., 1967), especially the Introduction and chap. 3. The literature cited in both of these books documents the origins and intellectual underpinnings of the argument.

12. The value categories are those of Talcott Parsons as modified by Lipset. See Lipset, "Values, Education, and Entrepreneurship," note 8, pp. 49–50, for the relevant citations to the work of Parsons.

13. Erik H. Erikson, *Young Man Luther* (New York, 1962), pp. 134–35. See also Erik H. Erikson, *Identity: Youth and Crisis* (New York, 1968), esp. chaps. 1, 5, and 6.

14. In an extreme statement and generalization of Erikson's position, Lucian Pye, in *Politics, Personality, and Nation Building* (New Haven, Conn., 1962), p. 288, has characterized one path to national development as follows: "The first approach is that of the grand ideological solution in which some leader, out of the depths of his own personal experience, is able to give his people an understanding of the new sentiments and values necessary for national development. This would be a solution according to the Eriksonian model of the relationship between ideology and personality which suggests that the struggle of the ideological innovator to find his own personal sense of identity may provide a vehicle for an entire people to find their collective sense of identity. If such a leader can fully and honestly face the problems of his times as they emerge in his own personality, he can give powerful and meaningful expression to new attitudes and values which can in turn inculcate in a people the feeling of a new order of legitimacy and redirect their feelings of trust and distrust, of aggression and anxiety, of repudiation and commitment." To the extent that any case has approximated this model during the past twenty years, it would be Fidel Castro and Cuba.

15. Rule by terror is defined and discussed in Hannah Arendt, *The Origins of Totalitarianism* (New York, 1958), esp. chap. 13, "Ideology and Terror," and in Carl J. Friedrich and Zbigniew K. Brzezinski, *Totalitarian Dictatorship and Autocracy* (New York, 1963), esp. section IV, "The Psychic Fluidum: Propaganda and the Terror." Although the models developed differ in emphasis, neither is applicable to Cuba.

16. Samuel P. Huntington, "Political Development and Political Decay," *World Politics*, XVII, 3 (Apr. 1965), 386–430. See also Samuel P. Huntington, *Political Order in Changing Societies* (New Haven, 1968), esp. chaps. 1 and 5. In a similar vein, Lucian Pye earlier suggested that

"it may be fruitful to think of the problems of development and modernization as rooted in the need to create more effective, more adaptive, more complex, and more rationalized organizations." Pye, p. 38.

17. The notion of the "living museum" as a description of the situation typically found in systems of governance in Latin America is taken from Charles W. Anderson, *Politics and Economic Change in Latin America* (Princeton, N.J., 1967), chap. 4.

18. Lee Lockwood, *Castro's Cuba, Cuba's Fidel* (New York, 1967), p. 180.

19. Herbert L. Matthews, in *Fidel Castro* (New York, 1969), elaborates this point at length and quite convincingly. Matthews, along with many others, calls this ideology Fidelismo and argues that it is Communist only because its author so designates it. See also Lockwood.

20. Certain critics see the continuance of revolutionary behavior outside the revolutionary environment as possible only with the establishment of tyranny. A variant of this position is taken by Eric Hoffer in *The Ordeal of Change* (New York, 1963), p. 33: "Much has been said by all manner of people in praise of enthusiasm. The important point is that enthusiasm is ephemeral, and hence unserviceable for the long haul. One can hardly conceive of a more unhealthy and wasteful state of affairs than where faith and dedication are requisite for the performance of unmiraculous everyday activities. The attempt to keep people enthusiastic once they have ceased to believe is productive of the most pernicious consequences. An enormous effort has to be expended to maintain the revivalist spirit and, inevitably, with the passage of time, the fuels used to generate enthusiasm become more crude and poisonous."

Index

Index